Private Utilities and Poverty Alleviation

Market Initiatives at the Base of the Pyramid

Edited by

Patricia Márquez

University of San Diego, USA

and

Carlos Rufín

Suffolk University, USA

Edward Elgar

Cheltenham, UK • Northampton, MA, USA

Published by
Edward Elgar Publishing Limited
The Lypiatts
15 Lansdown Road
Cheltenham
Glos GL50 2JA
UK

Edward Elgar Publishing, Inc.
William Pratt House
9 Dewey Court
Northampton
Massachusetts 01060
USA

A catalogue record for this book
is available from the British Library

Library of Congress Control Number: 2010929032

MIX
Paper from
responsible sources
FSC
www.fsc.org   FSC® C018575

ISBN 978 1 84844 538 3

Typeset by Servis Filmsetting Ltd, Stockport, Cheshire
Printed and bound by MPG Books Group, UK

Contents

Contributors

Gigo Alampay is a consultant based in Manila, the Philippines.

Scarlett Álvarez works for the AES Corporation.

Ariel A. Casarín is a professor at the IAE Business School of the Universidad Austral in Buenos Aires, Argentina.

Miguel Ángel Gardetti is Director of the Base of the Pyramid Learning Laboratory in Buenos Aires, Argentina.

Simone Lawaetz is an expert in energy and utilities at the United States Agency for International Development.

Patricia Márquez is Associate Professor of Management at the University of San Diego, CA, USA.

Francisco Mejía is the Principal Business Development Officer in the Opportunities for the Majority Office at the Inter-American Development Bank (IDB), in Washington, DC, USA.

Shawn Mendes is Director of Education at the Swedish National Agency for Education (*Skolverket*).

Francisco Morandi is a Managing Director at the Latin America and Africa Group at the AES Corporation.

Luciana Nicollier is a doctoral student at the University of Warwick in Coventry, UK.

Ivar Pettersson is the Chief Operating Officer Distribution Businesses at AES Eletropaulo in São Paulo, Brazil.

Carlos Rufín is Associate Professor of International Business at Suffolk University in Boston, MA, USA.

Cathy Russell works for the Global Partnership on Output-Based Aid, a partnership program administered by the World Bank.

Connie Smyser, founding partner of Smyser Associates in San Francisco, CA, USA, is a consultant specialized in energy access for the urban poor.

Patricia Veevers-Carter is Program Manager of the Global Partnership on Output-Based Aid, a partnership program administered by the World Bank.

Foreword

A few years into the twenty-first century, multinational corporations (MNCs) find themselves on the horns of a dilemma: shareholders expect double-digit returns while the global economy is growing at an average annual rate between 2 and 3 per cent. The answer may reside in focusing on emerging markets, but not the incremental market expansion targeted at the wealthy few; rather at the much larger base of the economic pyramid, the so-called BOP, where between 4 and 5 billion people (or two-thirds of humanity) live, work, consume and relentlessly try to improve their lives.[1]

The task of unleashing the economic potential trapped in the informal economy in which the majority of the world's poor operate is a challenge that MNCs, together with a myriad of for-profit and nonprofit organizations (NPOs), have begun to focus on. This change implies a basic challenge: shifting mindsets that traditionally considered that majority too poor to be viable customers of their products.

The challenges organizations face in providing utilities to the poor occur in broad contexts that differ among countries. Organizations need to respond to multiple stakeholders as they confront differing perceptions of the responsibilities of utility companies. Utilities must conform to varying regulations often developed amidst complex political interests. Thus far, articles and papers have centered mostly on how large consumer goods companies such as P&G and Cemex have turned their gaze to the BOP in search of profits, as ascertained by C.K. Prahalad in *The Fortune at the Bottom of the Pyramid* (2005). The book provided the initial explanations on how different businesses strive to approach this important segment. However, there is little mention of how utilities approach the BOP, managing to build successful commercial relationships that benefit all their stakeholders. Moving forward, in this volume a group of scholars and practitioners have come together to provide their analysis on utility experiences at the BOP worldwide. It brings together global experiences from MNCs, multilateral organizations such as the IDB and the World Bank, and NPOs providing a broad but actionable set of insights on the challenges and opportunities of providing utilities to the poor worldwide.

In the case of AES Corporation, some of our franchises around the world have developed programs to attend the BOP sector and a common ground found among them is the need for a holistic approach, where the utility company identifies the potential customer, and his or her socio-cultural context, his or her own and very particular consumer patterns and payment abilities, and then develops a comprehensive approach where all the influential factors shape the business model. The relevance of such a holistic approach is analyzed by the different contributors to this book.

As Stuart Hart and Eric Simanis, both from the Center for Sustainable Global Enterprise at Cornell University's Johnson School of Management, mentioned in an article on innovation,[2] '[g]ood ideas are dime a dozen – turning an idea into a profitable business is where the rubber meets the road. Within such a context, the linear and highly regimented planning models that constitute the heart of much of the managerial and administrative training are likely to fail. It takes a different kind of organizational strategy, one we should call a real options strategy.' Small-scale experimentation and low-cost trials are the tools that enable this real-option logic where organizational flexibility is of central concern. Following this approach, AES businesses have conducted a variety of BOP initiatives. Examples from EDC in Venezuela and Eletropaulo in Brazil are presented in this book. These experiences have provided the foundations of our global efforts to reduce non-technical electricity losses, and improve service reliability and quality to the communities we serve.

We understand the need for understanding the BOP consumers from a wide variety of perspectives. In 2004 AES started a series of discussions about the BOP market. We sponsored working group meetings that brought together managers working with BOP communities in their service areas; we reached out to practitioners from outside our industry such as Stewart Brand, author and founder of GBN Global Business Network, to share his knowledge on how megacities are being developed, and the implications of the seemingly unstoppable process of migration from rural areas to urban centers.

In countries like Argentina, Brazil, El Salvador and Cameroon we see a tremendous opportunity to increase our customer base: 'transforming consumers into customers', as we labeled the effort in AES; using a different approach that brings engineering and sociology together; serving the needs of this sector of the population with the right set of product and services, tailor-made for them; understanding their needs, circumstances and social conditions; building a partnership that will allow the utilities to be a key success factor in helping people in these communities improve their conditions of life. As one of my colleagues at AES, Ivar Pettersson, author of one of the chapters of this book, says: 'there is a market out there, we need to find it and design solutions that fit their needs. We should not adapt what we have, we should reinvent the way we provide services for this sector of the population, understanding the way they live and letting them be part of the design of the solutions.'

The rapid change in customers served signals the positive effect of changing mindsets, engaging stakeholders, and incorporating lessons into organizational processes. In São Paulo, we serve more than 5.9 million customers; in Rio Grande do Sul, 1.1 million; in El Salvador, 1.1 million; and in Cameroon 660000. We must prepare to serve well and sustainably new customers from the BOP, whether coming from rural areas in El Salvador or Cameroon or *favelas* in São Paulo. It all starts by learning how we do things in different places across our company but also how other stakeholders have found solutions around the world, especially on the ability of bringing these solutions to utilities' scale. This continued effort in finding the 'AES Way' to serve customers is a journey that continues by learning from other firms' experiences in the industry as well as in others. This is a joint effort that has started to see concrete positive results for companies, poor families, and communities.

In sum, utilities play an essential role in the alleviation of poverty and economic growth. With this book we hope to continue fostering the dialogue between key stakeholders in order to better provide utilities to BOP customers in sustainable ways. Conversations between different entities sharing best practices must go on. We are thankful to all the participants and to Dr Patricia Márquez and Dr Carlos Rufín for their efforts in organizing a workshop and then relentlessly producing this volume that, being a first of a kind, examines the many challenges and opportunities for utilities seeking to serve the BOP sector.

Andrew M. Vesey
Executive Vice President and President, Latin America and Africa
AES Corporation

NOTES

1. Based on Hart and London (2005).
2. Hart and Simanis (2006).

1. Introduction: utilities at the base of the pyramid

Patricia Márquez and Carlos Rufín

Omaira and Yesenia are neighbors in a Latin American shantytown. They are best friends, and dwell in hillside shacks reached by steep, uneven steps. Together with two partners, they signed up for a microfinance loan to buy equipment for their informal economy workshop: a computer and printer to stamp labels on their home-made clothes and coffee filters. Often the computer turns off because of a power surge. Once, a short-circuit caused a small fire in Yesenia's home. When it rains, their informal electricity connection often fails, they have to ask Wilmer – the neighborhood handyman – to reconnect wires to the nearby lamppost for a $10 fee. It is necessary for these two women to spend time at home as water service comes twice a week, and must be gathered in buckets by standing in line at a nearby pump. Both Omaira and Yesenia complain of the fetid smell outside when garbage piles up, as it is seldom collected.

This story is a snapshot of the drama of insufficient access to basic services suffered by the urban poor in Latin America. In other parts of the world, the poor endure even worse conditions as children play alongside human excrement, or electricity is not available even from illegal connections. Access to utilities is key for achieving economic growth and improving the lives of citizens worldwide. Polluted water is a major source of infectious disease, particularly diarrheal illnesses that are a major cause of infant mortality in many parts of the world (WHO, 2009a). As in the case of Omaira and Yesenia, obtaining clean water for household use consumes the scarce resources of the poor, particularly the time and energies of women and girls tasked with the chore of fetching water from communal sources (World Bank, 2004). Lack of electricity limits study and household activity after dark and contributes to deforestation and indoor pollution – with the attendant respiratory disease – by forcing recourse to alternative energy sources such as kerosene and charcoal (WHO, 2009b). Recent research has shown that access to telecommunications can have significant positive impacts on poverty, by increasing access to prices and other information that increase the bargaining power of the poor, while mobile telephony is helping bridge the 'digital gap' and giving the poor increased access to financial services (*The Economist*, 2009).

This book examines new business models for servicing the 4 billion people comprising the 'base of the pyramid' (BOP). Since this term was coined by C.K. Prahalad and Stuart Hart in 1999,[1] the idea that business models can mobilize social change by engaging profitably with the poor in the marketplace has caught the imagination of academics and practitioners alike. Companies today are seeking innovative models that can ensure both access by the poor and financial sustainability. This book identifies 'what is needed' for developing market initiatives bringing water, electricity, telecommunications and natural gas to underserved populations. It offers insights on the roles markets may play in attacking poverty, by highlighting how wealth creation can be effectively combined with social change. It is aimed at advancing knowledge on business at the BOP as well as influencing the development of new business models and management practices.

WHY UTILITIES?

Utilities are typically defined as products that share two characteristics: they meet basic needs – water, energy, hygiene, communications; and in densely populated areas, the most efficient technologies for utility supply are based on dedicated physical networks – mainly cables and pipes (Spiller, 1996). These characteristics have important consequences that set utilities apart from other products. First, because utilities meet basic needs, their market includes, at least potentially, the entire universe of households and establishments in a given area. Households and establishments, whether private or otherwise, require water for human consumption and other uses; they generate waste which can be discharged through sewers; they use energy for lighting, temperature control, mechanical needs and other applications; and they exchange information with other households and establishments. In turn, such massive consumption makes utilities highly visible. More specifically, deficiencies in access to utilities – whether regarding cost or quality of service – are often perceived by large numbers of persons at the same time, and can have significant social, political and economic effects. Second, the need for dedicated physical networks as means to reach consumers makes competition among alternative suppliers inefficient. Competing suppliers would have to build parallel networks, which in general results in higher unit costs than a monopoly supplier can achieve.[2] However, since a monopoly supplier can exploit its position to extract inefficiently high prices from consumers, utility prices must be regulated for the sake of economic efficiency. Hence, unlike most other products, utilities are generally subject to price regulation.

Providing utilities to the large poor populations in developing countries is a major challenge for the private sector. The construction or upgrading of utility networks entails heavy investments that cannot be easily recovered through sales to low-income consumers. In addition, privately owned suppliers face the challenges of clientelistic legacies in many countries, in which utility services were provided free or at highly subsidized prices under public ownership, and of ongoing regulation of utility prices, which create pressures and opportunities to hold prices artificially low for political gain or for the benefit of well-organized interests. Private utility supply is thus often enmeshed with social and political demands and constrained by concerns about profitability. Yet meeting the needs of the poor is not simply a growth opportunity for private utility companies, but a strategic imperative. The social and political aspects of utility supply imply that failure to meet the needs of the poor can threaten a company's entire investment in any one developing country.

On the other hand, there are few alternatives to private involvement in utility supply. Public ownership failed to provide service to the poor in most developing countries because of corruption, inefficiency and lack of financial resources exacerbated by heavy price subsidization. Accelerated urbanization in developing countries is creating the need for major investment in utility supply, but few governments are willing or capable to muster the required financial resources.

The emerging 'BOP paradigm' was first formulated in 1999 (Prahalad and Hart, 1999). It claims that new business models can allow companies to meet profitably the needs of the poor in developing countries. Yet most of the research conducted so far has concerned consumer goods.[3] Are the canonical elements of BOP business models – as identified so far – applicable to the case of utilities? Can utility services be profitably supplied to low-income consumers at regulated rates? In which ways do factors such as the environment, technology, the rise of civil society and sustainability affect answers to the previous questions?

This book seeks to examine new utility business models servicing BOP communities around the world, and generating economic value as well as social change. Our goal is to improve academic research on BOP, on the one hand, and expand the range of possibilities for meeting key service requirements, on the other. The specific conditions of utility supply previously described introduce the public interest and public policy in this type of activity in a very direct way that has so far not been addressed in most of the BOP literature. BOP models may need significant adjustment to accommodate the often politicized nature of low-income markets. At the same time, the BOP literature suggests the potential for organizational and technological innovations to overcome the constraints of dominant business logics. For example, access to telecommunications for the poor has been revolutionized by initiatives such as Grameen Phone, combining the ability of cellular technology to break the stranglehold of physical networks, with the organizational capabilities derived from Grameen Bank's microcredit experience (see, for example, Seelos and Mair, 2007).

KEY ISSUES

The intersection of the particularities of utility supply with the conditions prevailing at the BOP suggests several issues that practitioners and scholars must consider. To begin with, it is worth delving deeper into the degree to which utilities differ from consumer goods. How far does the 'tyranny of the network' set utilities apart from other sectors when it comes to providing service at the BOP? What elements of 'generic' BOP strategies, as elaborated since 1999, can be applied to utilities as well? Which ones are not applicable? To the extent that significant adaptations are needed, what are those adaptations? How do they modify and enrich what we know so far about doing business at the BOP?

A related question, concerning also the differences between utilities and other sectors, is to what extent is the BOP 'strategic' for utility suppliers, as we claim above. Are utilities also unique because of their widespread impact and visibility? Other products, for example foodstuffs (including bottled water), are also widely consumed, yet they seemingly attract less controversy than water supply, for instance. Why this difference? Perhaps the explanation lies in the lack of competition in utilities and thus, once again, the 'tyranny of the network,' rather than utilities being 'essential needs'. Consumers may be particularly sensitive to supply conditions when they lack alternative suppliers. But a more indirect mechanism may be at work, where regulation itself is the direct cause of the political visibility of utilities. Regulation may open the door to political opportunism by actors that find in regulatory policy a convenient way to attract low-income voters by pressuring companies to lower prices or to extend service. Identifying the source of political risk, like identifying technological constraints, is important because it can help decision makers understand how existing BOP frameworks must be adapted for utilities, and it can bring new insights for researchers concerning BOP frameworks and business models. For instance, the study of the BOP has so far paid little attention to political risk (Rufín, 2006), but political risk may actually be an important issue at the BOP because of concerns – perceived or real – about exploitation of the poor.[4]

The monopoly status of utility companies also affects them in other ways. One such effect is the impact on corporate culture, and especially on attitudes towards customers within the company (Gómez et al., 2006). With a monopoly status, utility companies have traditionally had an engineering orientation rather than a customer orientation. The focus of company managers has been on the deployment of equipment and technology to optimize operations rather than understanding and meeting customer needs. Changing such a focus can be expected to be particularly challenging when it comes to BOP customers. BOP customers pose additional difficulties to serve: they have limited and irregular incomes, live in hard-to-reach areas and in precarious conditions, and may in many cases be used to pilfering utilities. Utility companies thus face a complex task of educating their workforce, changing organizational culture and even changing fundamental internal processes in order to engage the BOP effectively. Understanding the extent and nature of these tasks is another key issue for research on utilities at the BOP.

The transformation of 'mental maps' is not limited to utility companies, however. It may also be necessary for their BOP customers, too. As mentioned, BOP customers are often used to consuming utilities without paying, or at least without paying utility companies. In some cases, this is due to prevalence of fraud and theft in the informal areas where the poor live (Smith, 2004); in other cases, BOP communities may have received free utilities under public supply arrangements. In either case, there can be a presumption that utilities are a right for which one should not pay, or at least a service that the government should provide for free to all citizens, just like public safety or basic education. Utility companies thus face a higher hurdle at the BOP than other types of suppliers: they have to make a convincing proposition to BOP consumers that the companies' services are worth paying for. The question is, how is this best done? Is there a difference between situations where utilities are seen as rights (which is often the case with regard to potable water supply) and situations where customers have simply come to expect free supply? How are claims of utilities as rights related to the political risks mentioned above?

We thus come back to politics when it comes to utilities at the BOP. This suggests that practitioners and scholars may need to invest in understanding politics and regulation (an extension of politics) more carefully than the BOP literature has done so far (which is not to say much). First, we should know how the cost of utility supply is apportioned, particularly for BOP consumers: is the cost recovered entirely from customers, or is some portion of it borne by taxpayers? How much of the burden falls on the

BOP under each case? In many developing countries, there are substantial cross-subsidies from large or better-off consumers to smaller or poorer ones, but taxes are regressive because of the complexity of income and corporate taxation. In these situations, the paradox is that placing the financial burden of utility supply for the BOP on the government may actually leave the BOP worse off than having the BOP pay, at least partially, for utilities: BOP consumers could end up bearing a higher burden via indirect taxation than if they paid cross-subsidized rates.

More generally, since utilities are usually subject to price regulation, we need to understand how regulation works. Who sets utility prices? What procedure is followed? Understanding regulation can also provide a big pay-off because company initiatives to work at the BOP may require regulatory approval, as in the case of prepayment meters (see Chapter 5 on the Buenos Aires case and Chapter 9 on the Caracas case). The key issue here is to look beyond the formal arrangements prescribed in the law to understand regulation in practice. In many developing countries, so-called 'independent' regulatory commissions may in fact be controlled by the government through a variety of means – appointment of commissions' members, control over the commissions' budgets, recourse to non-independent courts or even outright legislative changes, let alone refusals to enforce regulatory decisions. Where governments or elected politicians have influence over regulatory decisions, it may be particularly difficult for companies to raise prices or to charge for services previously provided for free; in fact, utilities are often important elements of clientelistic bargains, where politicians provide free or subsidized utilities to BOP communities in exchange for votes (Foster, 2002). The importance of utilities for meeting basic needs makes them valuable to BOP voters, who may thus be quite willing to trade their votes for lower utility prices. Where this is the case, politicians may be reluctant to give up control over regulatory decisions. What can utility companies do to alter such bargains? Finally, politics also enters into utility supply for the BOP through ideological battles about the desirability of private supply, particularly when undertaken by foreign companies. As the well-known controversies over water supply in Cochabamba (Bolivia) and Tucumán (Argentina) attest, the impact of private utility supply on the BOP is at the forefront of international debates about globalization and capitalism, with anti-globalization activists and governments inherently opposed to private supply in sectors such as water. We need to know more about the forces arrayed in these controversies and the responses that can be developed against accusations of exploitation of the poor.

A final set of issues that deserve to be highlighted here are those concerning the appropriate business models for utilities at the BOP. Since

1999, the BOP literature has developed a variety of elements that appear to be necessary to achieve the combination of profit and poverty alleviation: establishing partnerships with governments, NGOs and community organizations; co-inventing products and processes with BOP populations and partners; and acquiring a deep knowledge of BOP environments. A discussion of these elements lies outside the scope of this introduction. But their development suggests a fundamental question: to what extent are they applicable to utilities? Can utility companies make a profit if they incorporate these elements to their BOP strategies? To the extent that these elements have been developed in the context of other products and sectors, as previously mentioned, this question takes us back to the transferability of lessons from the extant BOP literature to utilities. But in addition to this general question, there are additional matters that must be addressed in order to create viable business models.

The first element of a business model is revenue generation. What is the appropriate pricing point and structure for utilities? Under price regulation these issues are, of course, in the hands of regulators, not of the companies. But companies can propose new ideas to regulators, particularly when convincingly formulated in the interest of BOP consumers. The traditional approach to pricing utilities for low-income consumers has been the use of cross-subsidies: customers with higher consumption levels, or classified (by territory or other means) as higher-income, pay prices above cost, which subsidize supply to BOP customers. Establishing criteria for cross-subsidization may be difficult, however; and in developing countries, where the total consumption by the poor may amply exceed that of the non-poor, cross-subsidization may lead to large differences in utility prices between the two groups, encouraging the non-poor to resort to fraud or other means to avoid paying the higher prices. At the same time, charging prices to BOP consumers that fully recover the cost of supplying them, as regulatory orthodoxy would have it, is sure to encourage theft and fraud, as well as invite political attacks, particularly when one considers that, because of economies of scale in utility supply, unit costs of supply for the BOP may actually exceed those of other consumers. Price structure, however, is not the only major issue concerning revenue generation. Utilities have traditionally billed on monthly or bimonthly cycles to reduce administrative costs, but for the poor, with irregular incomes and lack of access to financial services, monthly bills require unrealistic levels of cash accumulation. Innovative utility companies are searching for shorter cycles at a reasonable cost. Examples include prepayment meters (following the huge success of prepayment for cellphones), weekly payments collected by local shopkeepers and based on estimated or remote measures of consumption, or hiring of local agents for frequent measurement, billing and collection. Several of these innovations are discussed in the chapters that follow, and others are sure to come as experimentation continues in this respect.

An emerging alternative to reliance on external or cross-subsidies for BOP consumers is leveraging utilities as platforms for a variety of products, in effect turning the 'tyranny of the network' on its head. As Francisco Mejía discusses in Chapter 2, several highly successful experiences by utility companies and, once again, developments in the highly competitive cellphone industry, show that the high fixed investments in both physical infrastructure and organization needed to deliver utilities to consumers on a retail basis actually constitute excellent platforms for the delivery of other products at low incremental cost. Positive margins in these product lines can then provide additional return on the fixed investments and thus solve the pricing conundrum. In a way, this approach is not too different from well-known strategies such as loss leadership and maximization of revenue from by-products in other sectors. In fact, at the birth of the utility industry, natural gas companies relied on the provision of lighting, and electric utilities on running urban transport networks, to make ends meet. During the 1990s, the concept of 'multi-utility' companies became fashionable, based on the possibility of economies of scope among utilities: for example, a multi-utility company could send a single bill for water, gas, electricity, cable TV and Internet access. In practice, this concept did not work well, perhaps because regulatory risks were also compounded, or because other utility services were perceived as 'more of the same' and did not increase willingness to pay as much as selling significantly different products such as appliances. Accordingly, the idea of utilities as platforms is based on delivery of non-utility products, which are thus less subject to regulation. The experiences discussed in Chapter 2 show that we can expect much from innovations based on the platform concept.

On the cost side of the business model, given the paramount importance of the cost of the physical network, the major issue is: what is the potential for reduction of this cost? Other costs can be reduced through subcontracting services, particularly to BOP businesses and community organizations or individuals that may be able to perform a variety of services at lower cost. For instance, bill payment can be handled by local merchants, who constitute a readily available commercial network linking BOP communities and the broader economy. More generally, re-engineering of business processes may open up many opportunities to reduce costs, particularly in connection with the design of utility products to meet the needs of the BOP. This is a valuable avenue for practitioners and researchers to pursue. But where radical innovation can have a profound effect on utilities at the

BOP is in reducing the cost of the physical network. The experience of tele-communications shows what can happen if the 'tyranny of the network' can be broken. Although cellphone networks still involve investment in geographically dispersed physical plant – mainly transmission towers – the radically lower level of investment involved relative to landline networks has indeed eliminated natural monopoly in local telephony. Could this happen with other utilities? It is certainly possible to envisage a similar breakthrough in electricity, for instance, if solar and battery technology became so inexpensive, reliable and environmentally friendly that they could replace electricity distribution networks; low-cost water filtration technology could achieve a similar outcome for water supply, by allowing reuse of domestic water consumption. While we still seem to be far away from these possibilities, at least for utilities in urban settings where high densities make for lower relative costs of physical networks, their potential is only beginning to be explored. The tentative first steps on this path are already under way in Brazil, where AES Eletropaulo is replacing electric showerhead water heaters – common in Brazil, but very energy-intensive – with low-cost rooftop water tanks heated by the sun to help residents of the Paraisópolis slum reduce their electricity bills (Chapter 10).

APPROACH AND STRUCTURE

The book brings together the work of a group of researchers and prac-titioners working on utilities and the BOP in both academic and non-academic settings. The presentation of a number of papers on utilities and the poor at a Harvard Business School conference (December 2005) on 'Global Poverty: Business Solutions and Approaches' revealed a growing interest among academics and practitioners from different parts of the world in this issue, and with it, the generation of an increasing number of case studies and research papers. The strength of this interest was further ascertained at the conference on 'Research at the Base of the Pyramid' held at the William Davidson Institute of the University of Michigan in May 2006. Taking advantage of this interest, and mindful of the potentially significant implications for research in a number of fields, the contributors to this volume presented (with one exception) their recent research at a one-day workshop at the University of San Diego, California, on 2 May 2008. Their presentations, hopefully improved through discussions during the workshop and subsequent feedback from us, constitute the basis for the chapters that follow.

The core aim of the book is the advancement of academic research, while influencing practice. An explicit aim is to move beyond the analysis of specific cases to develop more robust generalizations, with potentially significant implications in a number of academic fields – particularly international business, business strategy, alliance management and business–society relations. This should be of interest to both academics pursuing applied research and practitioners engaged in supply, financing and management market initiatives with low-income sectors. More specifically, the chapters that follow offer valuable insights to a variety of readers: scholars working on the BOP, but also those working on relevant related areas such as alliances between business and non-profit organizations, corporate social responsibility and BOP market development, utilities and poverty alleviation, organizational change and innovation, and the implications of slums and urban development in developing countries, among others; the financial community, including microfinance, venture capital and multilateral financial institutions; international utility companies and other firms seeking to expand in emerging markets; non-governmental organizations and applied research institutions focused on international development; and, last but not least, multilateral and national development agencies. In addition, the book will be useful as a text on a variety of courses: at business schools, on courses in international business strategy, innovation and the social impact of business and corporate social responsibility, especially in view of the strong and growing interest in social issues at business schools around the world; at schools of public policy, on courses in poverty alleviation or social policy; and in international development programs dealing with the private sector and poverty.

Our book differs from other books published on the BOP thus far. *The Next 4 Billion* (Hammond et al., 2007) is a statistical exercise exclusively focused on the estimation of BOP market sizes across countries and major sectors of economic activity. C.K. Prahalad's *The Fortune at the Bottom of the Pyramid* (2005), by far the best-known and most influential work on the BOP paradigm, discusses business models and a number of cases, but does not address utilities specifically. In fact, none of the examples used by Prahalad deal with utility services (most cases are from consumer-goods industries) and few with peri-urban populations. *Business Solutions for the Global Poor* (Rangan et al., 2007) comes closest to the present book. Not only is it an edited book as well, but in fact both of us are contributors to the book, as well as several of the contributors to our book, since we first met many of them at the Harvard Business School conference which led to the Business Solutions book. However, where *Business Solutions* addresses a wide variety of sectors, issues, and perspectives, our book is much more focused. Our approach has been, indeed, to build on the research published in *Business Solutions* and take it to a more advanced level for the case of utility services. We thus see *Business Solutions* as a complementary work rather than a competing one. Finally, *Untapped: Creating Value in Underserved Markets* by John Weiser et al. (2006), explores barriers and challenges in developing market initiatives with underserved consumers, offering solutions and emphasizing the role of partnerships, but it provides very few examples of utilities, and those not fully developed as utilities are not the core of the book.

After this introductory chapter explaining the book's aims and motivations, setting out the key issues addressed by the book as well their context, examining the current state of scholarship and practice on these issues, and describing the book's structure, Francisco Mejía of the Inter-American Development Bank offers in Chapter 2 his answer to the question 'Why do utilities matter for the BOP?' by looking at utilities as platforms for the supply of valuable products to the poor. The next two chapters provide a variety of lessons from the field, drawing particularly on the experience of telecommunications – where the spectacular diffusion of mobile telephony among BOP populations has been balanced by concerns about the 'digital divide'. In Chapter 3, Shawn Mendes discusses the vast array of services that mobile phones are providing for the BOP in the Philippines, and their implications for Africa, where lack of landlines makes cellphones the key telecommunications technology. This contrasts with Gigo Alampay's account in Chapter 4 of the attempts by a variety of actors in the same country to bridge the digital divide in rural areas. Chapter 5 shifts from telecommunications to electricity and from Asia to Latin America, as Miguel Ángel Gardetti considers the degree to which efforts by electricity distributors in Argentina have really reached the BOP.

The central part of the book examines technological and managerial advances that are increasingly transforming the relationship between utilities and BOP communities. In Chapter 6, Ariel Casarín and Luciana Nicollier evaluate the use of prepaid meters in electricity distribution, a technology that has gained considerable attention in view of its vast success in making access to mobile telephony possible for lower-income users. Simone Lawaetz and Connie Smyser analyze in Chapter 7 a variety of innovations in electricity distribution at the BOP that draws on an ongoing multiyear effort by the United States Agency for International Development (USAID). On the financial side, Patricia Veevers-Carter and Cathy Russell of the World Bank describe in Chapter 8 the recent experience of the Bank with the use of an innovative formula, output-based aid (OBA).

Chapters 9 and 10 focus on emerging business models for utilities operating at the BOP, and more specifically on the experiences of a global utility with a deep commitment to the BOP, the AES Corporation. In Chapter 9, Scarlett Álvarez and Francisco Morandi of AES Corporation introduce

BOP-related initiatives in Latin America and Africa, presenting a broad perspective on company efforts to learn from its diverse experiences and to improve, refine and adapt its approach to BOP engagement. This is followed by Ivar Pettersson's presentation of the case of AES Eletropaulo's Loss Reduction Program in Paraisópolis, one of the largest *favelas* (slums) in São Paulo – itself one of the world's largest cities with some 16 million inhabitants. Lastly, Chapter 11 summarizes the main points raised by the contributors in their respective chapters, placing the various contributions in an overall framework that generalizes across industries and geographic settings, identifying the improvements and extensions to current research and practice offered by the contributions, and outlining further possibilities for research and practice suggested by the work presented in the book.

NOTES

1. One of the earliest papers to make use of the term 'bottom of the pyramid' in reference to opportunities for companies with regard to the world's poor is Prahalad and Hart (1999).
2. Also, to the extent that competing networks are not compatible with each other, competition can deny consumers benefits from being part of a larger network, 'network externalities' in the parlance of economists (Shy, 2001). In some instances, particularly telecommunications, such network externalities can be significant and provide, at the very least, justification for mandating network interconnection.
3. None of the examples in Prahalad's well-known book (2005) are about utilities. Widely cited case studies of BOP initiatives include the experiences of Hindustan Lever (consumer goods), ITC (commodities), Cemex (cement), Casas Bahia (retailing) and Aravind Eye Care (health care).
4. Karnani (2007) has argued that many BOP initiatives, such as Hindustan Lever's sale of Fair & Lovely skin whitening cream, exploit the poor's vulnerabilities for the enrichment of multinational corporations.

2. Reaching scale: utilities as platforms to provide opportunities for the majority

Francisco Mejía[1]

THE CASE FOR PLATFORMS

This chapter focuses on the potential of utility distribution networks as platforms to overcome barriers in improving the lives of millions at the base of the socio-economic pyramid, disrupting existing market conditions and leapfrogging existing competitors. Since the publication of Prahalad's and Hart's seminal article (Prahalad and Hart, 2002), the idea of developing appropriate business solutions that serve the poor, while staying profitable, has taken hold and developed into a new field in business strategy, public and social policy, and development economics.

Nevertheless, reaching these 4 billion neglected consumers, producers and suppliers in a fast, efficient and scalable manner remains a significant challenge. Companies that wish to reach scale fast and overcome competitors in the creation of new consumer bases have the option of tapping into existing networks. These networks have the potential of catalyzing and accelerating market penetration by leveraging their existing majority customer base and providing a platform to reach scale very fast.

In many urban areas in the developing world, the most ubiquitous services are energy (electricity and gas), water and sanitation, and telephony (fixed and mobile). These utilities have massive consumer bases. Offering additional and complementary goods and services by building on and leveraging this consumer base provides a unique opportunity for profits, growth, innovation and social impact. The pioneering models to provide access to financial services through mobile banking, or access to consumer and capital goods through energy distribution networks, or health services through water and sanitation provision, illustrate the potential that these innovations can have, not only in opening new markets, but also in addressing existing poverty and exclusion challenges. These new channels are potential disruptive technologies in providing new services for the majority. For instance, Codensa, the energy distribution utility in Bogotá, Colombia, in only seven years served five times more poor customers than all of the microfinance institutions in Bogotá together. The runaway success of Codensa in providing financial services to the majority offers an example for many other utilities both in Colombia and beyond.

The concept of leveraging platforms to provide access to goods and services is not limited to utilities. There are many other platforms with great potential in serving the poor in new and scalable business models. These platforms can be public in nature, such as Conditional Cash Transfer (CCT) programs, which can use existing financial distribution networks such as automated teller machines (ATMs), credit payment systems at the point of sale (POS) or existing technological platforms such as mobile phone networks to enable innovative payment and monitoring systems. Also, CCT programs can serve as a platform to introduce cheaper goods and services, leveraging their scale and scope. CCT can also serve as a platform to strengthen both its objectives and the supply of otherwise inaccessible complementary products such as health insurance or education and vocational training. Platforms can also can be based on private distribution and logistical networks, which have impressive reach and capillarity in low-income markets – one can buy a commercial soft drink or a cosmetic from major multinationals in the most remote and isolated locations. Microfinance organizations and non-governmental organizations (NGOs) also have important capillarity, particularly in poor and rural areas, where market access is hardest and most expensive.

The provision of financial services on top of mobile network grids exemplifies the potential disruption that platforms can achieve on a scale commensurate with the huge promise that majority markets offer. These platforms represent an opportunity to unlock a new uncontested market space, or 'blue ocean' (Kim and Mauborgne, 2005) and to think in billions of dollars and not thousands.

UTILITIES AS PLATFORMS

Traditionally, utility companies have perceived their core competencies to be strictly related with deploying their strategic assets in offering energy services at the lowest operational cost and technical and non-technical losses. Pioneering and innovative utility companies such as Codensa (energy), Promigas (gas) and Empresas Públicas de Medellin (energy, gas and water) in Colombia have combined their billing and collection capabilities, a core operational asset, with their client bill payment histories, a hidden asset, and created a new business line in financial services for the majority. In this process, they have transformed liabilities – unpaid utility bills and low customer loyalty – into a new asset: financial services. This blue ocean has become a significant source of consumer loyalty and income for the utilities, and has dramatically improved the lives of the poor by offering an entry point to an otherwise inaccessible financial system.

The majority of the population in most poor countries is 'unbanked'. Whereas more than 80 percent of households in most of Western Europe and North America have an account in a financial institution, in Latin America it ranges from 20 percent in Nicaragua to 60 percent in Chile. In Asia this estimate ranges from 40 percent to 60 percent and in sub-Saharan Africa less than 20 percent have accounts (Karlan and Murdoch, 2009). Furthermore, most developing countries lack credit bureaus and standard commercial credit scoring systems. The absence of credit bureaus and credit systemic information implies that most individuals, particularly the poor, have not had the chance to develop a credit history or a financial identity. As a result, one of the most relevant market failures in majority markets is the absence of reliable information about the customer. Utilities realized that they could unravel this conundrum by using the information that had been generated as a natural by-product of their operations to differentiate those clients that were trustworthy from those that were not.

By leveraging billing information and good payment histories, utilities are solving two different informational problems. First, they are overcoming adverse selection issues. This problem arises when the seller does not know the trustworthiness of the buyer. As a result, the buyer will have to sell to both reliable and unreliable customers and accept some losses, or not sell to any customer at all and withdraw from the market. However, by accessing this information, utilities could choose to serve only the reliable customers and often even lower the final retail price, since they did not have to cover any losses arising from unreliable customers.

The second informational problem that utilities overcome is moral hazard. Moral hazard arises when the reliability of the customer deteriorates after the product is sold. For example, a reliable customer may (consciously or unconsciously) take less care of their house after buying insurance, because now the losses will be borne by the firm, rather than the customer. This is also known as the principal–agent problem, because the seller cannot monitor the buyer's behavior and 'force' the buyer to take proper care of, in this example, their house. Nonetheless, it is in the best interest of buyers to be perceived as 'safe bets' also after the purchase because their credit history is being built and thus will have a decisive impact in future transactions they may want to conduct. This repeated games scenario is especially important in the case of low-income customers because of the sizeable amount of needs that still need to be met.

Utilities are particularly well positioned to take advantage of their informational superiority and leapfrog other companies thanks to their extraordinary capillarity, particularly in urban areas. The logistical structure that they have in place is instrumental in building and collecting the new operations required to offer additional financial products on top of the utility services they already offer. As a result from these new services, the firms involved not only increase their market penetration in low-income markets and improve customer loyalty, but also decrease default rates and non-technical losses and significantly improve reputation and corporate image.

THE CODENSA CASE: TRANSFORMING ACCESS TO FINANCIAL SERVICES IN BOGOTÁ

The Crisis and the Opportunity

By the mid-1990s the Empresa de Energía de Bogotá (EEB) was in crisis. EEB, owned by the municipal government, served a city of 6.8 million inhabitants in Santa Fé de Bogotá (Departamento Administrativo Nacional de Estadística, 2005). Between 1992 and 1995, EEB's losses amounted up to 25 percent of the energy distributed. Each percentage point represented over US$4 million in foregone income. The company was highly leveraged and projected debt service for 1995–2000 was 1.76 times internal income generation (Millán, 2007). In 1996, EEB reported total losses of close to US$200 million. EEB was not financially viable.

In 1994, national and local governments started a restructuring process that resulted in the creation in 1997 of a new corporate structure that included a limited partnership holding entity (EEB S.A. ESP), a generation company (Emgesa S.A. ESP) and a distribution company (Codensa S.A. ESP). In the resulting public tender, the Spanish energy company Endesa acquired 48.5 percent of both Emgesa and Codensa. The municipality, through EEB, maintained 51.5 percent. Endesa obtained operational control of both companies.

The restructuring and capitalization process was a success. Every financial and operational indicator improved dramatically. By 2006 operational losses dipped below 10 percent and reached best-practice levels both by Colombian and international standards. Service interruptions were reduced sixfold: from 30 hours per month to five hours per month (Millán, 2007). This success has been attributed to three factors: an institutional framework that shielded the company from local political interference; a world-class quality operator; and a concerted effort to

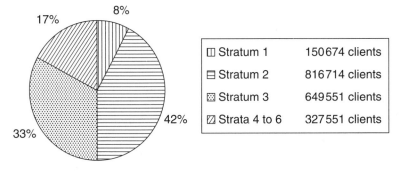

Source: Codensa (2007).

Figure 2.1   Codensa client base by social strata (2007)

add value to all consumers, particularly low-income consumers (Millán, 2007). By 2008, Codensa was serving approximately 2 million homes and 260 000 businesses, reported sales of US$942 million (7.307 Gwh), and had a 7.6 percent return on assets and 14.1 percent return on equity (Codensa, 2008a). A critical element in adding value to its majority client base was the introduction of the 'Easy Credit for All' program, later relabeled 'Codensa Hogar'.

Codensa's Clients: Poor and Unbanked

The Colombian population is classified in six strata, where 1 is the poorest and 6 the wealthiest. This stratification is used for various public policy purposes, including the definition of utility rates. The definition of each stratum is determined by national-level legislation (National Law 142, 1994). The specific location of customers by stratum is determined by local authorities. Strata 1, 2 and 3 pay subsidized rates, and subsidies range from 50 percent for strata 1 to 15 percent in strata 3. Strata 5 and 6 pay a utility surcharge of 20 percent. Stratum 4 pays full tariff. Almost 85 percent of Codensa's client base is classified in strata 1–3 as presented in Figure 2.1.

It is important to note that although it is generally acknowledged that lower-strata customers are poorer, they include some higher-income population. For instance, there is an 8.4 percent probability that a person in stratum 1 belongs to the highest 20 percent in the income distribution (Ramírez and Econometría, 2007). In 2004, approximately 40 percent of Bogotá's population lived below the official poverty line.[2] After 2004 this share decreased, to 24 percent in 2006 (Figure 2.2). Despite this reduction in poverty rates in Bogotá, the Codensa Hogar program maintained its

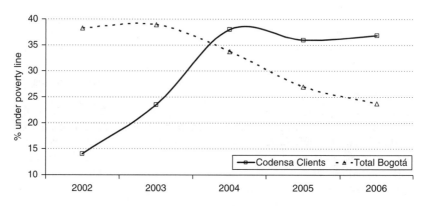

Source: Arbeláez (2007a) and Secretaria de Hacienda de Bogotá data.

Figure 2.2   Codensa's clients and poverty

focus on low-income customers. In its first two years of operation, less than a quarter of its customers were living below the poverty line. Then, as income increased for the population as a whole, Codensa maintained its focus on the poor. After 2004, more than 35 percent of its consumers lived below the official poverty line.

Access to financial services in majority markets in Colombia is low: according to the Colombian Banking Association (Asobancaria, 2008a), approximately 45 percent of the Colombian adult population have no access to financial services and are considered 'unbanked', and 87 percent have no access to credit cards or consumer loans (Asobancaria, 2008a). Access to credit services is very uneven across Colombia. Even when income-level differences are accounted for in a simple regression analysis, Bogotá still has twice the access to credit services that it should, according to its gross domestic product (GDP) per capita levels. Much of this difference can be explained by the introduction in 2001 and explosive growth of Codensa Hogar.

Financial exclusion increases transaction costs for the poor (Manroth and Solo, 2006) and impedes cash flow smoothing which lowers the probability that a transitory shock becomes a permanent one (Morduch, 1995). It is also generally associated with lower and more uncertain incomes and uneven cash flows, lower education, closer links to the informal sector and significantly higher interest rates on credit (Manroth and Solo, 2006). Over 70 percent of the unbanked earn less than the minimum wage, they have three times greater unemployment than the banked, are significantly more likely to be informal. It is estimated that 85 percent have incomplete primary education (Arbeláez et al., 2007a).

The unbanked make use of friends and family or informal money lenders as sources of credit, and end up paying significantly higher interest rates. It is estimated that among the lowest three out of six socioeconomic strata of the Colombian population (Ramírez and Econometria, 2007), 83 percent of credit operations are informal. Almost 75 percent of Colombians report a recent loan in the previous 12 months with a family member or a friend, 23 percent with a pawn shop and 25 percent with a local lender. In Colombia, annual interest rates in informal low-income markets range from 70 percent in loans from friends and family, to 213 percent in pawn shops and 274 percent in short-term day-to-day lending (USAID, 2007). The widespread use of informal credit markets and financial tools to cope with high levels of poverty, and lack of formal access to finance to manage uneven cash flows, was also recently documented for markets with opaque financial price-setting environments in Asia and Africa as well (Collins et al., 2009).

The Codensa Hogar Program

Codensa Hogar features
The Codensa Hogar program started to operate in 2001. It initially provided financing for white goods such as washers, dryers, refrigerators and heaters; grey goods such as computers and computing accessories; and brown goods such as televisions, and sound and video systems. It gradually incorporated five micro insurance products outsourced to the insurance company MAPFRE: accidents, funeral, small business insurance, life insurance, and home repairs. In 2006 Codensa Hogar introduced financing for home improvement projects including floors, walls, incremental construction, baths and kitchens, home furnishings and mattresses (Codensa, 2005, 2006, 2007, 2008a).

The program was originally conceived as a fidelity program targeted at low-income customers, and designed to enhance the value of Codensa's core product, energy, which had been perceived as low quality and unreliable prior to the restructuring of the company. Rufin and Arboleda (2007) call this 'innovating around the network'. Codensa understood that the poor quality of past services had been an important factor in generating a weak payment culture, which in turn contributed to high distribution losses. By adding a new attribute, small loans, which were seemingly unrelated to the core product – energy – and by providing new and previously inaccessible products to the majority, the company generated additional customer loyalty while developing a new profitable line of business in financial services. This innovation, although not a 'new' business model for utilities, profitably leveraged existing capabilities.

The Codensa Hogar business model and structure is organized in two layers. First, an internal division was created to develop and manage the whole credit process including client selection, credit origination and collections. This department, which reports to the commercial manager, is responsible for the development of customized credit-scoring methodologies, loan underwriting policies, risk management and leveraging the billing systems for collections. In this manner most credit competencies are kept 'in-house'. Nonetheless some very specific and non-core functions are outsourced to specialized companies.

Since its inception, and although it is not legally required to, Codensa Hogar has operated under formal market guidelines as established by the national financial supervision and regulatory body and reports performance data to the credit bureaus. Codensa typically offers longer-term loans (average 22 months) than alternative informal financial consumer products for the majority, which typically have weekly or even daily terms. Codensa's interest rates reflect formal regulated market conditions and fluctuate between 24 percent and 32 percent per year.

The second layer involves the channel definition for the product offer, including marketing and distribution. This layer was developed and implemented by external commercial 'allies', and includes a variety of formats: department stores, discount chains and specialized stores. The model has been successful because it uses existing technical capabilities and the monthly relationship the company has with its client base. It also combines this competence with external capacities in the physical distribution and marketing of the product offering.

Codensa Hogar results
Since 2001, Codensa Hogar has experienced explosive growth. In its first full year of operation (2002), it extended approximately 8800 individual credits for US$4.6 million. Five years later, in 2007, Codensa had almost 700 000 clients and approved approximately US$280 million in loans (Figure 2.3) (Arbeláez et al., 2007a, 2005, 2006, 2007, 2008a). More than 130 retailers participate in the program. In 2006, the program had proven to be so successful and profitable that Codensa sold a US$40 million tranche of outstanding loans to Citibank (Codensa, 2006).

In 2008, and as a result of the international financial crisis, Codensa Hogar's growth stalled and the portfolio quality deteriorated. The number of clients stabilized but the average loan disbursement decreased almost 25 percent from US$340 to US$240. Loan portfolio quality also weakened. In 2006, the 90-day delinquency ratio was between 1.7 percent and 1.8 percent (Millán, 2007). In 2008 this rate increased to 6.3 percent (Codensa, 2008b). Provisioning for loans in arrears tripled in 2008 as opposed to 2007

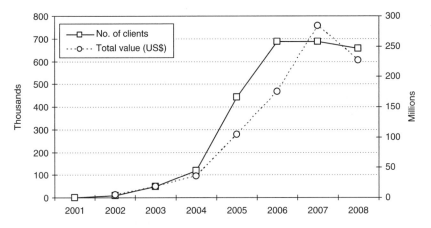

Source: Arbeláez et al. (2007a) and Codensa Annual Reports (2005–08).

Figure 2.3 Codensa Hogar loan portfolio

as a result of worse loan performance and more conservative underwriting and provisioning policies.

Codensa Hogar has had a major impact on access to financial services, appliances and home improvement goods and services for the majority in Bogotá. By 2008, Codensa Hogar was the largest financing source for home appliances in Bogotá, accounting for the financing of 30 percent of all appliances sold in Bogotá, and it was equal to more than 20 percent of the consumer loan portfolio of the largest bank in Colombia (*Revista Dinero*, 2009). In just seven years, the number of Codensa Hogar customers was approximately equal to all of the microcredit customers in Colombia and 4.5 times the number of customers in Bogotá (Asobancaria, 2008b).[3]

The Codensa Hogar program has also had a major impact on access to microinsurance products. As mentioned above, these products are provided through a strategic alliance with the insurance company MAPFRE. Between 2001 and September 2008, MAPFRE sold almost half a million microinsurance policies covering over 1 million customers. Over 70 percent of the policies were active in September 2008 (MAPRE, 2008). More than 90 percent of the policies were issued to the poorest three strata of the population (Figure 2.4).

The Codensa Hogar program (Arbeláez et al., 2007a, 2007b) has had a significant social impact on the poor in Bogotá (Figure 2.5 a, b, c). The average client has a median income of US$350 per month, 15 percent earn below the minimum salary, 95 percent of clients belong to lower income

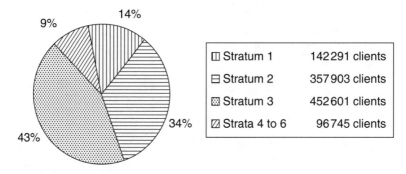

▥ Stratum 1	142 291 clients
▤ Stratum 2	357 903 clients
▨ Stratum 3	452 601 clients
▨ Strata 4 to 6	96 745 clients

Source: MAPFRE (2008).

Figure 2.4   Microinsurance through Codensa Hogar (2007)

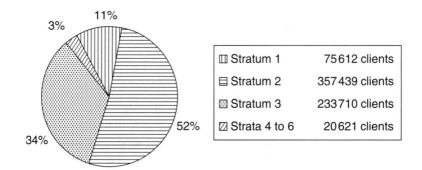

▥ Stratum 1	75 612 clients
▤ Stratum 2	357 439 clients
▨ Stratum 3	233 710 clients
▨ Strata 4 to 6	20 621 clients

Sources: Arbeláez et al. (2007a), Codensa (2008b).

Figure 2.5a   Codensa Hogar client base by social strata (2007)

levels (strata 1–3 out of 6), two-thirds were previously 'unbanked', and 87 percent have no college degree. The program accelerated access to banking services, since over 45 percent of the previously unbanked purchased other financial services, with a 60 percent probability of getting a second line of credit. It also reduced vulnerability to poverty by allowing this segment to accumulate assets and smooth out cash flows, and improved quality of life by providing access to durable goods which can significantly save time or increase income (washing machines), allowed purchases of lower-priced bulk items (fridges), and be a source of information and entertainment (TVs and computers).

A program such as Codensa Hogar improves the living conditions and the net incomes of low-income consumers in four distinct ways. First,

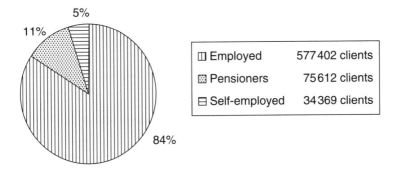

⊞ Employed	577402 clients
⊠ Pensioners	75612 clients
⊟ Self-employed	34369 clients

Source: Arbeláez et al. (2007a), Codensa (2008b).

Figure 2.5b   Codensa Hogar client base by employment status (2007)

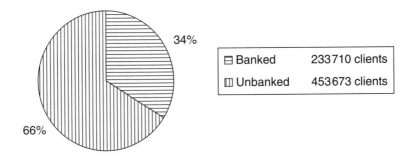

⊟ Banked	233710 clients
⊞ Unbanked	453673 clients

Source: Arbeláez et al. (2007a), Codensa (2008b).

Figure 2.5c   Codensa Hogar client base by banked status (2007)

it provides access to cheaper credit services at competitive market rates
to the poor. In Colombia, this unbanked population currently pays 70
percent to 270 percent effective interest rates in financing appliances and
other products in the informal markets, as opposed to the market rates
that Codensa charges.[4] Access to the Codensa Hogar program represents
savings on monthly payments of almost 16 percent of the minimum salary
for low-income consumers. In addition, it has provided financial services
to over 700000 previously 'unbanked' poor and increased their probability of accessing a second credit or opening a savings account. This scale
is only possible because Codensa, by leveraging and using good utility
payment histories of its massive client base, overcomes one of the main
obstacles to standard market-based microcredit programs: reliable individual credit histories. In just eight years (2001–08) one utility has served

more clients, with lower costs, than all microcredit institutions in the city together. In doing so, it has introduced a disruptive new business model that threatens the traditional microcredit business model (Christensen, 1997).

Additionally, lower-income segments have limited access to modern energy-efficient appliances. Old appliances are expensive to operate and are energy-inefficient. Replacing old appliances represents an opportunity to lower living costs significantly for the poor. Moreover, in the poorest segments, access to a new appliance can represent significant savings in time devoted to house chores (such as washing dirty clothes), and in the availability of fresh and healthier foods.

Finally, access to housing with good-quality characteristics and attributes (cement, tile floors or tiled bathrooms, for example) has two important effects on the poor: immediate positive impact on health and well-being, and improved medium-term asset accumulation and income generation potential. According to a recent study (Cattaneo et al., 2007) housing quality is critical for people's well-being, health and welfare. Replacing dirt floors significantly improves the health of young children by reducing the risk of parasitic infestations, anemia and diarrhea. As a result of healthier environments, permanent flooring is associated with a 36 percent increase in children's cognitive standardized tests. Regarding asset accumulation and income generation potential, housing is typically the main asset for lower-income segments. In the case of Bogotá, we estimated that a 1 percent increase in a housing quality index results in a 1.6 percent increase in asset value and a corresponding increase in potential rents. Furthermore, we have estimated that, in Colombia, households with a covered floor or remodeled bathrooms and kitchens experience a 15–20 percent increase in asset value.[5]

BEYOND CODENSA

By 2004, three years after its launch, the Codensa Hogar business model had shown that a utility can profitably leverage underused assets (the underlying payment information in its client base), while generating significant social and economic value to its various stakeholders, particularly the majority population. Five years later in 2009, there were least 14 similar programs in Colombia. These programs served 48 percent of the total urban population in the country, as shown in Table 2.1.

Most of these businesses followed Codensa's business model closely. In some cases, adjustments were made to further leverage existing capacities or to lower operational costs. Three innovations are particularly relevant.

Table 2.1 Utility credit programs in Colombia, 2009

Company	Program name	City	Start date	Population
Codensa	Hogar	Bogotá	2001	6 778 691
Electrificadora de Santander (ESSA)	ESSA	Bucaramanga	2005	509 918
Aguas de Manizales	Compractico	Manizales	2005	368 433
EDATEL	Cred1UNO	Apartadó, Turbo, Carepa and Chigorodó	2005	359 243
EPSA	Crédito Positivo	Popayán	2005	258 653
EBSA	EBSA es Hogar	Tunja	2005	152 419
Central Hidroeléctrica de Caldas (CHEC)	Pagos por cuotas	Caldas	2005	68 157
Promigas				
Gases de Occidente	Brilla	Cali	2007	2 075 380
Surtigas	Brilla	Barranquilla	2007	1 112 889
Gases del Caribe	Brilla	Cartagena	2007	895 400
EPM	Financiación Social	Medellín	2008	2 219 861
Electrificadora del Meta (EMSA)	EMSA Servicios	Villavicencio	2008	384 131
Total population covered				15 183 175

First, thanks to the Brilla program (see Table 2.1) Promigas strengthened the potential credit quality of the loan portfolio by bringing performance criteria from its own low-income residential gas connection financing facility, which had been operational for years. This allowed Promigas to go beyond clients in the formal sector and reach the informal client base, as it relied not only on credit scoring methodologies which apply only in formal labor market settings, but also on its own loan performance in the informal segment. By 2008, Promigas had extended loans totaling US$90 million to 270 450 clients with an average loan total of US$330 (Promigas, 2008). More than three-quarters of its client base belong to strata 1–3.

The second group of innovations involves the Financiación Social model introduced in 2008 by Empresas Públicas de Medellín (EPM). EPM, the second-largest utility in the country, decided to keep in-house critical credit decisions, but outsourced practically all of the financial and operational aspects of the credit origination, underwriting and disbursement processes. Although credit collections payments were kept in the utility bills, thus leveraging EPM's billing competence, the specific line item for the credit is kept separate in order to allow the customer to pay either or both. While Codensa, or Promigas, financed this operation directly from their balance sheet, EPM decided to structure it in an off-balance sheet vehicle, called *fideicomiso* (trust fund) and thus not directly affecting EPM's financial statements.

This trust fund was capitalized with an initial outlay from EPM and its subsidiary EPM-UNE and is treated as an investment in EPM's balance sheet. The trust returns are expected to be reinvested in deepening the program in lower-income segments. The trust is managed by a trustee consisting of two of Colombia's leading banks. This trust, in turn, contracted out the operational cycles of the credit origination and underwriting processes with a five-company alliance that includes: (1) the leading credit bureau, which is responsible for scoring and credit limits; (2) an information technology (IT) company responsible for integrating the technological backbone of all processes and the digitalization of all records; (3) the payments network (ATMs and POS systems) responsible for monitoring credit use, quotas and routing transactions; (4) the physical production of plastic credit cards; and (5) a leading law firm responsible for collections in delinquent accounts. By unbundling all of these processes, EPM retained control of critical processes in which it has a competence or in which it has reputational risks, such as initial client screening, the use of its communications networks and the billing cycle itself. The card can be used in a wide array of commercial 'allies' which include the biggest retailers in the area, thus leveraging economies of scale in purchases.

The third and final innovation is related to some of the smaller utilities in the country. In order to reap economies of scale in the financial and operational structure of their credit operations, they share a common financing vehicle and many operational tasks are performed by a common operator.

OTHER POTENTIAL PLATFORMS

Existing platforms, such as those provided by utilities or logistics companies, and even NGOs, can also be used as a launching pad to provide additional goods and services that serve the needs of the majority. Different platforms have unique characteristics that differentiate the competencies which may be leveraged when targeting low-income communities. Table 2.2 presents some examples.

One of the most important platforms by size and relevance are those of Conditional Cash Transfer (CCT) programs. CCT programs are a

Table 2.2   Platform possibilities for utilities

Platforms	Defining characteristics to be leveraged	Some key additional services and synergies with core competence	Some examples
Energy distribution utilities	Extended urban presence, billings and collections, client knowledge	Microinsurance, small consumer loans and microcredit	Codensa, Promigas, EPM
Conditional cash transfer programs	Capillarity and credibility among the poor with targeted subsidies, sophisticated logistical and information systems	Financial products, connectivity and information for underserved markets	Financial services in Familias en Acción in Colombia
Logistics companies	Capillarity among the poor thanks to collection and delivery points	Generation of purchase and payment history	Servientrega
Internal distribution networks	Ownership of the platform and decision about other stakeholders that may be included	Full control of scalability process. Enables appropriation of loyalty programs	Lojas in Doutores da Construção, Construya in Argos hardware stores
Direct distribution networks		Local information owned by sales network, often women ('consultants'or 'promoters'). Better education about product use and benefits	Natura, Belcor
Microfinance organizations	Microfinance technology with extensive networks and reach	Health and nutritional access	Grameen Danone in Bangladesh
NGOs and unions	Strong legitimacy in specific market segments	Health services, education and training	Salud a su alcance – Guatamala

powerful public policy weapon against poverty (Fiszbein and Schady, 2009). In Latin America, the region where these programs are most popular, it is estimated that they have benefited more than 15 million poor families and over 60 million low-income people. CCT programs have also generated between 7 percent and 25 percent increases in per capita consumption and improved child nutrition, health and school attendance. There is also ample evidence, particularly from randomized experiments, that CCTs have been very effective in improving health and educational long-term outcomes, as well as long-term living standards. For instance, Gertler et al. (2006) have estimated that five years after the subsidy, poor households were able to increase long-term consumption by more than 30 percent.

Many of these programs have been effective in developing sophisticated logistical and information systems for monitoring and informational purposes. In spite of the fact that some systems have introduced cheaper logistics with smart cards or mobile platforms, very little attention has been paid to how to leverage the impressive reach of CCT programs in providing additional value to low-income populations using market-based solutions. There is a lingering opportunity for the private sector to implement new distribution models or adapt successful external ones, thus taking advantage of their outstanding capillarity. Even when the subsidies are successfully disbursed, low-income communities still face high prices due to informality and lack of competition in local markets. This poverty penalty represents an additional option for the private sector to complement and leverage CCT programs offering cheaper goods and services alongside their subsidies.

Large logistics companies provide a similar opportunity based on the phenomenal capillarity of their platform that includes a wide array of collection and delivery points on which their daily operations depend. The defining characteristic of this platform lies in the type of information it generates about the customer. While CCT programs categorize the recipients on their income and so may enable a better fit between the type of private sector offering and the final customer, logistics companies accumulate information about the purchase and payment history of each individual customer. This second type of information can be very useful for private sector entrants in deciding customer trustworthiness and hence offering different types of financing options when marketing their products. This is the case, for instance, of Servientrega, a Colombian logistics company which handles approximately 1 billion packages per year, 40 percent of the package delivery market in the country. Servientrega has over 2000 microfranchises in its package-letter distribution network and an integrated information system that allows it to track live package routing. Servientrega holds a massive amount of payment and purchase information on its millions of costumers, and this can serve as a platform to introduce additional services to this clientele.

Company internal distribution networks can also be important platforms in their own right. The major advantage, when scaling up internal networks, is that the owning firm can take a driving seat in the expansion of products offered and fully control the scalability process. Being the player in control of the platform allows the firm to decide which other economic agents may or may not be included in the selling effort. For instance, it may decide to enroll the help of a financial institution to manage credits or installments better, as Argos, a Colombian cement firm, has done in its program Construyá. Additionally, having controlling ownership of the platform is pivotal in developing loyalty programs that may secure a portion of the targeted market. In this line, Doutores da Construção, a Brazilian alliance between construction companies and hardware providers and distributors, has managed significantly to increase sales and improve customer loyalty, by providing free certified technical training targeted at low-income construction workers in the hardware stores that participate in the program.

Massive distribution networks share many of the advantages of internal distribution systems. However, this type of network is much more geared to scalability than loyalty. For instance, in Latin America the Brazilian cosmetics company Natura and the Peruvian firm Belcorp have over 1 million and over 600000 saleswomen, respectively. Massive distribution networks often outsource a big portion of the final distribution or marketing stages to local agents which are usually in charge of offering the product to the final customer and collecting payments. In the scaling-up and effectiveness of these platforms women, as both customers and sellers, play an essential role. As customers they represent the entry gate to the household for many products. As sellers (or 'consultants' or 'promoters' as they are often called) they benefit from extensive informal knowledge about the purchasing power and reliability of the target market. The trust that the community has in 'one of their own' also allows these saleswomen to educate potential customers on the appropriate use of the product as well as the benefits derived from its consumption. Furthermore, they may provide useful suggestions in the process of improving the product or offering additional products and services to existing customers. In addition, the women that participate as promoters and salespeople themselves provide a largely untapped market for added value and services.

Microfinance as a platform is probably not as extensive as those belonging to utilities, but it certainly has distinctive advantages. First, it typically reaches poorer areas where utility grids do not exist, and so these and the platforms mentioned above may be complementary. Second, the platform is extremely flexible and evolves on the basis of the changing production and distribution of products. Third, it lends the support and legitimacy of a tried and tested business model that serves the poor while being financially sustainable. These three characteristics position microfinance platforms as an excellent partner to stimulate access to basic goods and services such as health and nutrition products. One of the leading pioneers in microfinance services, Grameen Bank, went down this road in 2006 by partnering with Danone to offer a special yogurt made of pure full cream milk with protein, vitamins, iron, calcium and zinc to fulfill the nutritional requirements of children of Bangladesh. The second generation of microfinance institutions goes beyond microfinance and is starting to provide access to health or educational services as an add-on or embedded in the microfinance product.

CONCLUDING REMARKS

Leveraging and developing platforms is clearly a promising avenue in providing access on a massive scale to goods and services in markets for those 4 billion unserved people that comprise the majority of the population of the world (Hammond et al., 2007). How do you reach these 4 billion potential customers and producers? How can you leverage a platform encompassing millions of poor customers into a proposition that can enhance your permanent competitive advantage? These challenges and dilemmas are similar to those faced by businesses in the last 200 years. As Peter Drucker (1994) says, missing critical opportunities is at the very essence of business history. These challenges also concern utilities, as they are particularly well positioned to leverage their client base and capillarity in the BOP, but face challenges in building new businesses and services in the BOP.

The first challenge for a utility developing a new and profitable business model in low-income populations is the need to adapt to BOP income streams, consumption patterns and price points. Utilities are a natural platform for credit services leveraging their collection and billings capacities. Typically, the utility billing cycle is monthly and credit collections are layered on this cycle. This has limited the scope of these microcredit programs to formally employed poor populations, excluding the informal (Arbelaez et al., 2007a). Income patterns in the informal sectors are typically unpredictable and irregular and customers face frequent cash constraints. In order to bridge this potentially devastating gap, the poor tap into informal credit markets whose financial instruments and products are adapted to this cash-constrained irregular economy. Evidence suggests that the poor use many of these instruments simultaneously (Collins et al., 2009), including family, friends, and savings and loan clubs. With most of these informal financial instruments, the poor are able to manage uneven flows since income cycles can be weekly or even daily. Nevertheless, although a daily payment can be perceived as having low impact on every-day cash flow, the effective interest rates are significantly higher than in formal markets, imposing a clear poverty penalty on the BOP.

In other markets, successful BOP strategies have adapted to local con-sumption patterns and lowered price points by using single-use packaging (sachets) and prepaid services, or by developing adaptive credit models. For instance, the Latin American cellphone market has grown from less than 10 million subscribers in 2002 to over 470 million subscribers in 2009[6] with a disruptive business model that introduced prepaid cards, no con-tracts, per-second billing and Internet recharges. This explosive growth can be explained not only by virtue of improved technology, but also by taking into account how this device can provide access to markets and information, thus lowering transaction costs and empowering millions. In the words of Robert Jensen (2007): 'The only sustainable way to end deprivation is to enhance earnings possibilities, with the invisible hand of the market becoming a helping hand to the world's poor.' This disruptive strategy is even extending its reach beyond its own industry. Cellphones are rapidly becoming the platform of choice to reach the poor for the finance industry. Mobile banking may be one of the most powerful means developed since 2000 to stimulate financial inclusion and to lower the cost of remittances. Many utilities can move forward in these informal seg-ments by leveraging their prepaid energy services and linking them with their emerging financial services. This can also be further enhanced by the use of mobile technology, which is increasingly used in prepaid utilities. The combination of mobile technology, the utility's massive customer base and prepaid systems is an opportunity yet to be explored.

The second challenge for a utility in providing non-energy services in low-income sectors is that success is very often contingent on a detailed understanding of the needs, characteristics and constraints faced by low-income customers. Often highly scalable product innovations can be unearthed by working together with communities in the search for a product that strongly fits their requirements, and can in turn represent a significant competitive advantage against possible entrants. Most utili-ties have significant presence in the communities, far beyond billing and collections, with maintenance, repairs and service installation work being done with local capabilities. The billing and payment information which the utility is leveraging in order to provide credit can be complemented with this local presence, empowering local communities in regular maintenance work or in involving them in the collections process itself, lowering costs. Furthermore, strategic alliances can be forged with local organizations in the development of these new products which generate fidelity and loyalty to the brand. This can only be undertaken if there is a deep common understanding and trust. This is the case, for example, of Gas Natural-Ban in Buenos Aires, which provides microcredit for gas residential installations with a close alliance with local NGOs, which helps organize demand and participate in the billing process, thus generating credibility in the process. Staying close to the customer, offering value-added and maintaining a continuous local presence can be prerequisites for a successful business model in very low-income areas.

The third challenge is a reputational one. In all countries, the provision of financial services, particularly for the poor, is strictly regulated and supervised by specialized government financial entities. This regulatory and supervisory framework serves two purposes. First, it protects individual financial institutions from excessive leveraging and credit risk exposure and positions with prudential regulations. Second, it protects individual consumers from predatory financial practices. In Colombia, utilities such as Codensa or EPM do not fall under the purview of the financial supervisory bodies as they do not receive deposits from the public and their credit services are provided by private-label credit cards. They are therefore not required to follow the prudential rules that apply in the financial system in areas such as provisioning and the writing-off of bad debts. To date, they have nevertheless voluntarily applied these rules recognizing both the business and reputational risks of overleveraging poor clients. Utilities that recognize the opportunity in leveraging their platforms into credit services have to understand these reputational and business risks, and operate within the applicable local prudential and financial regulations. Doing otherwise can very easily unravel into charges of unfair competition and socially irresponsible behavior.

The final challenge is that utilities might be perceived, internally and externally, as entering BOP markets in services that are not strictly related to their core product, energy. Nevertheless, in providing credit services, utilities are leveraging core competencies: their massive customer data payment information, and their billing and collection systems and processes. By leveraging this core competence, and providing access to otherwise unavailable financial services, utilities are not only contributing to the perceived value of the end product but unlocking a new business opportunity which can be extremely hard to imitate. This opportunity can become not only an additional income stream, but also a potentially significant source of customer loyalty and social impact.

NOTES

1. In drafting this chapter, I have greatly benefited from discussions with the organizers and participants in the Utilities at the Base of the Pyramid Research Workshop which took place at the University of the San Diego School of Business Administration in May 2008, particularly Carlos Rufín, Patricia Márquez and Jaime Millán. Maria Angélica Arbeláez from Fedesarrollo provided invaluable access to her research data on Codensa Hogar. I have also benefitted greatly from many discussions with my colleagues at the Inter-American Development Bank (IDB), particularly at its Opportunities for the Majority Office. This chapter would not have been possible without the resourceful and outstanding research assistance of Manuel Bueno, one of our 2009 summer interns. The views expressed in this chapter do not necessarily reflect those of the IDB. The material presented here represents my individual views and all errors are mine.
2. The proportion of households living below the poverty line is estimated as those that cannot afford a minimum basket of goods and services as established in the national survey of household income and expenditures as defined by the Colombian National Statistics Office (DANE).
3. This number does not include microfinance institutions not supervised by the Superintendencia Financiera de Colombia.
4. Interest rates in consumer loans are tightly regulated and capped in Colombia by the regulatory body Superintendencia Financiera de Colombia.
5. Internal IDB calculations based on the Sociometro database.
6. Source: GSMA Mobile Infolink Statistics.

3. The innovative use of mobile telephony in the Philippines: lessons for Africa

Shawn Mendes

In recent years there has been a growing realization of the critical role that information and communication technology (ICT) plays in development. Much of the focus of the role of ICT in development was traditionally on increasing the access to computers and to fixed-line telephones for people in developing countries, often through regional tele- and IT centres. However, these efforts have almost been overrun by the explosive growth of mobile telephony in many countries. Indeed, mobile phones are now the primary form of telecommunication in developing countries and they play the same role that fixed-line phone networks did in facilitating growth in Europe and North America in the twentieth century.

In developing countries a generation of people have grown up without computers and their creative energies have instead been focused on using mobile phones for communications, information and, more recently, access to a range of services from m-banking to m-education and m-governance. The transformation of society by mobile telephony, and especially mobile applications, is perhaps most profound in the Philippines, which makes it worthwhile to examine the Philippine experience further and identify best practices and lessons learned.

BACKGROUND

Access to financial and other basic services in many developing countries is limited, especially in rural and remote areas. Consequently, many do not have access to banking services and are forced to make all payments in cash, which is less secure and flexible than electronic payment forms. The Consultative Group to Assist the Poor (CGAP) estimates that almost 3 billion poor people lack access to the basic financial services essential for them to manage their lives. However, in the Philippines millions of people are now able to conduct basic banking tasks (for example, funds transfers between individuals, small purchases, payment of certain fees, and so on) via mobile networks (infoDev, 2006).

The fact that so many people in developing countries lack access to financial and other services, coupled with the dramatic growth of mobile phone access through most of the developing world, provides an opportunity to reach hundreds of millions of people currently outside the banking system. The costs of mobile telephony have dropped steadily, coverage has expanded and mobile phone subscriptions in developing countries have increased by over 500 per cent between 2000 and 2007 (Wireless Intelligence, 2007).

In the Global System for Mobile Communications Association's (GSMA) recent report on achieving universal access, it was found that mobile networks covered 80 per cent of the world population at the end of 2006, up from 40 per cent in 2000. This is mainly due to investments, which both respond to and drive consumer demand and typically generate profits, by mobile operators and the liberalization of telecom markets by governments. By 2010, 90 per cent of the world will be covered by mobile networks and the Association projects that mobile communication will deliver voice, data and Internet services to more than 5 billion people by 2015 – double the number connected today (GSMA, 2007).

The number of mobile phone subscribers will rise to 4 billion by 2010, thanks partly to the development of ultra-low-cost handsets to meet the demand from new subscribers in developing countries (PC World, 2006). The ultra-low-cost initiative started in 2005 as a way to connect people to existing networks. The GSMA launched the initiative after analyzing the extent of network coverage and determining that over 1 billion more people would use mobile networks if they could afford handsets. To support this, the GSMA challenged handset makers to design a phone in 2005 that would cost under US$30. This challenge was met and the GMSA launched a new contest to halve the price of mobile handsets again – to US$15 – by 2008. Another factor driving mobile phone prices down is the market for used phones in developing countries. In particular, older models exchanged for new ones with contract renewals in both developed and developing countries find their way to markets in the developing world at relatively low prices.

The availability of cheaper handsets will likely fuel mobile expansion among even poorer groups. This may, in turn, generate economic growth according to recent analyses, which find that increased access to mobile phones drives economic growth in developing countries. Research in China, India and the Philippines by McKinsey & Co. found that raising wireless penetration by 10 per cent can lead to an increase in gross domestic product of about 0.5 per cent. 'There's enormous entrepreneurship and creativity worldwide, and through mobile phones you're providing people with the tools – rather than aid – to earn a living', says Leonard Waverman whose study of 92 countries had findings similar to McKinsey's report (*Globe and Mail*, 2007).

THE POTENTIAL OF M-COMMERCE

The explosive growth of mobile phones offers an opportunity to extend banking and other services to millions of 'unbanked' and unserved. Over 60 per cent of the world's 3 billion mobile users live in developing countries and hundreds of millions of them do not have access to banking and other services. Conducting transactions with a mobile phone is often much cheaper than processing the same transaction at a bank, if a bank is even available. A recent report commissioned by the Information for Development Program (infoDev) finds that the use of mobile communications in developing countries has the potential to bring a range of financial services to previously excluded groups. The report examines the use of mobiles for payments in the Philippines, known for its intensive and widespread use of SMS,[1] and concludes that mobile-enabled financial services, or m-banking, can address a major service gap in developing countries that is critical to social and economic development (infoDev, 2006). The experience in the Philippines demonstrates that m-banking brings advantages to all stakeholders:

- For users: an opportunity to become engaged in the formal banking sector, facilitate and reduce the costs of remittances, and enable financial transactions without the costs and risks associated with the use of cash, including theft and travel to pay in person.
- For operators: an increase in SMS revenues and a drop in customer churn.
- For consumers: m-commerce is more secure and flexible than cash, allowing consumers to make payments remotely.
- For banks: an increase in customer reach and added cash float.
- For retailers: added business opportunities through the sale of prepaid account credits.
- For microfinance institutions: the ability to advance funds into remote areas and have regular repayments that do not inconvenience the user.
- For service industries and utilities: the ability to get payments electronically from a significant portion of the population (infoDev, 2006).

Given the experience the Philippines has had in extending, via mobile telephony, financial and other services to people traditionally excluded, there is a need to identify the underlining factors behind, and current reality of, m-banking and similar services in the country. This experience and some lessons learned from it are detailed on the following pages.

M-COMMERCE IN THE PHILIPPINES

The Philippines is the 'texting' capital of the world, known for deposing a president using SMS, and is ranked as the most SMS-intensive country in the world[2] (Wireless Intelligence, 2007). The use of SMS as a means of conducting m-commerce also originated in the Philippines, starting with the innovation of passing mobile phone airtime credits among subscribers in exchange for services (Lallana, 2004) and the development of 'mobile currencies' like G-Cash and Smart Money that are now used for more formal financial services, among them microfinance (Soriano and Barbin, 2007; Porteous and Wishart, 2006). Given this, there is growing interest in understanding how this phenomenon emerged (Lallana, 2004; Pertierra, 2004; Soriano and Barbin, 2007; Umali and Alampay, 2007; Porteous and Wishart, 2006; Proenza, 2007) and interest in identifying best practices and lessons that other countries can build upon.

To understand the success of mobile applications such as m-banking in the Philippines requires understanding the context of the entire telecommunications industry and the policies that surround it. It also requires understanding the role of technology in making this possible. As such, this chapter:

1. examines relevant telecommunications policies in the Philippines that contributed to access to information and communication technologies since the 1990s, especially the rapid growth in mobile phone access, and the factors that helped its expansion to the poor;
2. reviews mobile applications that have been developed in recent years in the Philippines with special emphasis on m-commerce; and
3. considers the implications of these developments in other situations and contexts, such as in Africa.

HISTORY OF ICTS IN THE PHILIPPINES

The increase in access to information and communication technologies in the Philippines has been influenced by government policies, corporate strategies and changes in technologies. Government policies include the establishment of its own network of public calling offices and, most importantly, the opening of the market for more telecommunication providers, which led to greater competition and spurred innovation to expand the market, and an increased variety of services offered. Further, many of these strategies would not have been possible had the technology not been present to allow the rapid roll-out of wireless services, thereby making the local telecommunications market truly competitive. In a way, these three factors converging at the right moment in time were crucial to the growth of access in the Philippines (Alampay et al., 2003).

POLICY FRAMEWORK

The 1987 Philippine Constitution recognizes 'the vital role of communications and information in nation-building'. This role can be best contextualized by considering how the country is composed of over 7000 islands, millions of overseas Filipino workers and one of the world's major players in the call centre and business process outsourcing industry. Information and communication technologies, as such, play a crucial role in linking Filipinos across the archipelago, linking their families around the world, and providing crucial support services to companies from different nations.

Telecommunications services in the Philippines had historically been provided by a private monopoly until the early 1990s, the Philippine Long Distance Telephone Company (PLDT). This was also complemented by a government backbone that provided limited services to underserved regions in the country. In 1990, the government's National Telecommunications Development Plan (1990–2010) sought to divest the state of its role in the delivery of telecommunications services through privatization and more competition. At the same time, the plan was for government to continue facilitating official development assistance for telecom projects in underserved and economically unviable areas (Abrenica, 2000: 150).

In 1995, the 'Public Telecommunications Policy Act of the Philippines' reiterated the policy of competition and the promotion of universal service in the country by saying that: 'the expansion of the telecommunications network shall give priority to improving and expanding basic services to areas not yet served . . . at affordable rates' (Philippine Congress, 1995). The Act also mentioned that only telecommunication entities were allowed to offer 'telecommunication services', which became a contentious issue years later, when new technologies that could deliver the same service were developed (for example, Voice over Internet Protocol).

The Medium Term Philippine Development Plan (2001–04) reflects the changes in universal access targets since the early 1990s. It also refers to new indicators of access to ICTs, such as the provision of high-speed, broadband transmission services in all cities; the installation of telecentres in all municipalities; availability of cellular mobile telephone service to all major highways and corridors connecting provincial capitals and cities; and the provision of public telephone service in all *barangays*.

The country's highest policy-making body for ICT, the ITECC (now CICT),[3] launched the ICT Strategic Roadmap in 2003. It outlined the strategic direction and identified critical projects needed to push information infrastructure development, electronic governance, e-business development, and human capital development in the country. The Roadmap was updated with the issuance of the Philippine ICT Roadmap 2006–2010, which re-emphasized that all citizens must have basic access to government services, information and quality education through appropriate and affordable ICTs. While the current Roadmap notes the outstanding increase in mobile telephone subscription over the years, it does not identify particular directions nor projects to support the utilization of mobile technologies for delivering government services, or spurring mobile commerce.

The liberalization of the Philippines telecommunications industry to competition was a critical point in increasing access to voice services. However, it should be qualified that real competition occurred with the emergence of more affordable cellular/mobile services, and not so much due to the competition provided by other landline providers.

GROWTH IN ICT ACCESS

The number of landlines and subscribers grew significantly between 1992 and 2002, from 744000 lines to 6.9 million. Landline subscriptions also grew in that span from 0.66 million to 3.3 million. From a landline telephone density of less than one (0.9) per 100 in 1990, it peaked at 9.1 per 100 in 1999 but then fell to 7.8 per 100 in 2005. This implies that population growth outstripped the pace of phone line installation during the period (see Table 3.1).

It is important to note that higher teledensity does not automatically mean that access has improved in unserved and underserved areas, because installed landline capacity is still concentrated in urban centres. For instance, in 2002, the national capital region (NCR) had 41 per cent of all installed telephone landlines and 51 per cent of all subscribers but only 14 per cent of the population (NTC, 2003), which clearly shows how services tend to be skewed towards urban regions.

Table 3.1   Philippine landline telephone density (1990–2005)

Year	Landlines (millions)	Subscribers (millions)	Population* (millions)	Teledensity†
1990	–	–	60.7	0.91
1992	0.74	0.66	61	1.17
1994	–	1.11	–	1.67
1996	3.35	1.79	–	4.66
1998	6.64	2.51	73.1	9.08
2000	6.90	3.06	76.3	9.05
2002#	6.91	3.31	79.5	8.70
2005**	6.54	3.37	84.2	7.76

Source: *NSCB (2001). †Alampay (n.d.) (lines per 100 people). # NTC (2003). **NTC (2006).

Teledensity data, however, are somewhat misleading because the number of available lines could increase even though the number of people using or subscribing to them does not grow. In fact, less than half of the 6.9 million landlines available in 2002 were subscribed. This implies that phones may not have been placed in areas where people could access them; or were placed in areas where there was already an oversupply (that is, the national capital region); or they may not have as much use or demand for them as previously thought (Minges et al., 2002).

PUBLIC ACCESS: PCO SERVICE/TELECENTRES AND PAYPHONES

There are two primary kinds of public access to phones: public calling offices (PCOs) and payphones. The difference between a public calling office and a payphone is that in a public calling office there are operators who can help clients with their calls and receive incoming calls. A public payphone, on the other hand, can be used independently any time of the day, but has no operator to assist customers and cannot ordinarily receive incoming calls. Thus, when deciding the preferred model for providing public access, whether a public calling office or a payphone, it is important to consider the advantages and disadvantages that each option provides. This is in contrast to much of Africa where stand-alone payphones are very rare, and public access is often gained through entrepreneurs selling wireless time on their mobile phones.

By the end of 2002, 96 per cent of all municipalities had public calling offices (NTC, 2007) and the government's target of having public calling offices in every municipality was close to being achieved. However, as with local exchange services, public calling offices also tend to be located in the centre of municipalities (Bongato, 2002). This means that considering the difficult terrain and poor road infrastructure in some areas, having a public calling office in a municipality does not translate into universal access.

The number of payphones rose from 4800 in 1990 to 15 200 by 2002 (Minges et al., 2002). However, available landline telephones for public use are actually more numerous than officially reported because of the practice of enterprising private individuals and private businesses making their phones available for public use for a fixed fee. Nonetheless, even considering this kind of public phone, the actual payphone penetration is still far below the ideal target of two payphones per 1000 recommended by the International Telecommunications Union (ITU).

Lastly, telecentres, like payphones and public calling offices, were also set up to provide community-based communications services. Moreover, telecentres were established to provide not only voice, but also a variety of data services such as fax and Internet access. In 2007 there were over 737 community e-centres established by government and the private sector in various locations such as local government offices, community centres and schools.

CELLULAR/MOBILE COVERAGE

The first cellular mobile phone service, PILTEL, was introduced in 1991 but the current leaders, Smart and GLOBE, entered the market in 1994. In 2003 a third provider, Sun Cellular, entered the market, offering lower-priced unlimited SMS and voice service (NTC, 2007).

As with much of the world, and especially among developing countries, mobile phones in the Philippines already outnumber landlines. In fact, while installed landline capacity declined by 3.7 per cent from 1999 to 2003, the same period saw cellular subscriptions increase eightfold (Umali and Alampay, 2007). By the end of 2005, the National Telecommunications Commission reported that mobile density had reached 41 per cent (NTC, 2007), the most accessible form of ICT in the country after radios and television. Mobile network coverage of major providers reach 99 per cent of the country's population, facilitating a market penetration rate of 60 per cent and household penetration rate of almost 80 per cent.

Mobile teledensity is more than five times the teledensity for landline services (41 cellphone subscribers per 100 people versus 7.76 landline telephones per 100 people) (NTC, 2007). By the end of 2005, there were almost 35 million cellular phone subscribers, up from 56 000 subscribers in

Table 3.2   Cell/mobile phone subscriptions (1992–2005)

Year	Cellular subscribers (millions)
1992	0.06
1994	0.17
1996	0.96
1998	1.73
2000	6.45
2002	15.38
2004	32.93
2005	34.78

Source: NTC (2006), although cellular subscribers may be slightly overstated since one person may own one or more SIM.

1992 (see Table 3.2). By 2007, it was estimated that every second Filipino had a mobile phone.

PHILIPPINES CELLULAR/MOBILE COVERAGE IN A REGIONAL PERSPECTIVE

Similar to most developing countries in Asia and around the world, the Philippines has experienced very rapid growth in mobile penetration. What distinguishes the Philippines from other countries is both the intensity of SMS use and the subsequent development of simple mobile-based applications such as m-banking. In Table 3.3, mobile market penetration in the Philippines is compared to various other Asian countries.

IMPACT OF TECHNOLOGY AND MARKET INNOVATIONS

When the market was opened to more players in the mid-1990s, the state made distinctions between landline services, international gateway facility providers and mobile operators. However, the extent of the competition that new technologies created due to convergence was not anticipated. Technology expanded the reach of telecommunication services and provided people with more alternatives. The choices people made were no longer limited to which form cost less to obtain and use, but rather, which one was most cost-effective based on the lifestyle they maintained. This section discusses how new technologies have helped in the expansion of

Table 3.3   Market penetration in select Asian countries, 2002–08

Market	2002 (%)	2003 (%)	2004 (%)	2005 (%)	2006 (%)	2007 (%)	2008F (%)
China	12.4	16.8	21.0	25.2	29.7	34.9	39.3
India	0.6	1.2	3.1	4.8	8.4	14.9	20.9
Indonesia	3.5	5.7	9.4	14.2	21.9	30.6	36.4
Malaysia	29.4	35.8	46.1	60.9	77.5	76.2	77.6
Papua New Guinea	0.2	0.2	0.3	0.5	0.7	0.9	1.2
Philippines	14.8	20.7	29.6	41.2	42.1	51.6	56.6
Sri Lanka	3.7	5.4	8.2	12.7	19.2	29.6	33.9
Thailand	17.4	31.2	38.3	46.0	51.9	69.4	78.9
Viet Nam	1.9	2.4	4.1	7.2	13.9	19.5	24.1

Note: Calculated data, 2002–07. Forecast data, 2008.

Source: Wireless Intelligence (2007).

access to basic telecommunication services, and how it allowed competition to thrive by giving people a choice among different service providers, how they would pay (prepaid or post-paid), and the manner by which they would communicate (that is, voice or text/SMS).

Expansion

The advantage of wireless technologies over 'landlines' is the cost and ease of network expansion in unserved areas (Hills and Yeh, 1996). Mobile telephony is an attractive alternative where it is difficult to install fixed-line networks because it can be installed more rapidly (Hamilton, 2003). In so doing, it can alleviate waiting time for potential subscribers and reduce unsatisfied demand. In this sense, developments in information technology have helped overcome assumed technological and financial barriers to universal access that prevent the public and private sector from providing services in isolated locations.

While it cannot be denied that competition played a part in the increase in access to ICTs, access would also have not increased without two important innovations that came with the introduction of mobile telephony in the Philippines: SMS and prepayment. SMS is the 'killer application' that helped make the GSM platform dominant in the market, and prepaid cards helped make communicating more affordable to the lower-income strata of the society (Alampay, 2006; Celdran, 2002; Minges et al., 2002). It should also be noted that credit loads (that is, loading calling credits onto a mobile/cellphone) went hand-in-hand with declining costs of the handset.

Short Message Service (SMS)

SMS was originally introduced in 1994 as a free service (Celdran, 2002). Only in 2000 did mobile providers begin charging for SMS use, but partly due to great consumer resistance and pressure, the prices have remained reasonable (Lallana, 2004). SMS allowed people to stretch their telecommunications budget given that it costs less to use than voice calls. The relative low cost of SMS in the Philippines has also helped foster a culture of texting.

It is difficult to overstate the impact of SMS in the Philippines, as evidenced by the sheer volume of messages sent by Filipinos. For example, in 2001, Smart and Piltel was already averaging 50 million text messages a day, six messages per subscriber per day (PLDT, 2002). Four years later, the figure had multiplied five times, with the National Telecommunications Commission (NTC) estimating that the Filipinos exchanged an average of 250 million messages a day in 2005. This shows that while cellular companies started charging for SMS in 2000 and have been reducing free text message allocation to their subscribers, the number of text messages exchanged continues to rise. As a result, text messaging-related services in 2005 amounted to about 45 per cent of Smart and Piltel's cellular revenues (PLDT, 2006a), while it accounted for about 36 per cent of Globe's wireless revenues.

This increase in use of text messages is also a result of increased competition. With the entry of a third player, Sun Cellular, text messaging reached a high in 2006 when Smart and Globe, following Sun Cellular's lead, issued unlimited text promotions for a low fixed price. By the end of 2006, there were approximately 500 million SMSs per day through Smart Communications (Wireless Intelligence, 2007) and the daily SMS total in the Philippines likely exceeded 1 billion – over ten SMSs per day for every person in the country. SMS remains popular today. A recent report by the GSM Association found that consumers in Asia still prefer text messaging over any other mobile data service (Ho, 2007).

In many developed countries the cost to send an SMS is equal to one minute of voice airtime (that is, a ratio of 1 to 1). In the Philippines the ratio is 6.5 SMS for every minute of voice calling. Therefore, it is possible that SMS intensity in the Philippines is more geared to pricing than to cultural factors, which suggests the experience could be replicated in other countries where the cost of sending an SMS is much lower than that of making a voice call.

Prepaid Cards

The prepaid option for telecommunications services was originally introduced for cellphones in 1998 (Celdran, 2002). Since then, over 30 million prepaid subscribers have been added and this option helped increase access to owning a cellular line by overcoming previous barriers to ownership. These include having a credit history, the need to go through tedious registration processes, and the whole market structure associated with paying the telephone operator. With prepaid, one simply has to have a cellular phone, secure a SIM card and be able to receive text messages and voice calls, even without credit (for an identified period before the account is activated). Neither identification, proof of credit history nor registration are required to purchase a cellphone and a SIM card. Moreover, SIM cards usually come with free text messages or credit. The new subscriber can then choose from a variety of amounts and promotional packages to load additional credit and start sending text messages.

With prepaid, people can better manage their consumption. They can also buy loads in any convenience store, and this is consistent with the local buying culture of 'tingi,' or incremental small purchases instead of wholesale. This is an important factor in explaining the popularity of prepayment methods in the Philippines and other developing countries. The introduction of prepayment changed the cost–benefit balance and perceived income threshold for consumers by reducing the barriers to universality in a way that traditional landline tariffs never did. Prepaid services made the cost of subscribing to a line cheaper. It also made the communication costs directly related to a person's actual use whereas 'landlines' have a fixed monthly rate regardless of use. The growth in low-cost prepaid services is the most critical factor in the growth of mobile use in the Philippines and other developing countries. It has led to a rapid growth in the market, growth largely driven by the lower-income strata of the population.

The company most dependent on this niche (that is, prepaid customers) in the Philippines is Smart. Indeed, by the end of 2005, 99 per cent of Smart Telecom's 20.4 million subscribers used prepaid (PLDT, 2006b: 36). In 2005, the prepaid segment comprised 96 per cent of Globe Telecom's subscribers, and grew by 27 per cent over 2004 (Globe Telecom, 2007: 19).

Because of its success in the cellphone market, the prepaid option was eventually offered for the landline market in September 2000. For fixed-line prepaid subscribers, PLDT charged Php1 per minute for local calls as opposed to unlimited local calls at fixed monthly charges for post-paid subscribers. However, international and long-distance calls for both prepaid and post-paid fixed line subscribers are charged the same rates (PLDT 2006b).

Despite the fact that mobile/cellphone prepaid cards were relatively inexpensive – originally priced at US$4.63 and US$9.25 and consumable over a two-month period – they were still too expensive for many of the poor. Therefore, another strategy was to provide for electronic loading of smaller prepaid rates that must be used up over shorter time periods (for example, three days to a week). This model of payment facilitated expansion of mobile phones to lower-income groups.

A further enhancement of the strategy to reach even poorer segments was to provide even smaller increments made possible by eLoad/'autoload' (over-the-air – OTA – purchase of credit) and Pasaload/'share-a-load' (over-the-air sharing of credit). Autoload/eLoad are easily available from retailers or microentrepreneurs with small stores located within the neighbourhood selling similar 'sachet' goods and items. Pasaload, on the other hand, refers to over-the-air sharing of credit from subscriber to subscriber within the same network, and is offered by both Smart and Globe. More recently, Globe has issued a promotion called 'Ask-A-Load', which allows a subscriber literally to request via SMS a particular amount of credit from another subscriber, which the latter could then choose to approve or disapprove. In this regard, the exchange of mobile credits, or 'loads', has become a de facto form of microfinance in the Philippines.

However, over-the-air purchases of credit-sharing normally have shorter validity periods. Also, higher-value credits exchanged over the air (that is, $2) do not carry with them the free SMS messages that are loaded for the same amount with prepaid scratch cards. Nonetheless, this scheme has become very popular because it enables the sharing of credit for as low as Php2 ($0.05) from one subscriber to another. Retailers prefer selling higher increments (that is, $0.50–$0.60 and above) in order to generate profit. Subscription to new promotions, such as unlimited text and calls (that is, unlimited SMS for $0.03 per day within the Smart network, $0.04 per day for Globe), are also possible through OTA purchases from retail stores. Two-thirds of Smart's prepaid users were loading credit electronically at the end of 2003 (Proenza, 2007). For Globe, on the other hand, Autoload max accounted for 90 per cent of reload transactions by December 2004 (Proenza, 2007; cited in Globe, 2007).

Clearly SMS and prepaid services have been instrumental in expanding the mobile market to less-affluent Filipinos. This is illustrated by the reduction, attributed to the changing demographic profile of PLDT's subscriber base, in the average revenue per user (ARPU) of PLDT's cellphone services. The most current monthly ARPUs, reported in 2005, are between $5 and $6, with the lowest monthly prepaid tariff for low-usage customers only US$1.24 (PLDT, 2006a; GSMA, 2007). These data suggest that an increasing number of lower-income households are subscribing to cellphones, and their average monthly consumption of services is lowering

Table 3.4   Comparison between fixed and mobile monthly charges

	PLDT fixed residential* (Manila)	Globe Mobile (Gtext)**
Installation fee	US$37	0
Monthly fee***	US$18	US$9
Free minutes	Unlimited	20
Free SMS	0	500

Notes: * From PLDT (2002); ** for this plan you already receive a free cellphone; *** as of 2004.

the ARPU. The ARPU for the prepaid option also shows that households are paying less on a monthly basis with this option compared to having a phone line with monthly fixed rates of approximately US$18 that they may or may not consume in actual services or calls.

New technologies have helped expand people's communication options. To illustrate, residential lines offer the convenience of unlimited minutes on calls to other landline phones, but their installation and monthly fee (see Table 3.4) make the cost prohibitive for many people (Garnham, 1997). These factor into how people choose the kind of ICT to use.

SUMMARY OF FACTORS LEADING TO INCREASE IN TELECOMMUNICATIONS IN THE PHILIPPINES

New government policies on the provision of basic telecommunication services coupled with technological developments since 1993 have helped contribute to the rapid expansion of ICT services in the country. First, higher teledensity has resulted from the early policy initiatives of the government to liberalize the sector by breaking up PLDT's monopoly; introduce more players in the sector; and impose mandatory service obligations to international gateway facility providers and mobile phone operators to roll out telephone lines under the Service Area Scheme (SAS). The notable increase in telephone lines coincided with the period that the SAS was implemented. Despite increased availability of landline services, however, subscription to government and private sector landline services did not grow as projected and regional distribution remained uneven.

Second, new technologies like the cellphone made competition in the industry possible by expanding alternatives for people to consider, helping companies to innovate and offer different payment plans, providing better services and expanding coverage. New services such as SMS and prepaid plans also made using telephones and mobiles more affordable to lower-income households. These two innovations helped push cellphone ownership to exceed both landline subscriptions and teledensity. This was also complemented by lower handset costs (GSMA, 2007) and a second-hand market for mobiles. As such, new technologies and the declining cost to acquire them have made universal access down to the *barangay* level more feasible.

Third, new technologies not only made competition possible in a telephone industry long considered as a 'natural monopoly', but it also led to the issue of whether basic telecommunication service should go beyond just voice to access to other value-added services such as the Internet and other data services like SMS and simple mobile applications, such as e-commerce.

OVERVIEW OF SIMPLE MOBILE APPLICATIONS IN THE PHILIPPINES

The widespread growth of access to mobile phones in the Philippines, coupled with the ubiquitous use of SMS among the population, government, business and non-governmental organizations, has motivated many actors rapidly to develop applications to take advantage of this medium for communication. As shown in Table 3.5, SMS use in the Philippines is very frequent when viewed in a global comparative perspective. Wireless Intelligence's list of reported SMS use per month per user indicates that intensity in the Philippines is more than triple that in the next-highest operator, in Denmark; ten times that of the largest operator in the US; and 20 times that of many operators in other countries.

Four main areas of mobile applications are discussed on the following pages:

1. citizen feedback mechanisms;
2. information dissemination;
3. service delivery; and
4. m-commerce.

Citizen Feedback

Among the first applications developed through SMS were mechanisms for providing citizens with the capability to air their complaints or commendations and requests for assistance. These types of citizen participation through SMS remain popular today. Current variants include citizen reporting of election irregularities (for example, Text COMELEC 2898),

Table 3.5   Global overview of SMS intensity

Rank	Operator	Country	SMS messages per user per month, Q4, 2006
1	Smart	Philippines	1008
2	Piltel	Philippines	446
3	Telia Denmark	Denmark	315
4	Maxis Malaysia	Malaysia	285
5	Movilnet Venezuela	Venezuela	136
6	Verizon Wireless	USA	102
7	O2 UK	UK	97
8	Netcom	Norway	94
9	O2 Ireland	Ireland	87
10	TMN	Portugal	67

Note: This table shows operators where we have data: reported, calculated, estimated or forecast. Some operators are missing from this list because there are no relevant data for them.

Source: Wireless Intelligence (2007).

emergency response (for example, Text 117) and reckless driving (for example, Txt LTFRB Hotline). It is also not only limited to national government agencies, as more and more local government officials provide numbers where their constituents can directly send their messages.

Information Dissemination

The other side of participation through feedback is the provision of information to the people. A commercial application that facilitates this is GiveMeUnlimited, which allows the user to send bulk SMS/text messages to mobile users via computers and the Internet. These kinds of applications are important for services that require quick dissemination of information to a large number of people (that is, in case of emergencies and so on). For example, the Department of Education has DE Text 2622, which provides the general public with announcements and advisories on test schedules, press releases, holiday announcements and the cancellation of classes.

Service Delivery

A convergence of technologies has allowed the mobile phone, through SMS, to become a medium for citizens to access informational databases through both public and private providers of public services. For example, in recent national elections both Smart and GLOBE were able to provide citizens with information about their voting precinct number. This type of information was crucial, as it had been a common complaint in the past that voters were disenfranchised because they did not know where to vote.

Another election-related service was developed by the National Movement for Free Elections (NAMFREL). In the 2004 elections, NAMFREL piloted an SMS-based system for a quick count (the Philippines is notorious for its lengthy national election tallying of votes). As a control measure, three different individuals would send electoral reports, and only when all three sources were in agreement were they tallied. However, while the initial pilot testing went well, its implementation on the national scale was problematic, as the system could not handle the resulting influx of data.

SMS has also been used for some health services. In Pasay City, it has been incorporated in its Community Health Information Tracking System (CHITS) to send clinical reminders. This service enables the staff in health centres to send SMS messages via computer system templates to patients for follow-up and medical intake reminders. It has been targeted for use in three areas: childcare for vaccination follow-ups; maternal care for prenatal follow-ups and anti-tetanus vaccinations; and the National Tuberculosis Program for the directly observed treatment, short course DOTS treatment protocol.

M-commerce

A subset of e-commerce that pertains to mobile ICTs is mobile commerce. Mobile commerce, or m-commerce, refers to the buying and selling of goods and services through wireless hand-held devices.[4] Mobile commerce involves the storage, payment, receiving and sending of 'electronic currency' through the use of mobile phones.

In the Philippines, m-commerce started in 2000 when mobile banking was introduced in the banking system. Mobile banking, or m-banking, refers to conducting bank transactions through wireless handheld devices. These transactions and services may include account balance inquiry, transfer of funds (from one's own account to another account or even between accounts at different banks), payment of credit card bills, water bills and electric bills, and purchase of mobile phone loads charged to a bank account or a credit card.

Prior to the creation of electronic currency for mobile phones, the seeds of m-commerce had already begun with the development of Pasaload, or the capability of individuals to transfer between users load credits (Lallana, 2004). Some non-profit organizations, such as Kerygma, have even expressed interest in exploring the possibility of converting these loads back to currency, thereby raising the possibility of raising donations through m-commerce.

Eventually, the two major mobile phone service providers in the country, Smart Communications and Globe Telecom, developed their respective models for m-commerce: Smart Money and G-Cash.[5] This is significant, because already in 2002 it was reported that 44 per cent of mobile phone users worldwide wanted the capability to use mobile phones for small cash transactions, and yet only 2 per cent had done so (Lallana, 2004).

SMART COMMUNICATION'S SMART MONEY

Smart Communications, in partnership with Banco de Oro, introduced Smart Money in 2000 (Proenza, 2007). It was considered a breakthrough in mobile commerce in the world. Smart Money is a debit card (prepaid card), which can be accessed using an automatic teller machine (ATM), a credit card terminal or a mobile phone. The Smart Money card allows users to withdraw credit or to charge purchases through any MasterCard terminal. It also allows users to conduct transactions using mobile phones such as sending cash credit from a Smart Money account to another person's Smart Money account. Subscribers are informed of their Smart Money transactions through mobile phone either for information or for transaction confirmation. Smart Money is a free[6] service for Smart subscribers, but it requires a minimum of 64K SIM memory.

However, there are several limitations to the uptake of Smart Money, mainly related to the high transaction cost in terms of time and money, as opening a Smart Money account requires going to a Smart Wireless Center, filling in a form and paying a fee for the plastic card. The card, in turn, is received through regular mail after a few weeks. Another barrier to the usage of Smart Money is the limited number of methods to load cash credits into the Smart Money card. There are three ways to load credit to a Smart Money card:

1. through mobile banking – from an enrolled bank account to Smart Money;
2. over the counter – through a Smart Wireless Center cashier; and
3. through Smart Money reloading centers – through merchant partners such as Tambunting Pawnshop and SeaOil Gas Station.

These different modes of loading credit, hand in hand with the Smart Money platform, facilitate its popular services for electronic loading of credit and cash remittance. Today, Smart Money is used between eLoad dealers and their retailers as it allows retailers to buy mobile phone loads from their retailers without needing to meet face to face. It was estimated that at the end of 2006, 20 per cent or 5 million of PLDT's total prepaid customers were registered Smart Money users (Proenza, 2007: 6). Smart Money transactions among these users averaged US$257 200 per day in 2006. In addition, US$28.9 million in remittances through Smart Padala were recorded for the same year.

GLOBE TELECOM'S G-CASH

In October 2004, Globe Telecom introduced G-Cash, an electronic money transfer facility that turns a mobile phone into an electronic wallet with the following services:

1. Purchasing of goods and services over the counter or remotely: G-Cash allows subscribers to pay for goods and services at G-Cash partner merchants using G-Cash. These G-Cash partner merchants can exchange cash into G-Cash ('cash-in') or G-Cash to cash ('cash-out').
2. Sending and receiving of money transfers locally or from abroad: G-Cash allows subscribers to receive domestic and international remittances. To accomplish this transaction, a sender goes to a remittance partner in the Philippines or abroad, fills in a form and gives the remittance to the remittance partner. The remittance partner sends the equivalent peso amount to the recipient in the Philippines. The recipient then receives G-Cash credits in their mobile phone that can be exchanged for money through G-Cash partner merchants.
3. Payment of utility bills and mobile phone airtime credits: G-Cash allows transfer of G-Cash from one subscriber to another. This is also known as P2P transfers, which stands for 'phone-to-phone' transfers or 'person-to-person' transfers. The payment of online purchases through fund transfers via G-Cash is also supported.
4. Other services: a few months after its launch, G-Cash extended its services to allow subscribers to purchase mobile phone load and online gaming credit, purchase Metro Railway Transit (MRT) tickets, payment of school tuition fees, loans and insurance premiums, donate to charities or pay for selected government services.

G-Cash is also used as a wholesale payment facility. As of 31 December 2006, G-Cash handled an average monthly transaction value of Php5.67

billion (US$123 million) and the registered user base of G-cash stood at 500 813 (Globe Telecom, 2007).

Registering for G-Cash is less cumbersome than registering for Smart Money. G-Cash allows registration through a mobile phone and the subscriber only has to submit registration information[7] to '2882', and then go to any partner merchant to exchange money for G-Cash.

COMPARISON OF CASH, G-CASH AND SMART MONEY

Smart Money and G-Cash each have their own pros and cons, depending on the user and their needs. Table 3.6, compares the benefits of using cash, G-Cash and Smart Money.

Both Smart Money and G-Cash services allow subscribers to pay for goods and services. The difference lies in how Smart Money and G-Cash accomplish these transactions. Smart Money utilizes a secure STK[8]-driven and card-based facility that also interfaces with ATMs and MasterCard terminals, while G-Cash utilizes basic SMS technology that can be used by any mobile phone subscriber of Globe.

However, there are also elements common to both Smart Money and G-Cash, which can be regarded as the essential components of m-commerce: value repository, management of currency, credit, debit and security.

Value Repository

M-commerce's electronic currency requires storage to ensure security. The storage of value or currency does not reside in the subscribers' mobile phones or in SIM cards. Instead, the electronic currency of an m-commerce user is stored in the telecommunications company's database (that is, the 'telcos' keep a record, or account, of the amount of electronic currency users have).[9] Therefore, even if a mobile phone or SIM card is lost or damaged, the funds value is retained.

Management of Currency

In a traditional (that is, non-electronic) commerce transaction, management of currency refers to the physical handling of cash. A person takes money from their wallet and hands the money to a seller in exchange for a product or service. M-commerce allows the user to manage their electronic currency with the use of the mobile phone. The user utilizes their mobile phone to check the amount of electronic currency available (balance

Table 3.6   Comparison of the elements and benefits of cash, G-Cash and Smart Money

Criteria	Cash	G-Cash	Smart Money
Customer sign-up	Not needed	• registration is required to activate account, over the air activation is possible • no charge for initial registration • initial cash deposit not needed but necessary before transactions can be made	• go to Smart centre to sign up for the service • may involve SIM change • initial cash deposit not required, but cash balance needed to be able to make purchases and withdrawals • optional debit card for Php220
Identification	n/a	• formal/acceptable IDs required for cash deposits and withdrawals as per Central Bank policy	• formal/acceptable IDs required for cash deposits and withdrawals as per Central Bank policy
Current usage	100%	• limited • estimated 30% Globe penetration among rural poor • faster growth in user base • 1.3 million registered G-Cash users; approx. Php3 million daily • 400 accredited partners, 3000+ outlets; also available in 16 countries	• limited • estimated 70% Smart penetration among rural poor • almost flat growth in user base • 3 million registered Smart Money subscribers
Liquidity	100 % liquid – use it anywhere	• low – need to go to Globe and other merchants to use it or to convert it to cash (cash-out) • use it for P2P (person-to-person) transactions	• moderate – use it at Megalink and ExpressNet ATMs • use it at any MasterCard terminal • use it for P2P transactions

Table 3.6   (continued)

Criteria	Cash	G-Cash	Smart Money
Security	As secure as your wallet	• uses an m-PIN in the message body of an SMS message; it is in clear view • m-PIN needs to be erased from the mobile phone to ensure that a lost/snatched mobile phone does not have the m-PIN in the SMS messages archive	• uses an STK menu where the m-PIN is never in clear view • uses encryption when sending transaction commands

Sources: Adapted from Soriano and Barbin (2007); and updated from Porteous and Wishart (2006).

inquiry), to pay for products and services and to send or receive electronic currency. After each m-commerce transaction, the user receives an SMS message stating information about the transaction and the user's balance.

Both Globe and Smart allow users to access their m-commerce account through mobile phones. However, Smart went a step further and gives m-commerce users a Smart Money card that serves as an ATM card, which allows users to withdraw cash from an ATM or purchase goods with the card. Thus, Smart gives users another way of using and managing their electronic currency.

Credit

There are currently three ways of crediting electronic currency into an m-commerce account:

1. Over the counter (OTC): this involves the physical handover of cash to an accredited partner and provision of m-commerce account information (a SIM number or an equivalent account number). The accredited partner will then use their network facilities to credit the electronic currency into the user's m-commerce account.
2. Phone-to-phone transfer (P2P[10] receive): this transaction requires a sender (an m-commerce user) to send electronic currency to a receiver (another m-commerce user).
3. Mobile banking (m-banking): m-commerce users may also transfer

cash value from a bank account to an m-commerce account. This can be accomplished via m-banking functions. To accomplish this kind of transaction, an m-commerce user needs to be subscribed to the mobile banking services of the telecommunications company.[11]

Debit

There are four ways of using m-commerce electronic currency:

1. Purchase of load. This is a simple m-commerce transaction involving users purchasing mobile phone credits ('loads') using their m-commerce account. The users have the option to credit the load to their own mobile phone or to another subscriber's mobile phone.
2. Phone-to-phone transfer (P2P send). P2P allows a user to transfer electronic currency from their m-commerce account to another user's m-commerce account. Both the sender and receiver of the electronic currency are provided with SMS records of the transaction.
3. Payment for product or service:
   - Over the air (OTA). This transaction involves the payment of a product or service using one's mobile phone to initiate or complete the m-Payment.
   - Via credit card POS. As previously discussed, Smart also lets users conduct transactions with a debit card. The debit card allows users to access an m-commerce account using point-of-sale (POS) machines also known as the 'swipe machines' used to validate credit cards. Some transactions require the user's confirmation. This confirmation is sent via the mobile phone.
4. M-banking transactions. M-commerce allows a subscriber to conduct banking transactions using a mobile phone. These transactions manage real (that is, brick-and-mortar) bank accounts. M-banking allows a user to transfer funds between their bank accounts.

Security

Security measures are put in place to safeguard m-commerce transactions. In the Philippines, m-commerce is regulated by the Bangko Sentral ng Pilipinas. The Anti-Money Laundering Act (AMLA) also comes into play as measures are entered into m-commerce transactions to prevent money-laundering activities. There are three levels of security mechanisms:

1. Technical. Examples are encryption, secure servers and security standards among others.

2. Operational. This includes the need for a user to enter an m-PIN (personal identification number). Operational security also includes the upper limits on transaction amounts per transaction or total transaction volume per day per user. These security measures are similar to ATM maximum withdrawal limit and ATM PINs.
3. Corrective. Corrective measures are taken when a mobile phone or SIM is lost or stolen or if human error leads to misdirected transactions. A user needs to report such instances so that corrective measures can be taken to secure the monetary value that could otherwise be used by an unintended recipient.

PRIMARY M-COMMERCE APPLICATIONS

M-banking

There is a strong potential for m-banking in the Philippines given the lack of banks and other financial institutions in rural areas of the country. ATMs are also predominantly located in urban areas. Access to Internet banking is also restricted, both by limited access to the Internet and, even more importantly, by a lack of bank accounts on the part of the poor. With over 40 million cellphone subscribers, plus access to cellphones via friends and relatives (and familiarity among most people with SMS and the passing of airtime credit), this method offers a clear advantage in terms of reach.

G-Cash has already been used as a payment channel for microfinancing. Specifically, a loan application payment service, called Text-A-Payment (TAP), has been piloted in a number of rural banks using this platform (Soriano and Barbin, 2007; Umali and Alampay, 2007). What it does is allow microfinance clients to make microfinance loan payments using their mobile phones. Once the e-Money is in the mobile phone account, the client can text the loan payment by keying in the amount and the rural bank's number. The transactions are made more secure with mobile PINs.

Complementary services to TAP include Text-A-Withdrawal, Text-A-Sweldo (text a salary), and Text-A-Deposit (Umali and Alampay, 2007). With Text-A-Deposit, for example, clients can make a deposit into their existing savings account with a rural bank using their mobile phone. Once the e-Money is in the mobile phone account, the client can make a deposit by keying in the amount and the account number. The bank will then verify account name, number, date and time of transaction and it is then immediately credited to the deposit account. Deposit instructions are encrypted and password protected.

Another example of how this can potentially be applied pertains to the government's e-Card program under the Government Service Insurance System (GSIS). However, in order to make withdrawals and cash advances through this system, the user must have access to ATMs. Teachers comprise one of the largest groups in the bureaucracy, but the Department of Education says that only 20 per cent of all teachers have access to ATMs. As such, a former Undersecretary of the Department says that G-Cash and Smart Padala may be a more workable option given its widespread use (Luz, 2007: A1, A13).

Remittance

A large number of Filipinos work abroad. In fact, dollar remittances of the huge migrant Filipino workforce has kept the economy afloat in times of hardship, and has helped keep the peso–dollar exchange rate stable. As such, one of the first m-commerce applications that was developed pertained to remittance services. Smart has Smart Padala, and Globe has Globe Quick Remit in addition to its ability for direct person-to-person money transfers.

Smart Padala is an international remittance service. This service accepts over-the-counter payments in remittance shops abroad and informs the recipient of the remittance through the recipient's mobile phone. The remittances are then cashed through Smart Padala partner establishments in the Philippines using Smart Money technology (Soriano and Barbin, 2007). Almost US$50 million is remitted each year to the Philippines through Smart Money (Porteous and Wishart, 2006).

Commercial and Charitable Transactions

An important application of m-commerce is the ability to conduct direct person-to-person money transfers. Providing this capability to ordinary cellphone owners can lead to more innovative transactions via SMS, and this is happening already with local auctions such as eBay.ph. Some online services, such as b2bpricenow, also have the capability to send money via SMS/text and may also be an avenue for generating funds for charitable organizations. One of the pioneers that offered SMS-based remittance services was RemitCard, and one of its offerings included an SMS-based donation system (Lallana, 2004). Its model required donors to purchase 'RemitCards' and text the required information to a specified number.

Prepaid Loading and Airtime Transfers

G-Cash and Smart Money can be used to purchase mobile phone credit or airtime. Over $18 million worth of transactions per month already passes through the Smart Load system (Wishart, 2006), and airtime transfers, or loads, are equally popular with other providers.

Retail Purchasing

Just as there are limitations in banking for the poor, so online commerce is also limited by the lack of access among many to credit cards that are often the mode of transacting online. Some auctioneers like Bidshot and eBay.ph, and online shops like Estore Exchange, accept payments using the mobile phone via G-Cash and Smart Money. M-banking can also be used for food deliveries, even when on the road (Porteous and Wishart, 2006).

Bill Payment

A recent innovation introduced by the Department of Trade and Industry (DTI) was to utilize the G-Cash payment system in mobile phones to pay for the online registration of business names. This method, used in conjunction with its current online Business Name Registration System (BNRS), makes its online services transactional. Under this model, the DTI does not pay the network provider for the use of the system, but registrants would be charged Php2.50 per text message as a value-added transaction fee. This is on top of the registration fees for the client or corporation's business name.

CONCLUSIONS AND LESSONS FOR AFRICA

Given all the information presented on the preceding pages, the key question remains: what can other developing countries, especially those in Africa, learn from the Philippine experience?

The Philippines is not the only developing country with the availability of m-banking. In fact, there are already m-banking services, or pilots, in African countries such as the Democratic Republic of the Congo (CelPay), Kenya (M-PESA), South Africa (MTN MobileBanking and Wizzit) and Zambia (CelPay). However, the Philippines has the most well-developed m-banking system and two major, and quite different, examples in G-Cash and Smart Money.

According to Castells: 'specific conditions foster technological innovation . . . . [and] the reproduction of such conditions is cultural and institutional, as much as economic and technological' (Castells, 2000: 37). These are caveats in any attempt to export lessons learned from the Philippine experience. As such, replicating the success of SMS applications in the

Philippines may require similar market conditions to those found in the Philippines.

The most important lesson from the Philippines is that it is possible to increase access to mobile phones, not only for the wealthiest in society but also for the poorer segments of the society. Crucial to the Philippines' success in this regard were appropriate regulatory policies that allowed for competition in the telecommunication industry, coupled with market innovations that made the technologies, such as mobile phones, more 'affordable', and the process of getting a line less restrictive. These forces are now well advanced in many countries in Africa, illustrated by the dramatic increases in mobile coverage and density in Tables 3.7 and 3.8. It is therefore concluded that this is not an insurmountable barrier for many countries in Africa.

Mobile innovations in the Philippines, however, were also built on existing consumer habits among the poor and a strongly established retail network of small village convenience shops or *sari-sari* stores. It is from these types of stores that the poor often buy *tingi* or sachets, or small increments, whether these be shampoo, fish sauce or soap. And it is through these stores that telecommunication companies were able to distribute their prepaid cards and, later, set up their network of credit load centres. Practically every village in the Philippines country side has a shop like this. This tradition of small retail shops also exists in much of Africa. Indeed, the mobile explosion in Africa has largely been fuelled by prepaid sales by micro retailers.

Another prerequisite to the Philippine experience with m-commerce may be more difficult to replicate because of its unique intensity in the Philippines. As Smart's Napoleon Nazareno points out: 'there must be an existing SMS habit' (Porteous and Wishart, 2006). M-commerce, at least in how it developed in the Philippines, was built on this very widely accepted mode of communication. SMS was initially provided for free, and only once a significant portion of subscribers were using it were charges introduced. The key is first to develop familiarity with the SMS process, and wider acceptance among subscribers.

The African experience is somewhat different. There are many who argue that much of Africa has an oral communication culture and that this is a barrier to the growth of SMS and, subsequently, mobile applications. However, SMS use is often driven by economics (that is, it is much cheaper than making a voice call) and in Africa one finds a similar low cost ratio of SMS to voice as in the Philippines. Earlier in this report it was noted that in the Philippines the ratio is 6.5 SMS for every minute of voice calling. Therefore, it is quite possible that the Philippines' SMS intensity is more geared to pricing than to cultural factors. This also

Table 3.7 Number of mobile connections in selected African countries, 2002–08 (000s)

Market	Q1 2002	Q1 2003	Q1 2004	Q1 2005	Q1 2006	Q1 2007	Q1 2008F
Africa	28 029 203	39 707 215	57 506 325	90 629 595	145 525 786	210 653 790	259 872 309
Congo (Kinshasa)	177 804	542 560	1 196 388	2 011 731	3 072 649	4 782 325	6 147 664
Ethiopia	31 385	60 000	132 000	223 683	343 016	528 242	815 874
Kenya	625 604	1 200 682	2 154 596	3 740 970	5 526 018	8 366 857	10 130 228
Mozambique	147 885	235 082	525 355	941 752	1 368 340	2 018 155	2 513 559
Nigeria	637 028	1 843 766	4 368 889	10 382 000	21 517 131	36 971 738	47 052 641
Rwanda	69 000	105 000	146 000	188 000	293 000	426 000	572 506
South Africa	10 660 847	13 738 042	17 895 000	23 169 913	32 435 534	38 680 922	42 259 804
Tanzania	455 845	854 010	1 303 765	2 252 500	3 874 175	6 223 585	8 213 914
Uganda	336 543	539 489	758 198	1 242 806	1 935 817	3 054 179	4 073 254
Zambia	123 688	191 286	360 055	592 548	1 011 469	1 787 914	2 389 747

Note: F = forecast data.

Source: Wireless Intelligence (2007).

Table 3.8   Mobile market penetration in selected African countries,
            2002–08

Market	Q1 2002 (%)	Q1 2003 (%)	Q1 2004 (%)	Q1 2005 (%)	Q1 2006 (%)	Q1 2007 (%)	Q1 2008 (%)
Africa	3.4	4.8	6.7	10.4	16.3	23.1	27.9
Congo (DRC)	0.3	1.0	2.2	3.5	5.3	8.0	10.0
Ethiopia	0.1	0.1	0.2	0.3	0.5	0.7	1.0
Kenya	2.0	3.8	6.7	11.5	16.8	25.1	30.0
Mozambique	0.8	1.3	2.8	4.9	7.0	10.2	12.5
Nigeria	0.5	1.5	3.5	8.1	16.4	27.6	34.3
Rwanda	0.9	1.3	1.7	2.2	3.4	4.8	6.4
South Africa	23.5	29.7	37.9	48.0	65.9	77.3	83.3
Tanzania	1.3	2.3	3.5	6.0	10.1	15.9	20.6
Uganda	1.4	2.1	2.9	4.6	6.9	10.6	13.6
Zambia	1.2	1.8	3.3	5.4	9.1	16.0	21.1

Source: Wireless Intelligence (2007).

suggests that the experience could be replicated in other countries with similar SMS to voice cost ratios. The largest operator in East Africa, Celtel,[12] charges approximately US$0.212 for one minute of voice time compared with US$0.036 for an SMS (Celtel, 2007), a ratio similar to that in the Philippines (that is, a ratio of 5.9 to 1). These pricing conditions have helped foster a culture of SMS in much of Africa. Therefore, the SMS culture factor in the Philippines is not considered to be an insurmountable barrier to exporting m-commerce lessons to Africa.

After SMS usage, the most important step towards m-commerce in the Philippines was the prevalence of prepayment. Consumers learned how to use cards, call numbers and enter codes in order to purchase credits. They also learned how to check their credit loads and balances. This made it easier for users to understand the concept of electronic loading, once this service became offered. Since people were already literally exchanging money for loads, it made it acceptable for some to use loads as a medium of exchange. As such, G-Cash and Smart Money were eventually built on this growing use of electronic loading of credit. It is in the practice of electronic transfer of loads and credits where the potential of m-commerce can be seen. This growing and seemingly sustainable practice was an important building block for the growth and advancement of m-commerce in the Philippines. Once again, similar conditions exist in Africa where prepayment is, by far, the dominant mode of mobile phone subscription.

Technologies, such as mobile phones, tend to be introduced with long lead times followed by explosive growth due to 'network externalities' (Torrero and von Braun, 2006). In this case people subscribe to ICTs such as mobile phones because other people subscribe to them. Therefore, the number of people using similar and compatible products affects the utility derived from the consumption of these goods. Likewise, m-commerce is affected by strong network externalities. Unless there is a relevant uptake in the number of users, its use remains irrelevant.

The key question is whether a critical mass of users can be achieved to enable network externalities to unfold, and if network coverage can be further expanded sufficiently to maximize service delivery. The challenge, therefore, is to obtain a critical mass of users upon which the market can build (Torero and Von Braun, 2006: 67, 339). Proenza (2007) argues that the urban bias of m-banking is largely driven by this network effect, as developing a network of merchants is easier and more profitable in the urban rather than in the rural areas. Aside from relatively lower mobile penetration, poverty is usually more concentrated in rural areas where potential customers may have a lower capability to pay for, and utilize, m-services. These externalities have fuelled the mobile revolution in the Philippines and are arguably driving an even more rapid spread of mobile telephony in Africa.

The same advantage m-banking has over traditional banking in the Philippines given the lack of financial institutions in rural areas also exists, to an even greater extent, in Africa.[13] As in the Philippines, ATMs are also predominantly located in urban areas in Africa and access to Internet banking is restricted by limited access to the Internet and by a lack of bank accounts on the part of the poor. There are now over 200 million mobile phone subscribers in Africa, plus tens of millions more accessing via friends and relatives. Africa is also the fastest-growing region in the world for mobile telephony and was projected to have over 300 million subscribers by 2009 (Gillet, 2007). This offers an excellent, and rapidly growing, base from which to build access to banking and other services through simple mobile applications.

Remaining Barriers

However, a number of barriers remain. One of the key barriers to entry for the poor, as far as m-commerce is concerned, is the need for proper legal identification to deposit and withdraw cash into and from its m-currency form (which applies to both G-Cash and Smart Money). This is the same barrier that many faced previously in obtaining a fixed telephone line, and is also the barrier to opening a bank account and a credit card account needed for Internet transactions. The absence of these requirements was also partly why the prepaid option became easily diffused. These requirements, however, are largely related to banking regulations; especially those that are meant to prevent money laundering through the banking system. As such, these regulations may be in place in most countries. Consequently, it may be necessary for less stringent financial regulatory regimes for small-value, low-volume users (the target of this chapter) in order to help unleash the potential of m-commerce in both the Philippines and Africa.

The issue of having proper identification also has implications for other applications, especially when considering SMS as a means for people to participate through elections or referenda. The idea of one vote for one person may require people to register their names and their phone numbers. This is a touchy issue in the Philippines, where people are wary about state control and privacy, and it may be an issue in other countries as well. However, having this information would be very helpful in delivering the right information for the right audience, and controlling fraudulent and illegal use of the cellphone as well as the false reporting that often comes with anonymous ownership.

At present, there is a divided market in the Philippines given the existence of two popular m-banking platforms – Smart Money and G-Cash. In the future, the two should be able to exchange one currency with the other, as this would help spur the growth of m-commerce transactions. Such a consolidation would be similar to how the telecommunication companies were required to interconnect. This, however, may be a regulatory question that both the Central Bank and the National Telecommunications Commission have to be involved in. Similar issues are faced in Africa where competing mobile network providers may not wish to cooperate to help m-commerce realize its potential.

In the long run, sustaining m-banking may also be dependent on the number of institutions, merchants and services that are willing to support or accept the currency. Unless people see the utility of m-banking in terms of diversity of applications, its usage will not become commonplace and sustainable.

In summary, to learn from the m-commerce experience in the Philippines, one must review the developments that led to where m-commerce in the Philippines is today. Even though the Philippines has mobile applications such as G-Cash and Smart Money, its success is still contingent on how successfully it builds on the existing culture and practices, especially with respect to cellphone usage and, perhaps even more importantly, SMS technologies.

Pushing m-commerce further will require compliance with banking regulations; the support of retailers in terms of accepting it as a currency;

the development of more content for m-commerce beyond what is already available to encourage use and create incentives for its use and create network externalities; and possibly the integration of existing m-currencies into one acceptable form, thereby making m-commerce exchanges as common as texting. It is also important to address banking regulatory issues in order to ensure that a mobile network operator has the right to engage in m-banking or if it must be in cooperation with a bank or through the creation of a bank-like subsidiary.

The Future for M-commerce in Africa

In Tables 3.7 and 3.8 the absolute number of connections and mobile density are shown in Africa as a whole as well as a number of African countries of interest for the Swedish International Development Corporation (Sida). Some of the more dramatic developments include a forecasted 1000 per cent increase in mobile connections in Africa between 2002 and 2008. In Tanzania, a country with a long and intense experience with Sida development cooperation, the growth of mobile telephony has been even faster – almost 1600 per cent between 2002 and 2008. The most dramatic growth has been in Nigeria – almost 7000 per cent over six years, increasing from a mobile penetration rate of 0.5 per cent in 2002 to a forecasted 34.3 per cent by the first quarter of 2008.

As seen above, the growth of mobile telephony in Africa has been breathtaking and far faster than the most optimistic of projections just a few years ago. Will this growth continue? The GSMA believes that the cost of mobile networks and devices will continue to fall, extending mobile services even to people on very low incomes. And, as noted earlier, Wireless Intelligence predicts that the number of mobile subscriptions in Africa will grow by over 50 per cent – from 200 million to over 300 million – by 2010.

Many developing countries have established universal service funds, which levy contributions from mobile and fixed operators, largely to subsidize the roll-out of fixed-line telecommunications networks in rural areas. The GSMA recommends that governments should regard market forces as the primary means to extend access and connections to mobile communications, and that the US$4.4 billion accrued by universal service funds should be invested in mobile coverage roll-out. They further conclude that universal service funds should be phased out over time and that universal service funds should be spent on the lowest-cost access technology, typically mobile networks, as the most efficient way to extend access to telecommunications (GSMA, 2007).

As African mobile coverage and density grow, it is important to note

that mobile phone networks in the Philippines have a very robust capacity for SMS traffic. Indeed, telecommunications giant Ericsson uses the Philippines as a test case to optimize networks to handle high volumes of SMSs. Therefore, mobile network operators in Africa intending to introduce m-banking and other SMS-inducing services need to ensure that their networks reliably support high volumes of SMS traffic.

There is another factor that makes much of sub-Saharan Africa, and especially East Africa, ripe for the expansion of simple mobile applications. The factor is a lack of Internet bandwidth. Specifically, East Africa is one of the few populated regions of the world without access to the global fibre pipeline (that is, Internet access is not through ultra-broadband terrestrial cable but instead through expensive, limited bandwidth satellite receiving stations). This situation led Engvall and Hesselmark to conclude that: 'ICT services are not likely to take off in Sub-Saharan Africa unless there is an ample supply of bandwidth at low costs' (Engvall and Hesselmark, 2007). In a sense, this lack of Internet bandwidth makes the region even more in need of simple (that is, low bandwidth) mobile applications than the Philippines, which is connected to the global fibre pipeline via undersea cables.

An African Pioneer?

Wizzit is a South African-based company targeting customers without bank accounts and has been offering cellphone-based financial services since 2005. A recent CGAP report examined Wizzit's m-banking services in South Africa and concluded that low-income people value the service and give it high ratings for convenience, cost and security. It was further found that although the lowest-income groups do not typically use the service, m-banking is opening banking to the poor and reducing costs and saving time for its users (CGAP, 2006).

Vodafone, which is investing heavily in Africa, is partnering with Kenyan affiliate Safaricom and the Commercial Bank of Africa to launch M-PESA, a mobile financial service that allows users to send and receive cash and perform other transactions. M-PESA was launched in Kenya in early 2007, as the first m-banking service in East Africa, and boasted over 100 000 users after three months. The service is open for those without bank accounts or bankcards and there are plans to launch M-PESA in Tanzania soon. Through PESA it will be possible to:

- deposit and withdraw money;
- transfer money (send) to another M-PESA customer or to someone who is not an M-PESA customer (they do not even need to be a Safaricom customer);

- buy Safaricom prepaid airtime; and
- manage M-PESA accounts (for example, show balance, call support, change PIN, language, and so on) (Safaricom, 2007).

In June 2007 there were 430 M-PESA agents where customers could buy and sell M-PESA e-Money. Agents are Safaricom dealers, operating one or more outlets around Kenya or other retailers with a substantial distribution network such as petrol stations. The agent's key tasks are to help register M-PESA customers; assist with deposit of cash into M-PESA accounts; process cash withdrawals for registered M-PESA customers; and process cash withdrawals for those who are not registered M-PESA customers. Registration for M-PESA is free at any M-PESA with a Safaricom SIM card, a mobile telephone and identification (Safaricom, 2007). In this regard, registration is more cumbersome than for G-Cash in the Philippines. To date, there are no regulatory hurdles for this type of service in Kenya but Safaricom is working with the authorities to ensure they stay abreast of regulatory developments.

In infoDev's report (2006) on micro-payment systems a South African m-commerce company estimated that the introduction of m-banking services could be profitable for mobile network operators with as few as 25 000 users. The report concluded that: 'it is not only technically feasible and profitable to deploy financial services over mobile networks, but there is a significant and growing demand. In fact, m-commerce may address a major service gap in developing countries that is critical to their social and economic development' (infoDev, 2006).

It is possible, even likely, that hundreds of millions of people in developing countries will have access to bank services through mobile phones in a few years. The biggest challenge may be to ensure that the positive effects of these new services are maximized. Will m-commerce merely benefit the 'haves', or will those currently outside the economy be brought inside through the mobile telephony revolution that we are witnessing in the first years of the twenty-first century?

NOTES

1. Short Message Service (SMS) permits the sending of messages between mobile phones and/or other devices. The term 'text messaging' is common in English-speaking countries and the Philippines, while most other countries use the term SMS. SMS can also be used to interact with automated systems to order products and services, participate in contests, access information and/or conduct financial transactions.
2. In the fourth quarter of 2006, Wireless Intelligence data showed that SMS use per user in the Philippines was more than double that in the next most SMS-intensive country.

Just one leading Philippine operator, Smart, with over 51 billion SMSs in the fourth quarter of 2006 – 500 million SMSs per day – registered more SMSs in the quarter than global giants China Unicom, Verizon Wireless and Cingular Wireless combined (Wireless Intelligence, 2007).

3. The Information Technology and E-Commerce Council (ITECC) was renamed as the Commission on Information and Communications Technology (CICT), merging the National Computer Center, the Telecommunications Office and the Communications segment of the Department of Transportation and Communications.
4. Whatis.com, 'm-commerce – Whatis.com Definition', http://searchmobilecomputing. techtarget.com/sDefinition/0,,sid40_gci214590,00.html; accessed 7 April 2005.
5. A third player, Sun Cellular, entered the market in 2004 but its e-commerce applications are currently limited to credit reloading.
6. Although Smart Money is a free service, there is a fee for the associated debit or credit card.
7. A four-digit m-PIN of choice, maiden name of the subscriber's mother, the subscriber's name, address and telephone number.
8. STK: SIM ToolKit; a menu-driven service built in to SIMs to access information or conduct transactions.
9. In contrast, the PLDT phone cards with SIMs 'hold' the remaining value of the card electronically in the SIM. Thus, if the card gets lost or physically damaged, the monetary value in the card gets lost or damaged with it.
10. 'P2P' is also used as an abbreviation for 'person-to-person' transactions.
11. This function is available for Smart. Although Globe has mobile banking services, it does not have the option to transfer money from a bank account to an m-commerce account.
12. Celtel is a major mobile network provider in Kenya, Tanzania and Uganda, a region where Sida has extensive development cooperation experience.
13. In fact, the Philippines has a relatively well-developed network of rural banks and associations. 'Not many examples like that in Africa, hence a more dire need for financial services. We keep our money under mattresses and in pots' (Ndiwalana, 2007).

4. Information and communication technologies and the base of the pyramid: lessons from the Philippines' Last Mile Initiative

Gigo Alampay

From March 2005 to July 2008, the Last Mile Initiative–Philippines (LMIP), a United States Agency for International Development (USAID)-funded project that supported the Philippine government's efforts to bridge the digital divide, set up and provided training for 30 telecenters in rural and underserved communities throughout the Philippines. LMIP was organized not so much to increase the number of such telecenters in the Philippines – indeed, the government's Community e-Center (CeC) Program had already committed to establishing at least 1500 such centers all over the country by 2010 – but rather to conceptualize, test, identify and document best practices that could both promote local development through CeCs and provide options to ensure the sustainability of such telecenters at the base of the pyramid (BOP) – that is, in poor, remote and unserved communities that, almost by definition, could not afford their services.

The experience of implementing LMIP provides lessons and validates the underlying premise that telecenters – even those established in poor and underserved communities – can be run sustainably, and perhaps even profitably, as pay-per-use facilities. Case studies from the program demonstrate how such telecenters can and do promote income-generating opportunities for distressed communities and their constituents.

Despite the successes, however, immense challenges remain for remote and small communities, even if they are connected to the Internet. Aggregation of CeCs may be one means of encouraging greater private sector participation and investment in them and thus enhancing their long-term sustainability.

WHAT ARE COMMUNITY E-CENTERS?

In the Philippines, Community e-Centers (CeCs) are self-sustaining, shared facilities designed to provide affordable access to information and communication technology (ICT)-enabled services and relevant information, particularly the Internet. They are also envisioned as conduits for delivering government services (such as health, education and other social services), as well as a potent tool for enabling the fuller participation of unserved and underserved communities in the country's economy. The Philippine government has identified CeCs as the principal vehicles for bridging the digital divide[1] and therefore now implements the Community e-Center Program under the auspices of its Commission on Information and Communications Technology (CICT).

CeCs go by a variety of names, such as telecenters, village knowledge centers, infocenters, community technology centers (CTCs), community multimedia centers (CMCs), multipurpose community telecenters (MCTs), common/citizen service centers (CSCs) and school-based telecenters, among others. But regardless of what they are called, such centers all have the same ultimate goal: to bridge the digital divide by providing universal access to information and communication technologies and services.

The Community e-Center Program (CECP) of the Philippines is based on the 1995 Philippine Telecommunications Law and the Medium-Term Philippine Development Plan of 2001–04. The law was enacted to enable residents in areas without any basic services to receive such services at reasonable prices. The medium-term plan was implemented to provide residents of any part of the country – through e-centers – with quicker access to a wider range of information. In addition to bridging the digital divide through shared ICT facilities and services, the CECP's other main objectives are to facilitate cooperation among local communities, to simplify business transactions by using market data, and to strengthen the social, political and economic power of rural communities.

Community e-Centers are outfitted with basic office equipment, such as computers, telecommunications equipment, copiers, fax machines, TV sets and digital cameras. They offer telephone and fax services, use of the Internet, seminars, copying and printing services, business support, and e-government service. CeCs can provide effective and affordable access to ICTs and can empower communities and residents by opening opportunities in education, commerce, tourism, public health and participation in governance. Subsidies from the central government and the proceeds from the various services offered are the main sources of revenue for the e-centers. Successful CeCs require the involvement of multiple stakeholders, including residents, non-profit organizations, private companies, local governments and others.

THE PHILIPPINES' LAST MILE INITIATIVE

From the outset, the Philippine government recognized that merely providing ICT equipment, facilities and Internet access would not by itself be enough either to ensure the long-term viability of CeCs or to achieve the broader development objectives of the CECP. Thus, the Last Mile Initiative–Philippines, a USAID-funded project, was implemented to support the CECP by providing technical assistance for the design, development, set-up and evaluation of sustainable CeCs in rural and/or underserved areas in the Philippines. LMIP was to work with community-based individuals and institutions and to identify specific advocates who could be recruited and trained to work for the success of the CeCs. The hope was that the CECP could then develop, replicate and even scale best-practice and proof-of-concept models that might emerge from its efforts throughout the Philippines.

The Key Word is 'Community'

Initially funded for only one year, LMIP was a modest undertaking. Its goal was simply to set up ten CeCs in rural communities throughout the Philippines. The relatively short period within which to identify locations for ten CeCs, set them up, train personnel and then monitor performance required not only advocates in the communities with whom LMIP could work, but also the involvement and significant participation of residents, community-based non-profits, private companies, local governments and others to ensure multisectoral stakeholder ownership of the CeCs.

The coastal town of Sogod, for example, was selected as a site for a CeC. Sogod is a fourth-class municipality north of Cebu City, and its economy is mainly centered on fishing, corn and vegetable farming, and making coconut products (such as edible oil), hog feeds and broomsticks. In 2005 the town's nearest Internet connections were two hours away by car, in Internet cafes in the outskirts of Cebu City. LMIP worked with several partners to set up Sogod's first CeC. Two non-profit organizations, World Vision Philippines and World Corps, provided computers and peripheral equipment (including an air conditioner), social preparation, business development and operations training, and technical support. The local government supplied the physical space (free for five years), office furniture and security, while LMIP furnished the server and six months of broadband connectivity and facilitated the provision of Voice over Internet Protocol (VoIP) services by local suppliers.

A second example of multisectoral public–private participation is that in Manolo Fortich, a predominantly agricultural town in the province of Bukidnon on the island of Mindanao. The local congressman for Manolo Fortich approached LMIP for assistance in creating a CeC for the town. The congressman's office provided five personal computer (PC) workstations, a printer, a webcam, a microphone, networking equipment and office suite applications; the local government supplied the physical space, furniture and staff support; a local telecommunications provider was tapped for Digital Subscriber Line (DSL) connectivity; and LMIP conceived and conducted an intensive two-week training for government employees and teachers in community development, enterprise development and operations management, as well as trainers' training in computer skills courses for the community.

The results of these ventures are discussed further below. What is important to note at this juncture is that fostering a sense of community is key to ensuring that as many people as possible feel not only a sense of ownership in the CeC but also, more importantly, a sense of responsibility for its long-term success. And this requires that the stakeholders make a tangible contribution to, or investment in, the whole effort, at least at the outset.

The short time-frame within which LMIP had to act forced the identification of communities with champions or actors willing and able to take the lead. While multistakeholder participation is critical, one champion has to play the role of catalyst and to bring – and hold – different community actors together.

People, even at the base of the pyramid, do not need to be convinced of the importance of bringing Internet access to their communities. They do, however, need to know or discover how exactly they can help make this a reality.

A champion, with a vision if you will, plays this role. In the case of Sogod, World Corps played that role – by first approaching the local government to identify out-of-school youth who could be trained to run the CeCs as entrepreneurs, and then recruiting help from the private sector for computers and software.

In Manolo Fortich, it was the local congressman who, in addition to approaching LMIP and procuring computers, also used his political clout to get the local government solidly behind the program to provide office space and guarantee payments to the telecommunications provider over the long haul.

The lesson then is that community-based initiatives to bridge the digital divide do not sprout naturally. Stakeholder participation comes only after someone to lead and encourage that participation is identified. From his or her lead, then, other actors can come to contribute, invest and commit, in the hope that these will then lead to a deeper sense of ownership within the community and among its members.

Can CeCs be Sustainable at the Base of the Pyramid?

Support from multiple stakeholders is a critical but insufficient prerequisite to ensuring the long-term sustainability of Community e-Centers. Although securing initial funding to set up CeCs (through corporate grants, private investments, government subsidies, and so on) may be relatively easy, ongoing costs are also involved, such as Internet subscriptions, operating and salary expenses, and equipment maintenance and upgrades. For LMIP, this concern was complicated by the fact that the areas in which it was to establish CeCs areas were typically poor and far from infrastructures that provide easy Internet access.

LMIP therefore embarked on a two-pronged sustainability strategy: providing capacity-building training designed to enhance the business, managerial and teaching skills of people who would run the CeCs; and encouraging the adoption of a pay-per-use model to generate continuing revenues that could cover operating expenses.

Promoting human capital development

LMIP created and provided two basic training packages. First, it helped CeC staff develop technical and entrepreneurial skills to prepare and implement viable business plans, identify and respond to the needs of the communities, investigate the market for services, promote the center's services to the community, and maintain the facilities and equipment. The first training package included these modules:

- Community Development and Understanding, which enabled the CeC more fully to engage community members at all stages of the CeC's set-up, thereby developing a sense of community ownership in the success of the CeC and hastening technology adoption and assimilation. This module included sessions on mobilizing the community, assessing community needs, understanding the social impact of new technologies, and exploring the role of the CeC in the community.
- Enterprise Development, which imparted creativity and innovative skills in designing products and services and emphasized that the CeC, although serving an undeniable social function, should be run

profitably and be able to generate revenues from its products and services. This module taught CeC staff entrepreneurial skills for turning demand into services, as well as how to sustain CeC operations by using business development tools such as simple market research and survey methods, cost and pricing calculations, business planning and time management, among others.

- CeC Operations Management, which ensured that the CeC, like any other profitable business, was imbued with a clear operating structure and was governed by policies, rules and responsibilities. This training helped the CeC establish policies and guidelines on staffing, daily operations, center use, and so on. Further, this module taught the CeC staff how to develop effective yet simple accounting systems, feedback schemes and a performance monitoring system.

The second LMIP package consisted of trainers' training – that is, teaching CeC staff to become trainers themselves on basic computer literacy and Internet use. They were then encouraged to offer free sessions on slow days to interested community residents – both as part of their social advocacy and as a way of introducing the facility to residents and increasing the number of trained people who might then become CeC customers. Trainers' training sessions included the following modules:

- Computer and Internet Trainers' Training, which equipped the community with skills for using a computer and the Internet, and for using basic productivity applications such as word processing, spreadsheets and presentation preparation. Staff were also taught how to tailor the training modules to make them more relevant to the community.
- Web Design, Graphic Design and Content Development modules, which were also given to a few advanced CeCs. Communities, through the CeCs, then learned to appreciate and establish a Web presence to broadcast information about the community and its people, products and services to the world. They were able to create websites for marketing products, services and tourism, and even for trading on the Internet. Local governments and non-profits learned how to post community profiles that included geography, climate, scenic spots and cultural traditions.

LMIP training used both proprietary software (donated by private companies) and free and open-source programs and online solutions. The advantages and disadvantages of both – going beyond the obvious cost differences – are discussed later in this chapter.

Encouraging an entrepreneurial approach to running CeCs

LMIP defined 'sustainability' as the capability to offer, on a cost-neutral or profitable basis, products and services that community residents were willing and able to pay for. All CeCs assisted by the Last Mile Initiative–Philippines were situated in rural and/or unserved areas with a population typically greater than 5000 people.

The CeCs provided a wide array of services to address information needs of the community. Internet surfing and the use of office applications such as word processing, spreadsheet and presentation programs were invariably the main applications that community residents looked for and used in the CeC. Users were charged by the hour at highly affordable rates (averaging US$0.40 to US$0.42 per hour). More often than not, computer and Internet hourly rentals were insufficient to cover all operating expenses. CeCs therefore offered other services, acting in effect as a one-stop business center for the community. For example, residents could go to CeCs to use the telephone, for which they were charged a modest fee; and in some CeCs, VoIP telephony enabled users to make inexpensive long-distance calls, with calls to relatives working or living overseas being especially popular.

CeCs typically offered the following:

- Basic Internet services – e-mail, research, web browsing.
- Business services – scanning, printing, copying and faxing; public telephone center; identification (ID) printing and lamination.
- Other services such as video editing and publication layout.
- Capacity building – hands-on computer literacy and skills development training.
- ICT services – troubleshooting, computer repair, technical services, Web development.
- Internet service provider functions – provision of Internet connectivity to local government units, schools, *barangays* (barrios) and households.
- Online advertisement of local products and local ecotourism.
- Access to e-government services – for example to obtain birth certificates, information on social security, permits, and so on.

An informal self-assessment conducted by LMIP generated these findings:

- E-Centers with multiple services tended to be more profitable and more innovative with their services.
- Internet service was the top revenue source for the CeCs.

- The use of office applications such as word processing, spreadsheets and presentations was the second-highest source of CeC revenues.
- Customers also frequented the center to print and photocopy documents and to use the telephony facilities; either public switched telephone network (PSTN) or VoIP.
- CeCs that offered basic ICT literacy training, including office applications and how to use the Internet, saw some benefits as a result – not only in terms of the social value of providing skills to the community but also in terms of increased revenues as the number of residents able to use their facilities increased.
- As with any business, location was a key factor. CeCs situated near schools, the local market, the local government building or other places with high pedestrian traffic were observed to attract more paying customers and therefore obtained higher overall revenues.

Some CeCs creatively offered additional services such as digital ID processing, compact disc (CD) burning, ink cartridge refilling and any other services that could enhance the value of the CeC to the community and that residents might be willing to pay for.

Finding the right people to run the CeCs, as with any other business, was often a major, if not the biggest, challenge. For the most part, LMIP worked with key contact people who had the prestige, resources or interest to make the CeC work – even if they did not necessarily run the CeC themselves. These included local public officials, such as the mayor or the congressman, who could provide start-up funds as well as assign personnel to attend LMIP training and to operate the CeC.

One interesting model was developed by World Corps, a non-profit partner of LMIP in rural Cebu that worked with the local government to identify promising out-of-school youth. These were young people who, for various reasons, never finished high school. Because the communities were very small (typically with populations of less than 5000 people), the local *barangays* were well placed and well informed to identify the most deserving candidates.

The identified youths were interviewed and shortlisted, and then trained in entrepreneurship and placed in competition with one another. The best candidates were 'rewarded' when, at the end of the training program, they were hired to become the managers of the new CeCs, with a chance to eventually own the CeC at the end of five years of successfully operating it. The promise of such a model is self-evident.

Unfortunately, LMIP was not implemented long enough to monitor and study how it would have worked out over a longer period of time.

Potential for Innovation by CeCs

Among the CeCs that LMIP established, three especially stand out for demonstrating the potential of CeCs as springboards for a variety of innovations within BOP communities.

CeCs for job generation: municipality of Manolo Fortich, Bukidnon, Mindanao

Manolo Fortich is the gateway to the vast province of Bukidnon in Mindanao. It is predominantly an agricultural town that generates a variety of products ranging from rice, corn and strawberries to pineapples from the vast Del Monte plantation.

LMIP worked with the local government of Manolo Fortich to help set up a CeC in a portion of its Public Employment Service Office (PESO). Already a collection point for résumés submitted by residents, the PESO was frequently contacted by companies seeking workers with various skills. The introduction of the CeC, it was hoped, would eventually allow citizens to go online to find jobs being offered by Manila-based Internet job sites.

Within two months of the CeC's launch, online interviews with Manila-based employment agencies using the CeC's webcams and VoIP facilities were successfully arranged. Fifty applicants from Manolo Fortich were interviewed by a recruiter in Manila, and ten were successfully hired by a company in Taiwan. Even those who were not hired came out ahead. In the past, all candidates would have had to travel by boat to Manila for their interview and to bear the costs of lodging and meals, only to be told to try again next time. Virtual interviews, conducted by Internet telephony, allowed everyone to save what would previously have been a sunk cost.

As a cautionary note, however, it remains to be seen whether this success is replicable or was merely the result of a lucky confluence of various factors (for example, a strong local executive who championed the CeC, the local government's prior relationship with a network of job recruiters, the availability of broadband connectivity). Indeed, the long-term viability of the CeC, given its reliance on political support from local officials who run for re-election every three years, has yet to be demonstrated.

Nevertheless, news of the services and benefits being provided by the CeC in Manolo Fortich traveled fast. Nearby municipalities in Bukidon and provinces such as Misamis Oriental have expressed interest in participating in or duplicating the practice in their own jurisdictions, indicating some promise of replicability and scaling of the Manolo Fortich experiment.

CeCs to promote ecotourism: municipality of Kiangan, Ifugao Province
The Ifugao Rice Terraces are 2000-year-old rice paddies, hand-carved into the mountains of Ifugao by early indigenous Filipinos. Commonly referred to by Filipinos as the 'Eighth Wonder of the World', the terraces are approximately 1500 meters (5000 feet) above sea level and cover 10 360 square kilometers (about 4000 square miles) of mountainside. They are fed by an ancient irrigation system from the rain forests above the terraces, and it is said that if the steps were put end to end, they would encircle half the globe.

Declared a World Heritage Site by the United Nations Educational, Scientific and Cultural Organization (UNESCO) and widely recognized in the Philippines as a national cultural treasure, this engineering marvel is nevertheless underpromoted and undervalued. The province of Ifugao remains among the poorest and most remote in the country, and the rice terraces themselves have suffered as the young Ifugaos move to other places in the Philippines in search of better economic opportunities.

Save the Ifugao Terraces Movement (SITMO), a non-governmental organization dedicated to preserving the rice terraces, sees the promotion of the area's ecotourism sites and the Ifugao people's unique and proud culture and heritage as a possible solution. And in this task SITMO, together with the municipality of Kiangan, saw the Internet as an important tool in their efforts to develop and increase global awareness, not only for the phenomenon of countless fully irrigated rice paddies carved out of mountains, but also for the rich cultural traditions, lush forests, pristine waterfalls, unexplored caves and other natural attractions that the site had to offer.

LMIP was able to assist SITMO and the local government in setting up the ePuggo (which translates locally as 'from the mountains') CeC, which was envisioned as providing the world with a virtual window into the rice terraces and their surrounding natural landscape. LMIP partnered with Microsoft and Intel to provide the center with computer equipment, software and broadband connectivity via satellite. LMIP then provided trained local staff to operate the CeC efficiently and sustainably, covering such topics as enterprise development, management, computer troubleshooting and trainers' training on a computer literacy course for the community. And finally, in line with the vision of using the center to promote the site over the Web, LMIP collaborated with the Center for Art, New Ventures and Sustainable Development (CANVAS, a non-profit organization dedicated to promoting Philippine art, culture and environment), to develop and implement a three-month intensive graphic design and Web development course for SITMO and the local government.

The results of the partnership have been impressive and encouraging. Within two months after the launch of the ePuggo CeC, Internet marketing efforts had drawn more than 100 additional tourists to two local festivals that, among others, allowed visitors to plant or harvest rice on the famed terraces and enjoy unique cultural performances by indigenous peoples. This increased tourism generated more than Php200 000 (roughly US$4000) in gross earnings for the community, from visitor fees alone.

In 2007, SITMO executive director Teddy Baguilat was elected governor of the province of Ifugao. Because of the success of the e-Puggo CeC, the new governor committed to establishing at least one similar CeC in every municipality in the province.

CeCs and telemedicine: Basak-Pardo, Cebu City

In June 2007, LMIP tested the use of CeCs as training centers for rural health workers in the small *barangay* of Basak-Pardo, on the outskirts of Cebu City. LMIP commissioned the production of a video entitled *Iwas Lason* (Poisoning Prevention), which was initially shown to 50 Basak-Pardo health workers to illustrate first aid and preventive measures to deal with accidental child poisoning, a leading cause of death in the Philippines. This was followed by online question-and-answer sessions and role-playing demonstrations – enabled by VoIP and webcams – with experts from the Philippine General Hospital Telemedicine Laboratory, several thousand kilometers away in Manila.

The possibility of extending this training to the tens of thousands of *barangay* health workers all over the country (nearly 400 health workers in Cebu alone) is tantalizing, and this pilot program demonstrated the promise of telemedicine as a cost-effective method of training health workers, especially in communities that lack ready access to doctors or hospitals.

LESSONS FROM THE LMIP EXPERIENCE AT THE BASE OF THE PYRAMID

Lesson 1: Setting up Sustainable CeCs – Even in Poor, Rural and Unserved Communities – Is Possible

LMIP's brief experience, however limited, in setting up CeCs in communities at the base of the pyramid indicates that such enterprises can be run in a sustainable manner. Awareness of the Internet, even where there is no access yet to speak of, is universally high. Indeed, residents in unserved areas have shown a willingness to travel for hours just to get to the nearest Internet cafe – to do research, to look for jobs, and even just to play online games. Clearly, residents – even in poor and rural communities – are willing and able to pay for services that CeCs offer. Simply put, it is possible and important that each CeC be set up from the start to pursue a demand-driven approach that responds to the particular needs of the community and to institute and follow basic business practices to ensure that it can cover its operating expenses over the long term.

Willingness to charge

Sustainability of the CeC requires a willingness to charge for services – something that CeCs, conscious of their social mission, may often find embarrassing or awkward to do. This is especially true of CeCs set up or managed by local governments that could be called to task by constituents who may feel that the services ought to be free. Simple information and education campaigns, even just through posters in the facility, to explain the need for a pay-per-use approach are often sufficient to address this concern and obtain the continuing patronage and support of the market.

Pricing

As with any enterprise, the success of the CeC depends on the demand for its services. Efforts to increase awareness and demand, therefore, are key. Hitting the right price points is important, and consideration of how much the competition (even if only potential competition) would charge is key. In this case, the rates charged by the nearest Internet access points are typically the main point of reference.

CeCs in previously unserved areas need to remember too that, even as they enjoy a first-mover advantage, they may not remain a virtual monopoly for long, especially as demand picks up and they begin to demonstrate the financial viability of their services. Barriers to entry are increasingly low, as major telecommunications companies aggressively roll out wireless broadband facilities throughout the country. CeCs need to remain conscious of the potential for competition that inevitably arises when broadband connectivity becomes available in their respective areas. Private companies are rolling out, mainly through wireless broadband, although the Philippine Long Distance Telephone Company (PLDT) has reported triple-digit growth in its landline DSL services as well.

Technology options

CeCs must continuously keep pace with technological developments and be conscious of local residents' expectations of CeC facilities. For example, an informal survey of LMIP-assisted CeCs revealed that a majority of customers used the facilities to engage in social networking and therefore expected that workstations would be equipped with webcams. The lack of a webcam was enough to motivate a resident to head off to the next-nearest Internet access point instead – even one several miles away.

CeCs also need to weigh the pros and cons of using proprietary software such as Microsoft products versus free and open-source software such as Linux and Open Office. The costs of licensing proprietary software are significant and require a much bigger start-up investment. But proprietary software is also typically easier to use and set up, and technical support is easier to obtain. On the other hand, open-source software is gaining ground and is often downloadable for free over the Internet. It generally requires more specialized skills to install and maintain, however. Moreover, LMIP CeCs that used open-source software sometimes encountered conflicts between the software and their peripheral equipment. It can sometimes be very difficult, for example, to find open-source drivers for crucial equipment like printers and webcams.

Multistakeholder ownership
A multistakeholder approach allows resources, funding and technical capacities to be pooled together to make CeCs more viable. Although entrepreneurial flexibility may be reduced under this ownership model, CeCs in rural areas usually consider this an acceptable trade-off in order to have multiple sources of resources and support to sustain the CeC. They view ownership by multiple stakeholders as vital to securing much-needed funding and allowing the risks to be shared, thereby attracting more investments and support for the CeC.

CeC managers in BOP areas therefore often work hand in hand with local government officials and community residents in creating applications, designing content and even laying out office space. This gives them the assurance that the CeC will be useful in their daily lives and not simply a provider of supplier-driven services. Since CeC technology is relatively new to most rural communities, a sense of community ownership also avoids technological alienation and even creates marketing opportunities.

For these reasons, LMIP sometimes supported the creation of a steering committee or an ICT council charged with monitoring the operation of a center, providing guidance and ensuring informed decision making. ICT councils were typically composed of representatives from local governments, non-governmental organizations (NGOs), the community and other private sector organizations.

Lesson 2: Remote, Poor and Small Communities with CeCs Remain Remote, Poor and Small

For all the promise that Internet connectivity offers individuals and communities, expectations especially at the base of the pyramid need to be managed and realistic. Internet connectivity does not immediately, or even necessarily, translate into significant results. Likewise, the presence of a CeC may not result in meaningful, measurable improvements in terms of quality of life or increased incomes.

Small, isolated communities have problems that Internet connectivity does not automatically alleviate. The market in such communities is so small that providers of useful applications such as Internet telephony often remain hesitant to provide services, regardless of the CeC's willingness to pay subscription fees. For the provider, going to the trouble of servicing such a small community can be costly and risky. If service breaks down, for example, the company will have to make a special trip to an isolated area.

Also, the Internet does open up possibilities for e-commerce and other online transactions, but BOP community residents attempting to generate an online market for their wares on their own are faced with nearly insurmountable challenges when it comes to gaining the trust of consumers and suppliers. Potential distributors, for instance, may have misgivings about the ability of such communities to deliver on commitments or to respond adequately if complaints arise. In the end, businesses may be more comfortable buying products from larger providers and middlemen, rather than directly from communities that could supply them more cheaply, simply because to them bigger equals more trustworthy.

Lesson 3: New Discoveries and Innovations Emerge from each CeC's Experiences

Servicing remote communities with access to the Internet results in innovations and applications that can hold much promise for replication and scaling, such as the examples of Manolo Fortich, Kiangan and Basak-Pardo. Learning from such experiences is very relevant because they pertain to the specific issues and dynamics of poor and remote rural areas. Documenting and sharing these best practices is therefore critical.

CONCLUSION: THE CASE FOR AGGREGATION

In summary, three lessons can be learned from LMIP's experience. First, CeCs – that is, shared Internet access points – can be self-sustaining even in communities at the base of the pyramid. If a CeC can contain costs, offer the basic services and expand its market (principally through training and fundamental business practices), community residents are willing and able to pay for the use of its facilities – at least enough to keep it going. Second, small, remote communities and their residents face overwhelming odds when they attempt to enter larger markets, principally because the private sector has little interest in investing in them or engaging in commerce with them. Access to the Internet by itself is not enough to overcome such odds and lift BOP communities out of their distressed situations. Finally, best practices and innovations can emerge from the communities themselves, and these need to be documented, shared and, ideally, replicated.

Thus, while the presence of CeCs in small and remote communities undoubtedly provides benefits for local constituents, their very small-ness and remoteness continue to limit the potential of such communities. Individual CeCs in far-flung areas find it far more difficult to attract private sector interest and investment, particularly relative to their urban counterparts. As a result, they offer fewer services and are less credible and interesting to the larger domestic and global markets that they seek to tap.

What, then, can be done to raise the level of CeC sustainability to a point that overcomes the drawbacks of the community's smallness and remoteness and possibly allows the replication and scaling of best prac-tices? The answer, proposed but untested by LMIP at the end of its run, may be aggregation. By using new information and communication tech-nologies to bridge CeCs under one platform, CeCs collectively may be able to provide various services and applications efficiently and to scale and, in the process, create a far bigger market that could be both more attractive to the private sector and more efficient for delivery of government services, especially in the countryside. Such a network or platform – if it were to be built – could provide the link or, more appropriately, the bridge to scale up best CeC practices and models throughout the country, as well as to allow the private sector to explore mutually beneficial possibilities for delivering its own products and services, especially to communities at the base of the pyramid.

To this end, LMIP proposed to explore, as a next step, the creation of such a network or platform, under the auspices of a new alliance led by the private sector or an organization of multisectoral stakeholders. This new organization would have the following goals:

- To aggregate Community e-Centers and other Internet access points in rural and unserved areas into a single market by establishing a central network, clearinghouse or portal.
- To assess opportunities for significant private sector investment and/or the efficient deployment of government services in rural and unserved communities through this aggregated market.
- To implement development-oriented and innovative applications and services that have been identified as potentially ideal for scaled

deployment through the aggregated market (without necessarily precluding services and applications that others may later propose as the portal or platform is used).

Innovative applications and services could be attempted, such as these:

- Expanded government insurance coverage. The platform would be developed to enable CeCs to act as registration points for the national government's insurance service (PhilHealth). The existence of such a facility could enable PhilHealth to expand efficiently to rural areas that otherwise would be difficult to reach. Incentive-based programs to encourage CeCs to act as such registration points, such as revenue-sharing from premiums paid by registrants, could be developed and agreed upon between the alliance and PhilHealth.
- Investment in human capital. With such a network, it would be easier for CeCs to establish relationships collectively with universities and other training institutions to develop and implement existing and additional training modules including, for example, remote training of rural health workers by experts through CeC facilities. The same model could be adapted for law training modules, as a means of enhancing legal protection and services in these areas.
- Participation of overseas Filipino workers in community development. The online platform could be used to match community-based development projects with interested donors, particularly the overseas Filipino communities.
- E-Commerce. Aggregation, as well as the participation of major private sector companies in the overall network of CeCs, could be the tipping point to engender market trust. With increased size comes increased credibility; in this case, buyers would find it easier both to locate sellers at the base of the pyramid and to trust them. The success of Kiangan in promoting ecotourism, for example, could be replicated by other similarly endowed communities in the Philippines. Each community could set up its own website and marketing campaign, but aggregation would make it easier for tourists to locate potential sites to visit, and for both government and the private sector to establish the infrastructures and services that would make such sites more compelling and attractive to visit.

Simply put, aggregation would enable individual and disparate CeCs (and the communities and residents that they serve) to pool their resources and work together. The resulting whole might very well be more successful than individual CeCs and communities could be on their own.

NOTE

1. Source: Philippine Commission on Information and Communications Technology (2006).

5. Power distribution in Argentina: are the strategies for the base of the pyramid actually BOP strategies?

Miguel Ángel Gardetti

The great disparity in access to electricity throughout the world, and the relationship between poverty and limited access to electricity, are well known. In 2000 the 1 billion richest people used 50 percent of the electricity generated in the world, whereas the 1 billion poorest people used only 4 percent (Leffler and Dagbjartsson 2004). Researchers, such as Clark and Wallsten (2003) and Komives et al. (2003), have also established that the poorest households have the lowest access rates to infrastructure services. The World Bank's *World Development Report 2004* considers access to basic utilities, including electricity, to be a public responsibility not exclusive to governments. According to this vision, the private sector is meant to play a major role in promoting power development (World Bank, 2004) and to join its efforts with those of the public sector (Inter-American Development Bank, n.d.; Hammond et al., 2007). The reasoning is that business-driven innovation, which contributes to economic growth, may also lead to both poverty alleviation and development. This promotion of increased access to electricity is reflected in the United Nations Millennium Development Goals (see, for example, UNDP, 2005).

Multiple points of connection between electricity consumption, poverty and the environment have been demonstrated. Although low electricity consumption is not a consequence of poverty, the void left by failure to render a sustainable electricity service is very closely related to several poverty indicators. For example, according to Vivien Foster (2000) these may be 24-hour exposure rates to indoor air pollutants and the proportion of households affected by energy-related incidents of poor health, such as respiratory illness, burns and paraffin poisoning (health); hours of reading by schoolchildren and grade completion rates of schoolchildren (education). And, along this line, the electrical power sector is essential to fostering the development of people living in poverty (World Resources Institute, 2004); according to Leffler and Dagbjartsson (2004), there is a great difference between education levels in children taught in areas with power supply and those taught in areas with no power supply.

This chapter examines the business strategies of three electricity companies in Argentina that seek to serve the so-called socio-economic base of the pyramid (BOP): Empresa Distribuidora y Comercialzadora Norte SA (EDENOR), in Buenos Aires City and northeastern Greater Buenos Aires; Empresa Distribuidora de Electricidad de Mendoza SA (EDEM), in Mendoza Province; and Empresa de Distribución Eléctrica de Tucumán SA (EDET), in Tucumán Province. Since organizations often mean different things when they refer to 'base-of-the-pyramid undertakings', this chapter reviews whether the strategies of these three Argentinean power distribution companies can be considered as 'BOP undertakings' from the perspective of the BOP Learning Lab Global Network. To conduct this research study, background information about the companies based on the work of the Argentina BOP Learning Lab was collected[1] and was supplemented with semi-structured interviews of company managers and, in the cases of EDENOR and EDET, with field visits to projects.

DISTINCTIVE FEATURES OF BOP STRATEGIES

The term 'base of the pyramid' was coined to designate an 'inclusive' form of capitalism, emphasizing the role of companies in poverty reduction (Hart and London, 2005) and giving rise to a new field of knowledge (Kandachar and Halme, 2007). In recent years, use of the terms 'base of the pyramid' and 'bottom of the pyramid' have proliferated quite impressively; however, their use remains inconsistent (Touesnard, 2008). Although 'base of the pyramid' is technically a demographic category rather than a market (Hart, 2008; Simanis and Hart, 2008; Simanis et al., 2008), when organizations refer to 'BOP work', 'BOP business' or 'BOP undertaking' it is not always clear what they mean or how what they are doing differs from other business activities in low-income communities (Touesnard, 2008).

For this reason, a key discussion topic at the first BOP Learning Lab Global Network Director's Summit, held in 2008, was the determination of the distinctive features of BOP strategies and undertakings.[2] Three critical factors typical of BOP strategies were identified:

- BOP undertakings are based on new business models, that require the development of new organization capacities taking into account different expressions and in-house stances (internal diversity) (Hart and London, 2005; London and Hart, 2004; London, 2007b), and these models should be transformational at a local level. That is, they should promote and develop local capabilities and socio-economic systems in order to create value for the parties involved (Simanis et al., 2005). This also means that the business, as a proactive partner, needs to leverage the local players' potential for developing success-oriented alliances between different sectors (for example, private sector, public sector and non-governmental organizations – NGOs) (Milstein, 2005). The reason for getting the experience and knowledge of local institutions involved (external diversity) is that some institutions can facilitate business in conditions that are quite different from those that executives are used to (Vachani and Smith, 2008; Gradl et al., 2008). Only by incorporating these concepts in a functional model will it be possible to develop solutions perfectly tailored to real problems in ways that respect the local culture and natural diversity (Gardetti, 2007; Hart, 2005).

- The 'triple bottom line' – sometimes referred to as 'people, planet, profit' – needs to be integrated into the strategy of any BOP undertaking. A better future will depend on the new paradigm of marrying business with development in ways that bring about social, environmental and economic stability (Boyer, 2003.)
- There should be aspiration and potential for scale and replication. If an undertaking is not able to help a business grow and expand, it has not met the BOP goal of transforming the local society and economy (Touesnard, 2008).

Two other critical factors discussed at the summit remain under review:

- The theory of disruptive innovation suggests that existing markets are the wrong place to search for further opportunities for development and that businesses should take a 'great leap' to the bottom of the pyramid to find new markets (Hart and Christensen, 2002). To meet the needs of people at the base of the pyramid, technological innovation should be regarded as a contextual process (Srinivasa and Sutz, 2008), for technological deprivation involves problems at various levels – namely, infrastructure, access to materials and products, institutional, people and economic resources (Kandachar and Halme, 2008).
- According to the principle of co-creation, which every BOP undertaking should adopt, the people living at the base of the pyramid should be viewed as partners and peers rather than as consumers and producers (Hart and Sharma, 2004; Simanis et al., 2005; Hart and London, 2005; Hart, 2005, 2007, 2008; London, 2007a; Simanis

and Hart, 2008; Simanis et al., 2008). That is, the local know-how of the poor has to be integrated, and it will deliver new capacities for building up new competencies that bring about the bottom-up approach (Waibel, 2009).

THE COMPANIES

The three companies in this study – EDENOR, EDEM and EDET – were identified and selected for several reasons. First, they are companies that distribute electricity to large, poor, population centers of different characteristics. Second, we selected them based on their background and the collection of information about them gathered by the Argentina BOP Learning Lab. The joint work between the above lab and two of the companies (EDENOR and EDET) was also considered.[3] And last, we considered the diverse shareholder structure of those companies.

As of September 2007, EDENOR distributed and traded power to 2 444 989 clients within an area of 4637 sq. km.[4] The concession area covers northern Buenos Aires City (corresponding to 25 percent of the city) and the northeast portion of Greater Buenos Aires, including Vicente Lopez, Escobar, San Fernando, San Isidro, San Martín, 3 de Febrero, Pilar, Moreno, Gral. Las Heras, Gral. Sarmiento, Gral. Rodríguez, Morón, Pilar, Marcos Paz and La Matanza (Figure 5.1). Note that Buenos Aires City and Greater Buenos Aires constitute 40 percent of the Argentinean power market. EDENOA's concession was granted for 95 years, divided into a period of 15 years up-front and eight renewal periods of ten years each. As of September 2007, the breakdown of the company's shareholding was as follows: EASA (owned by Pampa Holding), 51 percent; public shares, 48.8 percent; and shared ownership, 0.2 percent.[5]

The second company, EDET distributes and trades power to 385 026 clients. Its concession area covers Tucumán Province and is divided into five departments – Concepción, Monteros, Banda del Río Salí, Tafí Viejo and Metropolitan Area (EDET, 2007; see Figure 5.1). The company's shareholders are José Cartellone Construcciones Civiles SA, 45 percent; CGE Argentina SA, 45 percent; and Norelec SA, 10 percent (EDET, 2007). EDET was granted a concession for 90 years, beginning 4 August 1995.

The third company in the study, EDEM was created by Provincial Law 6498 – dealing with the streamlining of the Provincial Power Sector – and its Regulatory Decree 197/98.[6] In accordance with its concession agreement, EDEM is in charge of power supply and trade for 30 years as of 1 August 1998, to 353 000 clients in 11 of the 18 districts of Mendoza:

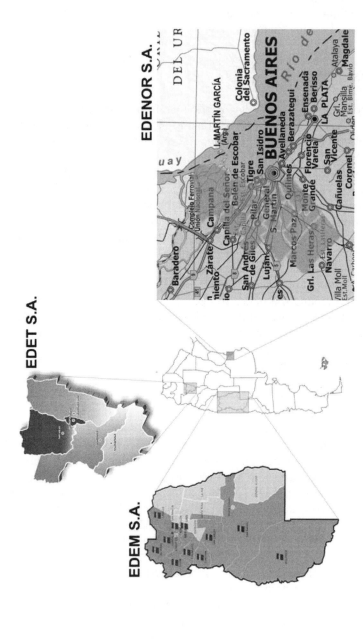

Source: Center of Study for Corporate Sustainability, Argentina; the area corresponding to EDENOR S.A. was adapted from a map of Buenos Aires Province by the Instituto Geográfico Militar (Military Geographical Institute) of Argentina.

Figure 5.1   Concession areas of the three companies

Capital, Guaymallén, Las Heras, Lavalle, Luján, Maipú, Tunuyán, Tupungato, San Carlos, San Rafael, and Malargüe (see Figure 5.1). The company's activity is regulated through the Provincial Power Regulatory Agency (Ente Provincial Regulador de la Energía Eléctrica, or EPRE). Its shares are held by the provincial government, 39 percent; the employees (of the former state-owned company EMSE), 10 percent; and private investors, 51 percent.[7]

THE SOCIAL AND ECONOMIC CRISIS OF 2001 AND ITS IMPACTS

In 2001 a social and economic crisis arose in Argentina that drastically worsened living conditions for the majority of the population. A survey by the National Institute of Statistics and Census (Instituto Nacional de Estadísticas y Censos, or INDEC) – whose figures were disclosed in July 2002 – showed that 21.5 percent of the active population was unemployed (INDEC, 2002). This rate translated into 3 038 000 unemployed individuals, representing a historical record. The impact of the crisis on the labor market was even broader, as an additional 12.7 percent of the labor force was underemployed (holding precarious or temporary jobs). The INDEC also reported that 52.8 percent of the inhabitants of the city of Buenos Aires and its neighboring area lived below the poverty line. That is to say, they did not have enough income to purchase a basic consumption basket of goods and services. Back in 2002 the basket was worth US$53 at the relevant exchange rate on 15 July of that year. Of the 6 048 000 inhabitants living below the poverty line, 2.7 million were indigent.[8] Overall, the poor quality of employment, along with inflation, which in the first quarter of 2002 reached 30.5 percent, pushed the poverty effect to the employed population segment, which did not receive subsidies from government plans even though the cost of living had increased so dramatically.

According to a Permanent Household Survey, from October 2001 to May 2002 the crisis was evidenced in many ways: restrictions to withdraw money from banks affected 2 million people, currency devaluation (260 percent as of July 2002), pesification (conversion of deposits and contracts that were denominated in United States dollars into Argentinean pesos), inflation and decreased actual salary (INDEC, 2002). These circumstances reflected another historical record: from October 2001 to May 2002, some 5.2 million people became poor; hence the skyrocketing poverty rate in urban areas.

As a consequence of these socio-economic changes, the three companies noticed a significant rise in the number of households that had to survive with no power or with illegal access to it, which is usually called 'hanging to the service'. For example, EDENOR's energy losses rose from 10.14 percent in January 2001 to 12.72 percent in April 2003; while EDET's climbed from 12.25 percent in December 2001 to 14 percent in January 2004; and EDEMSA losses went from 12.31 percent in December 2001 to 15.48 percent in December 2003.[9] In business jargon the electrical service providers refer to those who illegally connect to the service to obtain electricity at no cost as 'hanged'.[10] Because their actions are illegal, the 'hanged' are penalized with service cut-off.[11]

Being 'hanged' involves a risk of electrocution for the persons who hook up the connection, a risk that also extends to their families and to third parties because the connections are usually made with bare wires. When the number of 'hanged' people is high, it can also create an imbalance in the provider's installation; for instance, facilities are not prepared to address demand peaks resulting from large numbers of 'hanged' users. Carrying out power cuts according to the procedure designated for such cases was not a feasible solution for the three companies in this study, however; the sociopolitical cost of cutting off power to low-income people would have reinforced the public's general perception that companies privatized in the 1990s were corrupt.[12]

RESPONSE OF THE COMPANIES TO THE CRISIS

Given the effects of the economic crisis, as well as the public awareness and suspicion of the far from transparent privatization process that had taken place in the decade of the 1990s, the three power companies decided not to implement the traditional cut-offs. The companies then had to face the challenge of reconciling supposedly irreconcilable factors – for example, how to reduce the number of clients 'hanged' to the service (and their relevant risks), how to help such clients make more cost-effective use of power, and how to make them pay for the service when they could afford it.

Change and Innovation

EDENOR developed a program called Access to Power through Self-Manageable Systems (Acceso a la Energía por Sistemas Autoadministrables), which included a prepaid card-based power meter.[13] Not only did the company familiarize itself with poor people so that it could understand their needs, but it also made other changes that complemented the technological innovation of using the new meter for power distribution. It replaced the traditional payment commitment every 60 days (which

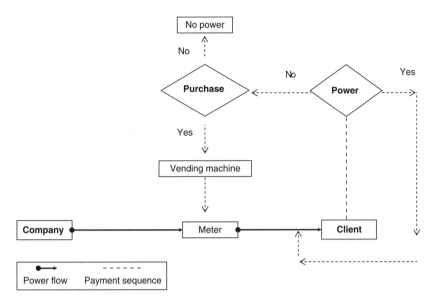

Source: Center of Study for Corporate Sustainability, Argentina.

Figure 5.2 EDENOR's new business model for the base of the pyramid

meant paying all at once for the previous two months' accumulated power consumption) by enabling fractionated, advance purchases of power from card vending machines; it transferred to the client the decision regarding times and amounts acquired in each transaction; and it fostered the efficient and sensible use of power (Figure 5.2).[14] These changes led the company to revise the rules concerning the attitude of 'hanging' debtors and households[15] (Gardetti and Lassaga, 2008). The project, which began as a pilot program with 100 prepaid meters in Escobar, was extended to Moreno, an area in the Greater Buenos Aires. There an additional 4668 prepaid meters were installed, thanks to the company's friendly relations with town councils.[16] With this project (and at scale) the company has an annual profit of US$39 600[17] based on the margin resulting from the electricity rate and exploitation costs. Should this project have not been in place, EDENOR would have losses of US$292 600, including exploitation costs and lost power.[18] Figure 5.3 shows EDENOR's previous BOP business model and the administrative burden (for example, billing, payment, warning notice) required for cut-off cases. A similar model was also used by EDET and EDEM.

EDET developed a project called Assisted Clients that was also based on a prepaid system (Figure 5.4). However, its execution was different

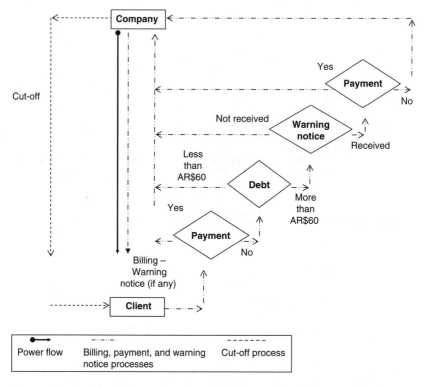

Source: Center of Study for Corporate Sustainability, Argentina.

Figure 5.3 EDENOR's traditional business model

from that conducted by EDENOR. The EDET project was conducted on the fringe of urban centers, in the settlements where the poorest segments of Argentinean society live. The company's most important innovation was the implementation of a case-by-case methodology that incorporated regular assistance visits to each household by a company agent, referred to as a proactive agent, who made the client aware of the efficient use of power and helped the client value the service received during the visit.[19] Additionally, during the visit, the agent informed the client of the household's consumption level expressed in kWh and its equivalent cash value. Based on this information, the client could make the payment as instructed by the agent at a government agency's office, such as the nearest police station, at times set by the company. These partial payments were subsequently credited to the client's personal account, and the company would send an invoice with the relevant credit or debit balance at the end

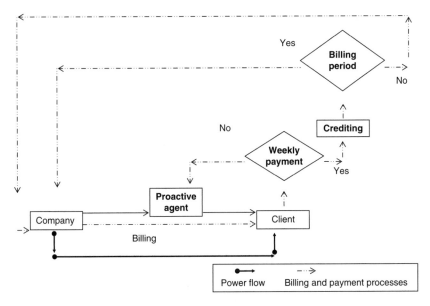

Source: Center of Study for Corporate Sustainability, Argentina.

Figure 5.4 EDET's new business model for the base of the pyramid

of the set period. This project reaches out to 21 000 clients and the annual average costs for execution amount to US$987 000;[20] while the company's annual revenues on average are US$1 298 000.[21]

The program set up by EDEM, called Light for Everyone (Luz para Todos), was developed in cooperation with the provincial government[22] and provided poor families with access to electrical power service, while taking into account their economic situation (Figure 5.5). To adjust each client's consumption level to his or her income, the company conducted a social field study with its own staff, including a survey of the client's living conditions, an inventory of the electrical appliances used, and the client's income. The company also taught and trained staff members in the efficient use of power, so that the staff could help raise clients' awareness about what it meant to pay for and access a basic service.[23] If the consumption level established by the social field study was exceeded for any reason, company staff would visit the client's house to discover the reason and would once again make the client aware of the responsibilities involved in accessing a basic service. Today the project reaches about 5000 clients with an annual investment for development of US$288 000.[24] This amount varies by year and relies on the number of clients who want

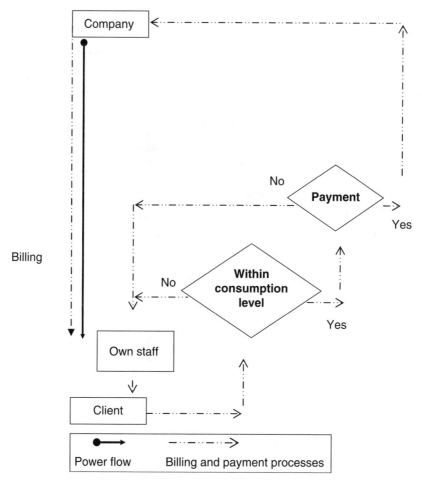

Source: Center of Study for Corporate Sustainability, Argentina.

Figure 5.5   EDEM's new business model for the base of the pyramid

to be in the system. The return on investment (ROI) for the company is three years.[25]

Beyond the First Steps

The first two companies – EDENOR and EDET – managed to go beyond the prepaid system framework. EDENOR supplemented its first program with one called Households for + Power (Casas por + Energía). By implementing social activities (workshops for neighbors on the sensible use of power) and sustainable technologies (architectural design focused on power efficiency), it promoted more efficient use of power, which was expected to result in a 30 percent reduction in current power consumption. The project included installing insulation to minimize power use for heating in winter, and removing humidity to avoid power waste. Additional significant energy savings were achieved by installing solar collectors to heat water used in the home, energy-efficient bulbs and intelligent refrigerators that did not emit polluting gases. This project was implemented in the town of Moreno (Greater Buenos Aires) which, through the Urban, Environmental and Regional Development Center (Instituto de Desarrollo Urbano, Ambiental y Regional, or IDUAR), supported and participated in the project. The project also received support from the Federal Secretariat of Energy through the Power Efficiency Project in Argentina (EDENOR, 2006).

EDET's program, called More Services (Más Servicios), was geared to provide proper electrical installation inside the houses. This program – implemented together with a local contractor and funded by the company according to clients' purchasing power – included installing circuit-breaker boards and outlets and replacing wiring. Taking into account its clients' needs, the company extended the improvements it provided to include gas installations and masonry work as well.

Some Considerations and Results Common to the Three Projects

In order to analyze the circumstances of different low-income consumers of electricity, the companies emphasized visiting poor communities. This process yielded a diagnosis that revealed the need to develop innovative alternatives. Based on the continuity of prepaid system programs, the companies, primarily EDENOR and EDET, took a proactive approach to go beyond those programs and offer alternatives to improve their users' lives. They changed their corporate vision from awareness of the finite nature of resources to social inclusion as a belief and value to be considered in their business decision-making process. They developed new management capabilities and learned to listen to the poor, acknowledging their real potential and the possibilities for improving their lives.

The access to a basic service, at no risk and without leaving anyone out, was undoubtedly a benefit for the base of the pyramid. But another benefit was just as important: the growing dignity and self-esteem that the poor experienced as a service became accessible and affordable to them. This improvement in their situation helped them avoid social exposure and uncomfortable events in their own primary and secondary social environments.

The reduction in power consumption was one of the most significant aspects of the three projects. The EDENOR project resulted in self-education regarding more efficient use of power, since users could know the consumption of their home meter and use that knowledge to make informed decisions. In this case, the average savings was 37.4 percent (EDENOR, 2004). In the other two projects, the reduction was even more significant because of the former 'abusive' use of the service through widespread illegal connections; in EDET the savings amounted to approximately 60 percent, and in EDEM approximately 50 percent.[26]

The clients who took part in EDENOR's project reaped an additional benefit. They experienced the feeling of being a citizen, because the card service purchase receipt was the only receipt they had, in case these clients wanted to apply for a loan to buy, for example, household gadgets, extended by the household gadget business.[27] (Di Natale, 2005). The main financial benefit for the company was saving costs associated with disconnecting bad debtors and illegal users. Even though this figure was not significant for the trial project, it was very significant when projected for those 200 000 users who had continuing difficulties in paying their bills (Di Natale, 2005).

Corporate Integration of the Distinctive Features of BOP Strategies

In implementing business models with their BOP bases, the three companies in this study varied in their deployment of the distinctive features of BOP strategies, as outlined by the 2008 BOP Learning Lab Global Network Director's Summit (see Table 5.1 for a summary). Two of the three companies – EDENOR and EDET – developed 'new' business models which, as noted above, required the development of new capacities taking into account different expressions and in-house stances (in-house diversity). These models differed in clear and significant ways from the previous business model applied to the base of the pyramid (compare Figures 5.2 and 5.4 with Figure 5.3), and they have a different value proposition. They involved moving from a service-centered to a community-centered proposition (Simanis and Hart, 2008). This required the development of new in-house capacities: trials, a search for ideas, patience for ideas to develop (and succeed), and flexibility were the factors the organization considered, factors that managers were not used to including. This approach was related to the 'revolutionary routines' described by Mark Milstein et al. (2007), which intentionally breaks the status quo, helping companies innovate. This can be seen when two companies become familiar with the BOP, understanding the needs and creating a new business model accordingly. Thus, the knowledge gained from implementing new

Table 5.1 Corporate deployment of the distinctive features of BOP strategies

	New transformational business models			Ecosystem (alliances)	Triple bottom line			Scale and replication	Innovation at the BOP	Partners and peers
	Business model	Development of capabilities	Creation of value for the parties		Environmental	Social	Economic			
EDENOR	New business model (community-centric and not service-centric) with the development of new enterprise capabilities	Only some capabilities of the BOP people were developed, to an unknown extent	Created value only for the directly involved parties (company and its BOP clients)	Only with town councils; no alliances with local players were promoted or developed	Power consumption reduction	Integration of BOP people into the legitimate service and promotion of human dignity; be a 'citizen'	Savings from the eradication of theft and/or fraud by those who were 'hanging'; cost savings from the elimination of the formal cut-off process, profit based on the electricity rate surcharge and operating costs	Restricted to the concession area and the clients who could be connected to the distribution network; also affected by political factors and the public perception of corporate corruption.	No new technologies developed, but the analysis and understanding of the BOP environment helped in the development of new business models	No co-generation principle in place

Table 5.1 (continued)

	New transformational business models			Ecosystem (alliances)	Triple bottom line			Scale and replication	Innovation at the BOP	Partners and peers
	Business model	Development of capabilities	Creation of value for the parties		Environmental	Social	Economic			
EDET	New business model (community-centric and not service-centric) with the development of new enterprise capabilities	Only some capabilities of the BOP people were developed, to an unknown extent	Created value only for the directly involved parties (company and its BOP clients)	Only with town councils and the provincial government; no alliances with local players were promoted or developed	Power consumption reduction	Integration of BOP people into the legitimate service and promotion of human dignity	Savings from the eradication of theft and/or fraud by those who were 'hanging'; cost savings from the elimination of the formal cut-off process; profit from the difference between project development income and execution costs	Restricted to the concession area and the clients who could be connected to the distribution network	No new technologies developed, but the analysis and understanding of the BOP environment helped in the development of new business models	No co-generation principle in place

EDEM	Incremental adaptation of the traditional business model	Created value only for the directly involved parties (company and its BOP clients)	Only the provincial government. No alliances with local players were promoted or developed	Power consumption reduction	Integration of BOP people into the legitimate service and promotion of human dignity	Savings from the eradication of theft and/or fraud by those who were 'hanging'; cost savings from the elimination of the formal cut-off process; annual investments for developing a 3-year ROI project	Restricted to the concession area and the clients who could be connected to the distribution network	No new technologies developed, but the BOP analysis helped make an incremental improvement to the traditional business model	No co-generation principle in place

Source: Center of Study for Corporate Sustainability, Argentina.

models changed the traditional paradigms, which evolved into new beliefs rooted in the project's[28] performance (Di Natale, 2004, 2005). In connection with the new value proposition, the two new models were innovations that combined business development and sustainability, whereas the traditional model was applied to the same clients and was based mainly on economic aspects.

In contrast to the first two companies, EDEM developed a business model that merely adapted the pre-existing model to the local conditions, thus indicating that the company was more committed to evolutionary routines and geared toward an 'incremental' adaptation (Milstein et al., 2007). However, according to Vermeulen et al. (2008), this degree of change is not enough to achieve success at the base of the pyramid.

While there is evidence that the three models (mainly two of them, EDENOR and EDET) created value only for the directly involved parties – that is, the company and its clients – they did help develop certain abilities in poor people. The education that people received about both the service and its more efficient use is an obvious example. However, the extent to which the development of abilities in poor people is achieved by these models is not yet clear.

The creation of an 'ecosystem' of alliances[29] is not a trivial aspect of the BOP strategies; the dynamism of such an ecosystem, just like the focus on the local level, is essential both for development (Elliott, 1999; Wheeler et al., 2003) and for understanding the local culture (Johnson School of Management, 2005). For their part, Rondinelli and London (2003) argue that these alliances can provide information on the local context, legitimacy and easy access to resources. The three companies in the present study promoted and created only public–private alliances. This is not surprising, given that all three of them at one time belonged to the public sector and participated in the privatization process. In addition, the provincial government was a shareholder in EDEM. Other players who might expedite the development (Hammond, 2004) such as non-governmental organizations (NGOs) and social entrepreneurs, were not included.

All of the projects showed results at the environmental, social and economic levels. The significant savings in power consumption related to the environmental field; the integration of people into the legitimate service and the promotion of their human dignity (through a sense of belonging) related to the social aspect; and the profits for companies related to the economic aspect (see the economic results – for the three companies – in each project description).

For the three projects, scale and replication were aspects inherently restricted both to the companies' concession areas and to the clients in those areas who could be connected to the current distribution network.[30]

One of the companies, EDENOR, faced other limiting factors. The first one, political in nature, was evident in a statement by Representative Hector Polino, of the Free Consumers Association; he said that: 'instead of installing these types of [prepaid-system] meters, a social rate should be set for low-income or unemployed people' (Clarín.com, 2004).[31] The second factor was the widespread public perception that companies privatized in the 1990s were corrupt. On 20 October 2003, a person wrote in an opinion forum in the Energy Crisis Portal: 'The company is seen as the great philanthropist providing access to basic utilities and "tailored" to the population that has unmet basic needs. The connivance between governments and privatized companies has not ended' (Crisis Energética, 2004).[32] These are not isolated voices and, within the frame of 'populist' government, this project may jeopardize scaling up. In fact, the EDENOR Access to Power through Self-Manageable Systems (Acceso a la Energía por Sistemas Autoadministrables) project could not be further developed as a result of the above.

None of the three companies developed specific technologies to provide access to power at the base of the pyramid. However, their thorough analysis and understanding of the living conditions of their BOP clients helped them devise and develop new or modified business models.

The co-creation principle is essential for every project at the base of the pyramid. According to this principle, the new value propositions are jointly developed by the company and the community, and business models are creatively combined with both partners' abilities (Simanis and Hart, 2008). None of the three companies in this study considered this principle in their BOP projects.

CONCLUSIONS AND LESSONS LEARNED

In modern times, no country has witnessed a reduction in poverty without a significant increase in power consumption (DFID, 2002; UNDP, 2005). The three cases under review here are characterized by an understanding of the local conditions, which gave rise to a new or streamlined business model in an internal context (internal diversity). Although these cases may share a similar motivation, the internal processes that led to the business models differed according to the historical development of internal capabilities, provincial contexts, and shareholders' culture and practices. The impacts of the three models were limited, however, mainly because they lacked an 'ecosystem' developed through alliances with a variety of parties and did not adhere to the co-creation principle. Both factors are related to external diversity (London, 2007b).

Several authors have argued and empirically proved that access to the base of the pyramid requires a new capability – the native capability (Hart, 2005, 2007; Hart and London, 2005; London and Hart, 2004; Sánchez et al., 2007). According to Hart and London (2005), native capability involves participation in mutual business associations, based on long-term trust and understanding, to combine creatively the capacities and technologies of all players, including fringe groups and communities. This concept has also been referred to as 'business intimacy' by Simanis and Hart (2008), a term that implies a deep interdependence whereby both the company and the community nurture a shared commitment to long-term growth and development for each of them. These concepts, which regard people at the BOP as partners and peers, mark the differences between the 'early' BOP strategies (BOP 1.0) and the 'new-generation' strategies (BOP 2.0) (Hart, 2007; Simanis and Hart, 2008; Simanis et al., 2008). EDENOR and EDET – through their supplementary projects Households for + Power (Casas por + Energía) and More Services (Más Servicios), respectively – now had an opportunity to evolve new-generation BOP strategies, because these programs had helped the companies gain a more thorough knowledge of BOP needs by facilitating a closer relationship between the companies and the BOP communities they served.

Over the next 40 years to 2050, the global population is expected to grow by 2.2 billion, reaching 8.2 billion people, most of whom will live in developing countries (World Bank, 2006). It is also anticipated that many of these people will lack access to products and services through traditional business models. Therefore, scalability is a significant element of exploring the opportunities at the base of the pyramid (Mutis and Ricart, 2008). Achieving scalability requires clear policies and regulatory structures to drive BOP integration into power distribution systems.

Local entrepreneurship and bottom-up development are both regarded as fundamentals of the BOP conceptualization. Although the poor are considered to be active agents with valuable insights (Chambers, 1997; Hammond, 2004; Sen, 1999), this realization is seldom put into practice, because traditional strategic and innovative approaches are not suitable for BOP undertakings (Gardetti, 2007). Although the development of the three models in this study was based on the companies' knowledge of BOP conditions – which are co-creation (bottom-up approach) instances – a more suitable approach would have been what recent literature has described as 'an emerging and creative innovation process' that emphasizes bottom-up joint efforts (Hamel and Prahalad, 1991; Alvarez and Barney, 2007).

NOTES

1. The lab was set up in Argentina in September 2005. One of its activities – the multisector meeting – brings together companies, non-governmental organizations (NGOs), and members of both the government and academia who are concerned by the huge existing inequality in Argentina. The parties work together to determine the best way in which the private sector can eradicate poverty as a proactive partner, betting on the potential of local players to cooperate in fostering and jointly promoting local development. Other activities of this lab include the development of Regional Mini Labs; research and case study development in collaboration with companies, civil organizations, and public administration and multilateral organizations; education and training for the development of strategies and models of inclusive business; publications; and participation in congresses, conferences, forums and other labs.
2. This event was held at Tilburg University (The Netherlands) on June 3–4 2008. The participating institutions and organizations included, among others, Fundação Getulio Vargas (Brazil), Tilburg University, Instituto de Estudios para la Sustentabilidad Corporativa (Argentina), Cornell University (USA), IESA Business School (Venezuela), Confederation of Danish Industry (Denmark), the University of Halle-Wittenberg and TU Munich Business School (Germany), Chambers of Commerce SA (South Africa), CHOICE Humanitarian (USA), ESSEC (France) and Deutsche Gesellschaft für Technische Zusammenarbeit (GTZ) GmbH (Germany).
3. The examples relate to study and learning cases developed with EDENOR and used in academia. Two cases were developed with EDENOR: a teaching case (Gardetti and Quiroga Furque, 2005) and a case study (Gardetti and Lassaga, 2008).
4. Subgerencia de Gestión Entes y Análisis Regulatorio de Edenor SA.
5. Ibid. Pampa Holding SA is the largest integrated power company in Argentina; through several subsidiaries it is involved in power generation, transmission and distribution in Argentina.
6. Company presentation, Institutional Relations Manager's Office.
7. Ibid.
8. The 'indigence line' concept was defined by the INDEC, based on whether households had enough income to purchase a 'basic consumption basket of food to meet their minimum power and protein needs, or not'.
9. These companies calculate their losses of electrical power as the difference between purchased and sold power; these losses include technical loss (inherent to the business and electrical systems), non-technical loss resulting from administrative errors, power theft and fraud.
   In this note, should 'sold power' perhaps be something like 'generated power'? I do not quite understand how it is 'sold' power if it is not 'purchased'. In connection with this note, during the privatization process the government divided the electricity sector into three 'legs' – generation, transport and distribution – to avoid monopolies. The three companies in this study are 'distributors', that is, they purchase electricity to the generator and they sell it to end users. The difference between purchase and sale is the losses.
10. People who are designated as 'hanged' are part of both the structural poverty and the 'new' poverty in Argentina. In an EDENOR video, one of the dwellers of such a district, Sergio, refers to the fragile nature of life in that area of Greater Buenos Aires: 'Our situation is different now. Before, you could get $43 [US$11.82 at the July 2002 exchange rate] to pay for electricity. If you have a job, you can manage to get that money, but if your child gets sick and you need to feed him or her, that is the top priority. It is a very common situation that leads you to be "hanged"'.
11. The typical penalty is service cut-off.
12. President Carlos S. Menem, who took office in July 1989, firmly led Argentina to a free-enterprise and open-economy system, pushing an extremely strong privatization process designed to separate the government from its historical involvement in the

economy and generate revenue to deleverage both domestically and abroad. In the first half of the 1990s, the country experienced very important growth, evidenced by an increased gross domestic product (GDP). However, growth did not translate into development, and the inequality gap significantly widened. For example, according to Gasparini et al. (n.d.), the gap – inequality between the rich and the poor, estimated on the average income of the 10 percent richest population versus the average income of the 10 percent poorest population – for Greater Buenos Aires went from 17-fold in 1990 to 26-fold in 2000. Meanwhile, investigations of several officials of President Menem's Cabinet clearly raised the public's awareness that the privatization process had not been entirely transparent.

13. The technology used in this project included a prepaid card-based power meter with a 'dual body'. One part of the meter – installed within the house – has a keypad and a viewer, where the customer enters the code contained on the ticket provided upon purchasing electricity service. The other part of the meter is installed outside the house, usually on a high line pole. Purchasing the card is simple, since vending machines are located, at most, 15 blocks (1500 meters) from individuals' homes.

14. For more detailed information on this case, see Gardetti and Lassaga (2008).

15. This means that with this project, EDENOR had to review its stance on the 'hanged' or in-arrears clients (see the discussion of the changes in the company's corporate vision and the development of new management capabilities elsewhere in this chapter).

16. There are three reasons why the company decided to test the pilot in Escobar District (Buenos Aires Province). First, residents of this area represented the types of clients eligible for the company (of the 100 selected clients, 14 percent were 'lent power', 6 percent 'did not have electricity', 50 percent had a debt with the company and 30 percent were 'hanged'). Second, these clients tended to remain within the formal system and not in an illegal system. Third, the town council and the company had a good relationship.

17. This corresponds to AR$151 297 at a 3.82 ARS/USD exchange rate.

18. Data provided by the company.

19. Visits were daily at the beginning of the program, and later were reduced to once a week, as clients' awareness and knowledge increased.

20. This corresponds to AR$3 770 000 at a 3.82 ARS/USD exchange rate.

21. Data provided by the company.

22. The government did not make any economic contribution but rather facilitated carrying out the program.

23. In most cases, the electrical service is the only service the BOP can access. Therefore, raising awareness of the importance of getting access to this service and its efficient use is essential in these models. In conversations with such users, they often make statements such as: 'I didn't know how much electricity I used. It was just plug and use. Now I take precautions', or 'I want to pay for electricity and don't want to be hanged as most people in my neighborhood do.'

24. This corresponds to AR$1 100 000 at a 3.82 ARS/USD exchange rate.

25. Data provided by the company.

26. Interview with EDET marketing manager; EDEM presentation, Institutional Relations Manager's Office.

27. Usually, in order to have access to a line of credit to purchase a household gadget, the business selling those products requests a utility receipt to have access to the credit line. As those people do not have access to drinking water or a household gas system they do not have those utility receipts. The only receipt they might show to meet this requirement is the ticket from the vending machine; otherwise they will not have access to the loan.

28. The created knowledge changed the traditional paradigms and evolved into new beliefs that supported the execution of projects.

29. A BOP ecosystem is made up of companies of different sizes (large domestic companies, multinational corporations, small and medium-sized enterprises, and small undertakings) NGOs, academia, local government and the wider community.

30. An exception was the alliance EDET formed with the provincial government of Tucumán to supply power through the 'distributed generation' (solar energy) system to users not living near the current distribution network.
31. Within 'populist' frameworks, utility prices get a lot of attention, especially when it comes from congressmen.
32. This statement expresses the underlying idea that the poor are being exploited with the government's consent.

6. Prepaid meters in electricity: a cost–benefit analysis

Ariel A. Casarín and Luciana Nicollier

The concerns for universal service in utilities have motivated firms and regulators to identify technological and regulatory options aimed at encouraging access, and making it easier for consumers to pay for their services. In both cases, Latin America has pioneered the adoption of innovative mechanisms.[1] The improvement of access to infrastructure services has led to industry restructuring, private sector involvement and consequential regulatory reforms. Higher access rates have then been encouraged with the identification and imposition of connection targets, the creation of community involvement and microcredit programs, as well as the use of new technologies. Following this, higher levels of affordability have been sought with the use of instruments that ease the burden of bills via cost and tariff cutbacks, and the introduction of alternative payment means.

Indeed, most efforts to secure higher levels of affordability have consisted of mechanisms aimed at reducing the cost of services, either affecting their quality or reducing their demand. Other efforts, however, have targeted the adoption of various subsidy schemes, either directly or through tariff structures (Gómez-Lobo and Contreras, 2003). In general, experiences with policies that adopt alternative payment methods for utilities have been scarce. The simplest alternative which is often suggested consists of increasing the frequency of billing to low-income users.[2] However, a disadvantage of this mechanism is that it would increase administrative collection costs, which would ultimately result in higher tariffs (Estache et al., 2002).

Since the middle of the 1990s, and probably following their rapid adoption in the UK, prepayment meters – either in electricity, water or piped gas – have been proposed as an innovative solution aimed at facilitating affordability and reducing the cost of utilities. This mechanism, essentially, requires that users pay for the delivery of goods or services before their consumption. In this way, consumers hold credit and then use the service until the credit is exhausted. Prepayment systems have been introduced for the first time in South Africa, but are now widely used in the

UK, Turkey and India (Tewari and Shah, 2003). Yet, their use is still controversial. On the one hand, those who support the diffusion of prepaid meters claim that they benefit both consumers and utilities because they help users to consume more efficiently and to improve the management of their budget, while allowing firms to reduce financial costs, as well as the costs of operation and bad debts. On the other hand, those who are against prepaid meters argue that their adoption is expensive for firms and risky for low-income consumers, as the insecurity and volatility of their income may force them to make little use of the service, or ultimately bring about involuntary self-disconnection.

In spite of the rapid diffusion of prepayment systems, the arguments in favor of or against prepaid meters have not been comprehensively examined before, and neither has their welfare impact. This chapter contributes to the literature of affordability in utility services because it uses social cost–benefit analysis to evaluate the adoption of electricity prepaid meters in the first municipality to have adopted them in Argentina. The fact that the district's utility has offered prepaid meters to all users since 1996 creates a data-rich experiment to apply cost–benefit techniques to evaluate the adoption of prepayment systems. The chapter contributes to the analysis of policies oriented to ease affordability for at least two reasons. First, because it conducts a complete analysis that factors in the end results of prepaid meter implementation in respect of users, the utility and the government. Second, because it makes it possible to identify the components of the results – that is, where gains and losses come from – and through this process, to help establish regulatory definitions concerning prepaid meters, which in many cases have yet to be made. Despite the fact that the cost–benefit analysis is based on a very particular experience – that of a small local community – its results provide useful insights into the possible implications of prepaid meters from a social perspective. The empirical evaluation is also complemented with an examination of the results of a survey that explores the perception of users about prepaid meters.

The results indicate that prepaid meters bring about a favorable change in social welfare. For consumers, the benefits of the system originate from a better allocation of resources, while for utilities, the advantages derive from the reduction of arrears in accounts receivable and of operational and financial costs. The government, however, sustains a loss generated by lower tax revenues related to changes in electricity consumption and tariffs. Moreover, the increase in social welfare evolves across time in a way that is typical of investments with high sunk costs, which here relate to the investment in the new meters. A simulation exercise confirmed the system's potential as a means to increase social welfare, but highlights the role of tariff discounts and the importance of defining whether new meters are paid for by consumers of the firm. In addition, the results of a survey conducted in the district among residential users suggest a generalized level of satisfaction among prepayment users, and highlight the importance of the variables linked to the cost of the service, both directly through lower tariffs and indirectly by way of the enhanced control of consumption, as allowed by the prepayment technology. The survey also indicates that self-disconnection does not seem to be a major issue.

The chapter is organized as follows. The next section describes the main features of prepayment meters in electricity. Then we present the cost–benefit model, its implementation and the data used in the analysis, followed by the main findings. The findings section also reports the results of several simulation exercises that explore the sensitivity of results to changes in the implementation of prepaid meters. Another section summarizes the main findings of a survey carried out among the district's electricity users. The last section concludes.

THE TECHNOLOGY AND ECONOMICS OF PREPAID ELECTRICITY

Prepayment systems refer to the outlay made by a consumer for using goods or services before consumption. In the case of electricity, the distinctive feature of the prepayment system is the reversion of the conventional commercialization system: whereas in the latter consumers hold a consumption credit because they pay for their energy bills periodically and after consumption, in the prepayment system such credit is not available, because the purchase and payment of energy are made prior to consumption. Thus, prepaid systems allow users to consume energy only when they have credit in an electricity account, as supply is discontinued when such credit is exhausted.

The prepayment technology was initially developed in South Africa in the late 1980s with the objective of supplying energy to a large number of low-income and geographically dispersed users. The system was initially intended to minimize the difficulties arising from users' irregular incomes, and to overcome the limited development of the infrastructure required for the dispatch and reception of credit slips. By the late 1990s, prepayment systems were very popular in India and in some Organisation for Economic Co-operation and Development (OECD) countries (Estache et al., 2000), and had probably reached their highest development in Great Britain (Waddams et al., 1998). In Argentina, prepayment meters were firstly introduced in 1993, when Energía Mendoza Sociedad del Estado (EMSE) placed a small number of meters in small shops at the

Mendoza Bus Central Station.[3] The experience was soon extended to other communities in the country.

From a technological point of view, the prepayment system consists of three well-differentiated components. The first is a service meter installed at the unit where energy will be consumed, such as a household dwelling or a store. In general, these meters are of the 'two-gang' type, and consist of a user's interface unit and a current measuring set. The interface unit is a device installed inside the building, which allows the user to 'interact' with the meter. The metering unit, on the other hand, is the intelligent component that stores credit and consumption information, and makes up the element that either clears or switches off electricity supply. The second component of the system is the so-called credit dispensing unit, which is the vending machine where consumers can purchase electricity credit. In general, these sales outlets are located at the utility's commercial offices, as well as in stores with long opening hours. The third component is the supporting device that links the various sales outlets to the utility's management system.

The way the system works for the user is simple. The user purchases energy at the sales outlet and, as part of the operation, receives a credit slip and a supporting device that identifies the operation, which may be a voucher with an identification code or another with magnetic support. The user then utilizes the device to add on his or her new consumption credit, either by entering a code or inserting the magnetic medium into the interface unit, which in both cases will be possible only if the device identification matches that of the meter.[4] The measuring unit then clears consumption of the amount of energy purchased and also displays, in real time, the available credit remaining for consumption. The meter switches off when credit is exhausted, and it switches on again only when the device corresponding to a new purchase is inserted.

From an economic perspective, the reversion of the commercialization system, as implied by prepaid meters, translates into changes in the cash flow of the utility and in consumers' behavior. In the case of the firm, prepayment systems may result in a decrease in metering, billing and disconnection and reconnection costs. The fact that payment is made prior to consumption implies both a significant improvement in the collection of revenues and a reduction in working capital. Moreover, prepaid systems may constitute a way to provide more flexible payment options to users with minimal or unreliable income streams, without increasing transactional costs to the firm. From the consumer's perspective, prepayment systems may result in a better understanding of how much energy is being consumed, inducing more control of energy use and budget management (Tewari and Shah, 2003). However, these apparent improvements are not cost-free, as the change from conventional to prepaid electricity implies a change in consumption habits which may reduce consumers' utility. Prepaid electricity changes the consumer's budget constraint, and so modifies the quantity of electricity he or she is willing to consume. The change from conventional to prepaid electricity implies that the cost of electricity faced by consumers includes not only the price of electricity itself, but also the opportunity cost of reload time and of advanced payment. This change in the price of electricity relative to other consumption goods may result in too little electricity consumption, or even to self-disconnection among poorer groups. Moreover, the system may result in a socially inefficient distribution of risk between consumers and the utility, as the latter eliminates the uncertainty in the collection of revenues while the former bear a higher risk of lack of energy and disconnection.[5]

THE MODEL

We examine the adoption of prepaid electricity using social cost–benefit analysis techniques. Jones et al. (1990) set out the method we used below, and Galal et al. (1994) and Newbery and Pollit (1997) apply it to examine privatization policies. The method compares the performance of the electricity distribution system in the local district after the adoption of prepaid meters (the factual scenario) with what that performance would have been had prepayment meters not been adopted (the counterfactual scenario). Thus, we construct for the utility a counterfactual scenario that serves as our control. The welfare gains (or losses) that we estimate below are then the difference between the level of welfare in factual and counterfactual scenarios. The basic notion behind this partial cost–benefit analysis is simple: the adoption of prepayment meters should be encouraged if benefits exceed those of the best available alternative, which is represented by the counterfactual, but not adopted in the opposite case.

The model is based on the assessment of social welfare for each scenario, and its distribution among groups. The model requires an appreciation of the difference between two results: the social value of the system under the prepayment system and its social value if that innovation had not been adopted. The net effect on social welfare can thus be estimated by adding up the net welfare changes of each group. These changes can all be expressed as $\Delta W = \lambda_c \Delta C + \lambda_\pi \Delta \pi + \lambda_G \Delta G$, where ΔW represents the total net social welfare change, ΔC the changes in consumers' welfare, $\Delta \pi$ the changes in the firm's profits, ΔG the changes in the government income, and λ the weighing of each component on welfare.[6] Thereby, the cost–benefit analysis requires the construction of a simple model for each of the groups involved and the calculation of the changes in each group's welfare. The aggregated results for each group lead to a final outcome for all groups.

Changes in Consumers' Welfare

Consumers switching from the conventional to the prepayment system face two types of costs. One refers to direct monetary cost, while the other refers to differences in habits that result from replacing a post-consumption and single monthly payment with more frequent payments, which occur prior to consumption.[7] The main direct monetary effect is the cost of the new meter and its associated opportunity cost – which we proxy using the interest rate for savings accounts deposits. Other direct monetary effects include possible changes in the cost of electricity due to tariff differentials. In this case, consumers benefit from a 5 percent discount on the final unit price of electricity consumed. Finally, users pay the opportunity cost arising from advance payment of consumption, which is estimated by relating consumers' average expenditure to a rate capturing the opportunity cost of money.

Periodic purchases of electricity imply a change in consumer habits, because they have to incur the extra costs associated with the time spent on additional buys. The extent of this cost would vary with the periodicity of energy reloads (it would be neutral if reloads occurred once a month, as this would demand an effort similar to that incurred when paying the conventional monthly bill), and it would be directly dependent on the user's salary; it is possible to presume that the higher an individual's salary, the higher the opportunity cost of their time. We therefore estimate this cost by firstly computing an average hourly cost, which we approximate using census income data for the district, and then multiplying that cost by both the estimated time incurred in each reload and the average number of yearly purchases made by each household using the prepayment system.[8]

Changes in Utility Profits

The effects of introducing the prepayment meters on the firm's profits were estimated as $\Delta\Pi = \Delta R - \Delta C - r^F\Delta F - r^V\Delta V$, where ΔR sums up income changes, ΔC the change in operating costs, $r^F\Delta F$ the changes in the cost of fixed capital F at an r^F rate, and $r^V\Delta V$ those in net working capital V invested in electricity distribution at a rate r^V. Economic profits differ from accounting profits because r^F includes not only depreciation and the cost of debt, but also the expected return of shareholders, and it is also different from accounting profits because it factors in the opportunity cost of net working capital $(r^V V)$.

Income changes ΔR_t for each year t were obtained by breaking them down into price P and quantity Q components for each user category i registering prepayment users using the formula $\Delta R_{it} = \Delta P_i \cdot Q_{t-1} + \Delta Q_i \cdot P_t$. Then, $\Delta R_t = \Sigma_i \Delta R_{it}$. Income changes were then computed using tariff and demand data for each user category that come from the firm's annual reports. The prepayment system may impact the firm's operating cost associated with meter readings, dispatch of correspondence, collection costs, invoice claims and disconnecting service. Cost changes could be obtained through an econometric estimation of the firm's cost function, which in this case was not possible because of the limited number of observations. Therefore, cost changes ΔC were estimated by linking an estimation of the amount of inputs applied in those activities to their cost, which were estimated with data from the firm's financial statements (see Ofgem, 1999 for a similar approach).

Cost changes due to bad debts were estimated by collating for each year a rate for bad debts for each scenario, which was then multiplied by total sales. For the factual scenario, the bad debts rate was obtained from the quotient between the costs of bad debts (resulting from the sum of all charges to profit and loss in concept of allowances for this concept plus court costs) and sales, while in the case of the counterfactual scenario, they were projected using average rates over the years prior to the adoption of the prepaid system (1992–96).

Changes in working capital ΔV were estimated for each scenario by applying an opportunity cost rate r^V to the difference between the product of each year's sales and the cash conversion cycle. In the factual scenario, the latter was obtained by multiplying the sum of the inverse of the rates of cash turnover, accounts receivable and accounts payable times 365.[9] The counterfactual scenario was projected using average rates over the years prior to the adoption of the prepaid system (1992–96). Opportunity costs for both scenarios were approximated by the average rate for current account advances to the private sector. However, if the cash conversion cycle was positive, the opportunity cost for each year was estimated by the average rate for saving account deposits. All series come from the Central Bank.

Changes in fixed assets ΔF are of two types. The first consists of the cost of new prepayment meters, which in this case affects the firm only as regards depreciation charges, as meter costs are incurred by users, although replacement costs at the end of their useful life are considered as the utility's responsibility. The second type of change is associated with the new equipment needed to operate the system (the equipment to issue vouchers for reloading at the sales outlets and to link this information to the utility's operation systems). These costs stem from the incorporation of computer equipment, and their magnitude was obtained during interviews held with the firm's management. Estimations assume the useful life of such assets to be seven years, which together with an opportunity cost r^F equivalent to 14 percent results in an annual cost for their use equivalent to 30 percent of their value.

Changes in Government Revenue

Changes in government revenue result from the effects that adoption of the prepayment system cause on fiscal revenues at various levels of government. Tax receipts are affected not only because consumption of electricity is variously taxed, but also because the sale of prepayment meters implies an increase in the collection of value-added and income taxes.

Federal taxes on power consumption are the value-added tax (VAT) and the Santa Cruz Provincial Fund (Law 23681) tax. The tax rate of the former is 21 percent, while the latter – aimed at financing the works of interconnection to the national grid and to subsidize the cost of electricity in Santa Cruz Province – is 0.6 percent. Provincial levies, on the other hand, are the Special Fund for Major Provincial Power Projects (Law 9038), the Province's Electrical Power Development Fund (Law 7290), the Law 9226 Fund and the Law 11969 tax.[10] The former two are applicable to residential users only, with rates of 5.5 percent and 10 percent, whereas the other two are applicable to all users (except municipal distribution utilities and public lighting) with rates of 6 percent and 0.6 percent, respectively. Electricity consumption is also taxable for the Provincial Rate Equalization Fund, which with a 5 percent rate seeks to balance final prices in the Buenos Aires province by compensating cost differences among suppliers. Changes in government revenue were thus estimated by applying the aforementioned rates to the changes in the utility's income, as explained above. Changes in receipts relating to the sale of prepayment meters were estimated by applying, respectively, value-added and income tax to sales and the supplier's estimated profit.

THE ADOPTION OF PREPAID METERS IN A LOCAL DISTRICT

Carmen de Areco

Carmen de Areco is a small municipality in the Buenos Aires Province that was the first to widely adopt electricity prepaid meters in Argentina (Table 6A.1 in the Appendix provides comparative socio-economic data of the district). The district's power distribution company, CELCA,[11] made prepayment electricity optional to all consumers within its franchise area in 1996. CELCA was created in 1945 and is one of almost 200 municipal electricity distribution utilities operating in the Province of Buenos Aires. These utilities – most of which are organized as cooperatives – were traditionally allowed to set their own tariffs until 1996, when privatization of the then vertically integrated electricity operator of the provincial state, called Empresa de Servicios Eléctricos de la Provincia de Buenos Aires (ESEBA), resulted in the creation of independent power producers, three new regional electricity distribution utilities – in whose exclusive franchise areas municipal utilities operate – and a new provincial regulatory authority, named Organismo de Control de Energía Eléctrica de la Provincia de Buenos Aires (OCEBA). Following privatization, local electricity distributors purchase energy from one of the three regional utilities at OCEBA's regulated tariffs.[12] This agency also regulates the final tariffs local distributors charge to final consumers.

Table 6.1 summarizes some economic indicators for CELCA before and after the implementation of prepaid meters. By 1996, when the system became available, the utility had 4888 users, three-quarters of which were residential. (Note that Table 6A.1 in the Appendix shows that access to electricity in the district is almost universal.) A total of 134 users switched to prepayment during 1996. The series show that average demand has remained roughly stable except for those using prepaid meters, for which demand has increased since 1996. Figure 6.1 shows that by 2003, the average demand of residential users for prepayment converged with those of the conventional system. It also illustrates that the number of residential users of prepaid meters increased steadily, reaching about 45 percent of total residential users by 2003.

Table 6.1 also summarizes some performance indicators of the utility. The data show that the average tariff increased 40 percent between 1992 and 1996, since when it has reduced slightly. CELCA encouraged the prepayment system by granting those that switch a 5 percent discount on unit charges, despite that fact that switchers had to pay for the new meter and its installation costs. The data show that revenues, assets and the firm's equity all increased much faster between 1992 and 1996 than between 1997 and 2003, when prepaid meters were in use. It is interesting to contrast, however, the composition of the firm's asset structure before and after the implementation of prepaid meters. The data show that liquid assets and investments increased markedly since the adoption of the prepayment, reversing the deteriorating trend that prevailed before. Moreover, the figures display that the upward trend of accounts receivable was reversed, to the extent of allowing the firm to reduce significantly the total amount of unpaid bills.

Table 6.1   *Major economic indicators, CELCA, various years*

	1992	1996	2003	Δ annual average 1992–96 (%)	Δ annual average 1996–2003 (%)
Conventional users					
Residential	3 197	3 563	2 360	2.7	−5.7
Industrial	50	110	84	21.8	−3.8
Other[1]	1 197	980	931	−4.9	−0.7
Prepayment users					
Residential	0	184	1 974	268.3	40.4
Industrial	0	3	11	31.6	20.4
Other	0	48	302	163.2	30.0
Total	4 444	4 888	5 662	2.4	2.1
Average annual consumption (kW)					
Conventional users					
Residential	1 214	1 458	1 322	4.7	−1.4
Industrial	22 213	54 605	56 723	25.2	0.5
Other	5 374	5 040	4 887	−1.6	−0.4
Prepayment user					
Residential	0	795	1 407	431.0	8.5
Industrial	0	25 343	62 595	1 161.7	13.8
Other	0	2 671	4 324	618.9	7.1
Average tariff	0.10	0.14	0.13	8.2	−0.8
Revenue	1 814 343	2 392 419	2 871 011	7.2	2.6
Assets	2 192 814	3 615 308	3 689 441	13.3	8.7
Cash and equivalents	29 987	21 580	85 662	−7.4	21.8
Investments	20 123	14 040	118 712	−8.6	35.7
Accounts receivable	602 681	1 235 519	813,840	19.7	−5.8
Fixed assets	1 183 528	2 034 615	2 201 509	14.5	1.1
Inventories	245 012	248 463	414 948	0.3	7.6
Other assets	111 484	61 090	54 769	−13.9	−1.5
Equity	853 761	2 303 861	2 974 780	28.2	3.7

Note: 1.   Includes business and rural users, the waterworks firm and other government agencies as well as non-paying users and the utility's own consumption.

Source: Own estimates based on CELCA's Annual Reports, 1992, 1996 and 2003.

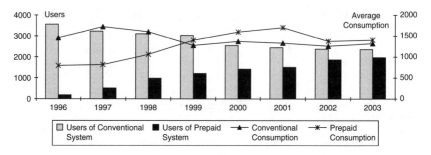

Source: Own estimates based on CELCA's Annual Reports, 1996–2003.

Figure 6.1   Residential users of energy and mean annual consumption, CELCA, by type of system, 1996–2003

Results

Table 6.2 summarizes the results (in 1996 constant pesos) of the cost–benefit analysis of the adoption of prepaid meters, and the distribution of net welfare changes across consumers, the firm and the government. The rows in the table distinguish each element that was considered to compute net welfare changes. The series also displays the distribution of these results over time, and distinguishes those of the 1996–2003 period from those projected for future periods, which consist of adding the results projected for each year between 2004 and 2008 to those projected for the years following 2008, which in turn were obtained by calculating the present value of a perpetuity that assumes 2008 values will remain constant.[13]

Results suggest that the policy leads to an increase in overall welfare equivalent to AR\$214 200, or AR\$38 per user.[14] Results differ across groups, as users and the firm both benefit from implementation of the system, whereas the government does not. Data in the first column show that until 2003, the policy did not result in improvements for any group. A breakdown of results indicates that users bore the largest losses, as the benefits of those using prepaid meters originated from tariff discounts and tax savings were not sufficient to make up for the meters' costs. The following columns, however, show that this result is overturned when one takes the projections into account. In the case of users, projections indicate that the benefits from lower prices and associated taxes exceed the costs associated with the advanced payment of electricity, the time incurred in recharging the meter and the meter cost.[15] Thus, the last column shows that adoption of the system results in a total benefit to consumers of AR\$125 000, or AR\$55 per user. In the case of the utility, projections indicate that losses of

Table 6.2   Distribution of profit and loss in the prepayment electricity system

Concept	1996–2003 A	2004–08 B	Perpetuity C	Projection subtotal D = B + C	Total Present Value E = A + D
Prepayment users					
Tariffs	123 681	130 234	644 564	774 798	898 479
Taxes	53 471	57 623	286 107	343 731	397 202
Reloading time	−19 471	−16 699	−64 036	−80 735	−100 206
Advance payment	−9 488	−9 393	−46 534	−55 926	−65 415
Meters	−531 463	−100 878	−372 619	−473 497	−1 004 960
Subtotal	−383 270	60 887	447 483	508 370	125 100
Utility					
Revenue	−123 681	−130 234	−644 564	−774 798	−898 479
Running costs	131 369	109 464	413 619	523 083	654 452
Working capital	106 322	47 037	230 763	277 801	384 122
Bad debts	−77 227	94 880	465 481	560 361	483 134
Bad debt taxation	−37 610	46 207	226 689	272 896	235 286
Fixed assets	−81 771	−70 010	−267 453	−337 462	−419 233
Subtotal	−82 598	97 345	424 535	521 880	439 282
Government					
Fiscal revenue	−21 309	−54 360	−274 513	−328 873	−350 182
Subtotal	−21 309	−54 360	−274 513	−328 873	−350 182
System total	−487 177	103 872	597 505	701 377	214 200

Source: Own elaboration based on survey results.

tariffs discounts are overturned by the benefits incurred in the reduction of operating and financial costs. The net benefit for the firm is AR$439 000, or AR$78 per user. The last column indicates that the utility benefits the most. Finally, the table shows that the government loses in all cases.

Figure 6.2 breaks down the net benefits for each group across years. In the case of users, the figure shows that investment in meters generated losses in the first years that gradually decreased, becoming gains in 2001. In 2002, the net gains increased remarkably as that year's economic crisis seemed to have prompted many users to opt for the prepayment. The series indicate that as from 2004, users obtained benefits from using

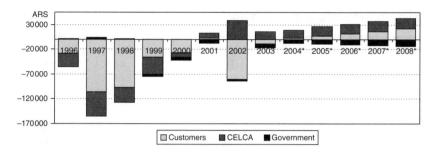

Note: Present values in 1996 ARS; * projected values.

Source: Own elaboration based on survey results.

Figure 6.2   *Evolution of costs and benefits: prepayment system, 1996–*
                2003 and projections

prepayment. Estimates also show that the evolution of the firm's net
benefit is similar, as original losses linked to investment in assets and tariff
discounts are followed by benefits arising from the decrease in bad debts
and from lower running and finance costs, which originate from improvements in working capital.

Results also indicate that the implementation of the prepayment system
generates losses for the government, as the increase in revenues associated
with the sale of meters do not compensate for the decrease in revenues
linked to tariff discounts. It is evident from the data in Table 6.2 that some
results come from transfers between different groups. Thus, user benefits
generated by lower tariffs and taxes (both totaling AR$1 295 600) are
equivalent to losses carried by both the firm and the government.

It is also possible to examine the sensitivity of these results vis-à-vis
changes in some parameters and distinctive features of the policy. A few
simulation exercises were conducted for this purpose. The aim of the first
simulation was to identify the discount rate at which the implementation of
this policy makes no change at an aggregate level, while the second simu-
lates the discount rate. The third scenario conjectures that the use of the
prepayment system is not associated with a tariff discount, while the fourth
envisages that the provider of the service bears the cost of the meters. The
fifth scenario explores the options regarding the latter two in conjunction.
The exercises for scenarios six and seven therefore assume that the utility
bears the cost of the meters and seeks a tariff discount that makes the adoption of the policy for the users in one case, and the utility in the other, economically neutral. Table 6.3 shows the results of those simulation exercises.

Table 6.3   Results for alternative scenarios, prepaid electricity system – Carmen de Areco

Concepts	Base Scenario	Scenario 1	Scenario 2	Scenario 3	Scenario 4	Scenario 5	Scenario 6	Scenario 7
Parameters to be simulated								
Discount rate	5%	6.5%	8%	5%	5%	5%	5%	5%
Tariff discount	5%	5%	5%	0%	5%	0%	0.64%	3.09%
Who pays the meter?	Users	Users	Users	Utility	Utility	Utility	Utility	Utility
Prepayment users								
Tariffs	898479	641836	494851	0	898479	0	114849	555230
Taxes	397202	283361	218185	0	397202	0	50773	245457
Reloading time	-100206	-73766	-58371	-100206	-100206	-100206	-100206	-100206
Advance payment	-65415	-46852	-36210	-65415	-65415	-65415	-65415	-65415
Meters	-1004960	-833867	-729218	-1004960	0	0	0	0
Subtotal	125100	-29287	-110763	-1170581	1130060	-165621	0	635066
Utility								
Revenue	-898479	-641836	-494851	0	-898479	0	-114849	-555230
Running costs	654452	483182	383329	661429	654452	661429	660537	657117
Working capital	384122	290340	236033	384122	384122	384122	384122	384122
Bad debts	483134	302275	200153	483134	483134	483134	483134	483134
Bad debt taxation	235286	147208	97475	235286	235286	235286	235286	235286
Fixed assets	-419233	-309585	-245954	-419233	-1204430	-1204430	-1204430	-1204430
Subtotal	439282	271584	176184	1344739	-345915	559542	443801	0

Table 6.3 (continued)

Concepts	Base Scenario	Scenario 1	Scenario 2	Scenario 3	Scenario 4	Scenario 5	Scenario 6	Scenario 7
Government								
Fiscal revenue	−350 182	−242 298	−180 930	47 020	−350 182	47 020	−3 753	−198 437
Subtotal	−350 182	−242 298	−180 930	47 020	−350 182	47 020	−3 753	−198 437
System total	214 200	0	−115 509	221 178	433 963	440 941	440 049	436 629

Source: Own elaboration based on survey results.

The data show that the elements of the model are sensitive to the discount rate employed to standardize each year's results. Results from the first exercise indicate that there are no benefits when a 6.5 percent discount rate is used to standardize the basic scenario's annual operating statements, while results from the second show the importance of decline in social welfare when an 8 percent rate is used. The third scenario makes it clear that the users' benefit depends on tariff discounts only. These results show that in the hypothesis where users were obliged to use the prepayment system without the benefit of a discount, they would suffer a loss, although both the utility and the government would obtain substantial benefits. The results of the fourth scenario differ from the previous one because it shows that when the firm bears the cost of the meters, it incurs net losses, but the users benefit to a considerable extent. This situation is reversed in the case of the fifth scenario, as the firm bears the cost of the meters but does not grant tariff discounts.

The last two exercises identify implementation alternatives whose results may benefit a given group but without disturbing the welfare of another. The sixth scenario thus indicates the minimum discount that leaves users' welfare unchanged, with the utility bearing the cost of the meters. Results show that in such a case, a tariff discount lower than 1 percent is enough for the policy to make no difference to users, for the utility to obtain profits and for overall welfare changes to be positive, albeit with losses for the government. The last scenario indicates that if the firm bears the cost of the meters, any tariff discount above 3.1 percent will generate a welfare loss. The government position, on the other hand, will be similar to that of the utility, in that any tariff discount will be translated into a decrease in its welfare. The simulations highlight the importance of tariff discounts and of payment for meters in the distributive effects from implementing the system, since although in almost all scenarios a net increase in social welfare occurs, the distribution of benefits and costs associated with the system differs from one scenario to the other.

THE PERCEPTION OF CONSUMERS

The results of the cost–benefit analysis seem to suggest that adoption of prepaid meters leads to a welfare increase, not only to users adopting the system but also to those that do not. Such economic analysis ignores, however, how consumers evaluate the system. The views of consumers are thus relevant not only because they might be highly correlated with changes in their welfare – and so they might give additional support to the findings of the economic model we used above – but also because they become a relevant factor behind the success of prepaid systems. Indeed, some observers argue that a key potential of prepaid systems is that their implementation in small communities helps reduce the level of confrontation between the local utility and consumers (USAID, 2004).

Nevertheless, previous studies indicate that prepaid meters are not necessarily a well-received innovation in some segments of society, to the extent that in some cases, society as a whole is reluctant to implement the system (Tewari and Shah, 2003). In general, the arguments against prepaid meters are based on the belief that their adoption is risky for low-income consumers, as the insecurity and volatility of their income may force them to make little use of the service, or ultimately bring about involuntary self-disconnection. In this section we summarize the results of a survey conducted in November 2004 among residential electricity users in Carmen de Areco. The survey examined the main characteristics of households that switched to prepaid meters and explored their satisfaction with the system. A total of 90 users were surveyed: 47 percent stated that they had adopted prepaid meters, while the rest indicated that they had remained with the conventional system.[16]

Table 6.4 summarizes some socio-economic features of households that use prepaid meters and that do not. The data show that households that adopted the prepayment system have, on average, both a larger number of members and of minors, and that such differences are statistically significant. The data also indicate that adoption of prepaid meters does not differ, statistically, according to the occupation of household heads except for unemployed households, retirees and beneficiaries of social plans, as most of them had opted for remaining within the conventional system. It is thus possible to speculate that the argument that the lower or more unstable the family income, the stronger the tendency to use prepaid meters might hold,[17] up to the point where income instability makes the prepayment increase the chance of self-disconnection, in which case consumers seem to prefer the conventional system and to expose themselves to a disconnection triggered by the utility.

This finding illustrates a relevant dimension of prepaid meters that was not considered in the cost–benefit analysis above, and that it relates to the redistribution of risk between consumers and the utility. Indeed, if consumers are risk-averse (their utility function exhibits diminishing marginal utility – that is, is concave) and the firm is risk-neutral (that is, it optimizes according to expected values), prepayment meters bring an inefficient redistribution of risk, as the firm eliminates uncertainty in the collection of revenues while consumers bear a higher risk of lack of energy and disconnection.[18] Our computation of consumer welfare may therefore overstate our estimates of consumer surplus.

Table 6.4   Socio-economic features of residential users – Carmen de Areco
           District

Status	Prepayment users	Conventional users	Mean difference test[1]
Number of household members (average)	4.1	3.3	**
Number of minors (average)	1.3	0.6	**
Occupation of household head (%)			
Worker or employee	48.8	35.4	
Self-employed	31.7	25.0	
Manager or employer	4.9	2.9	
Other[2]	14.6	37.5	**
Housing tenure (%)			
Owner	77.5	89.6	**
Rented	20.0	6.2	*
Other[3]	2.5	4.2	
Distance to top up/payment center[4]	6.11	7.57	
Telephone (%)	80.5	68.1	
Air conditioning (%)	9.8	14.9	
Number of bathrooms in dwelling (%)			
One	63.4	82.9	**
Two	34.1	14.9	**
More than two	2.4	2.1	

Notes:
1. The symbols * and ** indicate that differences are statistically significant at 1% and 5% significance levels, respectively.
2. It includes retirees, beneficiaries of social plans and unpaid workers.
3. It includes company-owned homes and other unspecified options.
4. Average distance, in number of blocks.

Source: Own elaboration based on survey results.

Going back to the survey data, Table 6.4 also displays some variables that can be considered as imperfect approximations of households' income, such as ownership of the household's dwelling, the availability of a fixed telephone line and of air conditioning equipment, and the number of bathrooms in the residence. Results indicate that the use of prepayment in electricity varies according to housing tenure. Households owning their home are more inclined to remain within the conventional system, whereas households renting their home are more prone to use prepaid meters

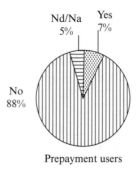

Prepayment users

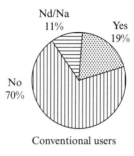

Conventional users

Source: Own elaboration based on survey results.

Figure 6.3   Willingness to switch, % of total users for each system

(probably because of the imposition of property owners, as prepaid meters reduce the risk of unpaid bills). The average distance to outlets where regular bills can be paid or electricity be purchased is similar to most consumers. The data show that ownership of a fixed telephone line and of air conditioning equipment is not statistically different between the two groups. This result contrasts, however, with the fact that the proportion of houses with more than one bathroom – a variable that is suspected to be positively correlated with the dwelling's total built size – is statistically higher among users of prepaid meters. These findings may suggest that the potential existence of a direct relationship between household income and use of prepaid meters is not conclusive.[19]

Survey results also suggest the presence of an apparent equilibrium between the number of users of the prepayment and conventional systems, as most users manifest a strong preference to remain with their system. Figure 6.3 shows that 88 percent of prepaid meter users are not willing to switch back to the conventional system, whereas 70 percent of conventional

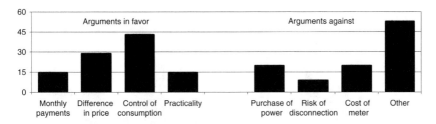

Source: Own elaboration based on survey results.

Figure 6.4   *Switching to prepayment system: arguments in favor of and against switching*

meter users are not willing to switch; only 19 percent of the latter would consider switching to prepayment.

Figure 6.4 summarizes the reasons that would motivate users of the conventional system to remain in this system, or to switch to prepayment. In the first case, the survey data indicate that the inconvenience involved in the advanced purchase of electricity and the cost of the meter are important reasons for not switching. Other arguments against switching include the fact that tariff discounts are not large enough – given consumption levels – to warrant switching, and that advance payment for a utility is not sound practice. In the second case, the reasons that favor switching include the possibility of exerting better control over consumption and the perception that the prepayment involves lower expenditures. Results suggest that over 70 percent of users interested in switching to prepaid meters would do so for reasons associated with the cost of electricity. In addition, almost 15 percent of users willing to switch consider that the prepayment is practical and convenient – a percentage that is higher than the proportion of users who prefer the conventional system owing to the risk of being left without electricity.

Survey data also reveal the advantages and disadvantages of prepaid meters as identified by users. Figure 6.5 summarizes these results. The main advantages refer to electricity expenditure, as the tariff differential between the two systems is considered an advantage by more than 20 percent of prepayment users, while 45 percent value the opportunity of a better control of consumption. Indeed, more than a half of prepayment users consider that their electricity consumption has decreased since they adopted the system in their homes.[20] Other advantages include the possibility of purchasing electricity according to the availability of money, which is closely linked to the advantage of not having to make fixed monthly payments. It becomes apparent that the advantages identified

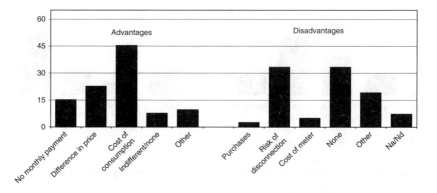

Source: Own elaboration based on survey results.

Figure 6.5   Prepayment electricity system: advantages and disadvantages

by users are very similar to the reasons cited for having installed prepaid meters: more than 70 percent of users had adopted prepaid meters because they expect to reduce their expenditure in electricity.

The main disadvantage reported by one-third of users refers to the possibility of disconnection. The data also underline the low relevance that prepayment users attach to the cost of the meter, as well as to the necessity of making more frequent payments, despite the fact that 23 percent of users report topping up electricity meters at least once a week (recall that average distance to electricity retail outlets is about seven blocks).[21] It is noteworthy that a high proportion of prepaid meter users find no disadvantages of the system whatsoever.

The risk of disconnection does not seem to be too much of a problem. Results in Table 6.5 indicate that 45 percent of prepayment users report to have been disconnected at least once during the last year. The data also show that for 62 percent of users disconnected, the lack of energy lasted less than seven hours; in 80 percent of the cases, disconnection occurred due to user neglect. The opposite situation occurs, however, in the case of disconnections over periods longer than seven hours, for which the main cause is lack of money to reload the meter.

CONCLUSIONS

Prepayment systems have been proposed as an innovative solution to the problem of affordability in utilities services. In spite of being a popular system in European and African countries, the use of such mechanisms

Table 6.5 Lack of electrical power for prepayment users: frequency and reasons

	Number of users (%)
Lack of electricity	
During the last year	45.2
During the last month	16.7
During the last week	7.1
Reasons for lack of electricity	
Less than seven hours	62.0
Not enough money	16.7
Neglect	83.3
More than seven hours	42.0
Not enough money	66.7
Neglect	33.3

Source: Own elaboration based on survey results.

remains controversial. Among the main arguments in favor of its dissemination are the advantages concerning lower costs of arrears, running costs and finance charges for the service provider, and the better allocation of resources it implies for users. The arguments against prepaid meters are based on the higher cost of the technology and the possibility of self-disconnection of low-income users. This chapter contributes to the debate because it uses cost–benefit analysis to examine the adoption of the prepayment electricity system in the first local district that has adopted it in Argentina.

The case study makes it possible to identify the change in aggregate welfare resulting from the adoption of the prepayment system, as well as in each of the groups concerned. The figures show that the adoption of this system involves a favorable change in social welfare, which expressed in 1996 constant prices reaches AR$38 per user of electrical power. The increase in social value is not distributed in a constant way among the various groups involved, as while the distribution utility and the users obtain a net profit, the government sustains an important loss generated by lower tax revenues related to changes in electricity consumption. In addition, the increase in social welfare exhibits an evolution over time which is typical of investments with high sunk costs, because the results show that in the first years of implementation the system generated losses owing mostly to the high cost of the technology involved. These results are, however, reversed and more than compensated for when the period of analysis is longer.

The analysis was complemented with those corresponding to the model's sensitivity to changes in some distinguishing parameters and features of policy implementation. In general, the simulations confirmed the system's potential as a means of increasing social welfare, highlighting at the same time the role of tariff discounts and payment for meters in the distribution of the generated benefits. The importance of those simulations for regulatory purposes is due to (at least) two reasons: on the one hand, because the possibility of replicating the policy depends on the positive results of its implementation being maintained under different scenarios; and on the other hand, because the definition of regulatory policies in respect of prepayment systems should be based not only on the added welfare change but also on the identification of winners and losers.

The analysis is also complemented by the results of a survey conducted among residential users of electrical power in the district. The data show a generalized level of satisfaction among prepayment users, and highlight the importance of the variables linked to the cost of the service, both directly through lower tariffs and indirectly by way of the enhanced control of consumption as allowed by the prepayment system's technology. The survey also indicates that, at least in the case of Carmen de Areco, self-disconnection does not seem to be a major issue. However, it is important to point out that even if the results of this work highlight the potentialities of the prepayment systems as a tool to facilitate the affordability of public services and enhance social welfare, they partially depend on the particular socio-economic characteristics of the context of the study. Further studies remain to be conducted in the future on the extension of this analysis to different locations.

NOTES

1. See Estache et al. (2002) for an account of experiences in several Latin American countries.
2. This system has been adopted, for example, in the concession of water services in La Paz-El Alto. In this case, the utility opened commercial offices in low-income areas to facilitate payment of services, so that users could cancel the cost of their consumption at least once a week.
3. EMSE was privatized in 1998. This first experience consisted of the installation of 100 meters to commercial users only.
4. In this way, theft or loss of bills already paid can be avoided.
5. This would be the case if consumers are risk-averse (their utility function exhibits diminishing marginal utility – that is, is concave) and the firm is risk-neutral (that is, it optimizes according to expected values).
6. This formulation allows each group to carry a different weight, which may stem from either efficiency or equity considerations (thus, the existence of taxes or other distortions may imply that one additional dollar of government revenue may displace more than one consumption dollar).
7. The results of these changes could be examined with an econometric estimate of the

users' indirect utility function, which in this case was not possible because the number of observations was insufficient to obtain reliable results.

8. Unfortunately, the unavailability of data at the household level prevented us from accounting for income differences across households to estimate this cost.

9. The cash flow was obtained for each year by dividing sales by average cash balance; the accounts receivable turnover was calculated as the quotient between sales and the average balance of such accounts; and the accounts payable turnover was estimated by dividing the cost of sales and the running costs by the average balance of the accounts payable.

10. Receipts of the Special Fund for Major Provincial Power Projects and the Province's Electrical Power Development Fund are intended to expand the service and finance investment related to electricity generation, while revenue from the other two taxes is assigned, in the latter case, to the collecting municipality, and in the former, to the province's Treasury Department.

11. CELCA stands for Cooperativa de Electricidad de Carmen de Areco.

12. Alternatively, local electricity distributors can purchase power from the Wholesale Electrical Market (MEM), in which case a transportation cost should be added. By 2003, about 20 percent of local distributors were members of MEM.

13. Present values were computed using a 6 percent discount rate. The computations assume that all l's equal 1.

14. AR$ refers to Argentinean pesos.

15. Projections consider that the proportion of users in the prepaid system will remain constant at 2003 values.

16. These proportions are similar to those observed for the district's residential population in 2003. The size of the sample n was estimated with the formula $n = (N*Z\,2*p*q) / [d2*(N-1)*\,Z\,2*p*q]$ where N is the size of the population, Z the level of confidence, d the level of accuracy and p and q the proportion of the users' population with and without the prepaid system. The values employed were $N = 4.34$ (the number of residential users), $Z = 1.96$, $d = 0.10$, $p = 0.46$ and $q = 0.54$.

17. This is usually the case when minimal or unreliable income streams make it hard to make a monthly payment (USAID, 2004).

18. We do not approximate the social cost of disconnection.

19. This finding should be interpreted with caution, because it could result from the reduced dispersion of households' income within the district.

20. This relationship between the prepayment and a low demand contradicts the average demand data reported in the third section of the chapter.

21. This result differs from those of other communities where prepayment meters have been installed. For example, many users in Johannesburg have declared that it is 'a big hassle to buy electricity frequently' (Tewari and Shah, 2003).

APPENDIX

Table 6A.1   Demographic and socio-economic data

	Carmen de Areco	Greater Buenos Aires				Rest of Buenos Aires Province				Total national
		Max.	Min.	Avg.	Total	Max.	Min.	Avg.	Total	
General Characteristics										
Population	13876	1255288	118807	361852	8684437	560666	1709	46086	5142766	36260130
Households	4211	333688	29561	99337	2384089	177019	487	13968	1536507	10075814
Population density (inhabitants/km^2)	13.0	163.6	10068.5	4213.7	2394.4	654.8	0.9	60.2	16.9	13.0
Unemployed[1] (%)	23.4	35.6	13.5	25.71	36.4	42.7	14.2	23.5	27.0	28.5
Retired heads of household (%)	18.3	24.6	10.1	17.24	18.3	28.9	0.2	21.0	21.0	18.9
Education (%)										
Illiteracy	2.4	2.6	0.5	1.5	1.6	3.9	0.6	1.9	1.6	2.6
Educational level of employed population										
Without schooling or unfinished primary school	15.5	15.8	2.9	9.7	9.5	24.5	4.7	12.5	10.1	12.4
Finished primary school or unfinished secondary school	55.6	58.4	23.1	46.1	45.4	59.4	32.7	51.5	46.4	42.2

Finished secondary school or unfinished secondary school/university	18.6	43.5	20.3	31.3	31.9	38.1	13.2	22.9	27.9	29.6
Tertiary education completed	6.5	10.5	3.8	6.3	6.4	11.9	3.8	7.7	7.6	7.2
University education completed	3.9	19.8	1.7	6.5	6.7	16.8	1.4	5.4	8.0	8.5
Public services (%)[2]										
Sewage	61.0	98.4	4.3	14.7	50.0	87.3	1.9	53.5	50.3	54.8
Running water	74.4	100.0	9.3	65.3	75.0	99.4	24.0	79.9	75.1	84.6
Electricity	97.7	99.7	9.3	97.2	97.0	99.2	64.4	93.3	96.8	95.5
Piped gas	50.2	98.6	44.0	82.0	78.0	93.6	1.1	63.1	78.5	65.5
Pavement	76.2	99.1	67.6	86.1	82.0	96.9	35.2	69.2	81.7	72.8
Public transportation	11.5	98.9	80.0	92.5	84.0	89.5	2.5	44.2	86.9	79.3
Garbage collection	85.8	99.6	88.9	95.5	94.0	99.7	49.5	86.6	93.7	89.8

Notes:
1. Population 14 years old or older.
2. This refers to households where the service is available.

Source: IN DEC (2002).

7. Challenges and opportunities in electricity service provision for urban BOP communities*

Simone Lawaetz and Connie Smyser

BACKGROUND

As slum communities expand with increased urban growth, there is a growing market for service provision. The number of slum dwellers is expected to rise to 1 billion (one out of three city dwellers) by 2010 and this could double by 2022. In some countries, such as Brazil, Pakistan and Kenya, there are more children growing up in slums than non-slums. Households at the base of the pyramid (BOP) devote about 7 percent of their expenditures on energy, with this share slightly increasing as incomes diminish. (BOP households are defined as households earning less than US$3000/year in local purchasing power parity.) In Africa, Eastern Europe and Latin America, energy ranks third in BOP household expenditures, following food and housing. In Asia, energy ranks second, surpassing housing. Globally, the BOP households total about 4 billion people and constitute a $5 trillion global consumer market, of which energy's portion is $220 billion and growing (Hammond et al., 2007).

Historically, electric utilities have expected low or negative returns from expanding service to low-income customers, given their relatively low consumption levels and the added problems and costs of electrifying these mostly informal areas. However, as slums have grown, utilities have increasingly focused on these areas to reduce their commercial and technical losses as well as fulfill any universal service requirement policies. With increasing experience, utilities are acquiring knowledge on effective ways to improve relations with communities, prevent theft and dramatically increase collections, realizing the market potential of informal slums. Nonetheless, as described below, formidable challenges remain in designing and implementing effective programs that yield results that can be sustained over the medium to long term.

After a brief description of the global opportunities for regularization programs, the remaining sections discuss the specific challenges faced by utilities in designing and implementing regularization programs that are financially viable for the utility and customers, and presents solutions that have been successfully tried in addressing these challenges.

OPPORTUNITIES AND CHALLENGES

Like other communities, slum neighborhoods require electricity service to light and cool residents' homes and businesses as well as to power appliances and equipment. Where legal service is unavailable or costly, residents have used neighborhood electricians to tap illegally into nearby lines, steal from neighbors or tamper with meters. The subsequent web of long distribution lines illegally strung from poles to households creates a dangerous environment for the community and raises both technical and non-technical losses for the electricity provider. Although the service provider is not being paid for its service, those who facilitate electricity theft and the households that on-sell service to others often make electricity service more costly for slum consumers than if they had had legal service.

Electricity utilities are grappling to find effective ways to tap into this ready market of consumers and transform or 'regularize' these non-paying consumers into regular, paying customers who will use electricity rationally. Regularization programs have become a key component of larger loss reduction initiatives, and have been shown to have attractive returns on investment. However, as described below, there are many challenges throughout the stages of a regularization program, particularly in sustaining results over the longer term. Based on United States Agency for International Development (USAID) experiences, the stages of a regularization program can be described as follows:

- Pre-regularization involves first contacting the community leadership and other stakeholders, such as non-governmental organizations (NGOs) and community-based organizations operating in the community, to gain support for the project; plus any pre-project baseline surveys, customer mapping and registration, and community campaigns to prepare the population for the upcoming changes.
- Regularization comprises two components: (1) upgrades to the distribution system and installation of new service drops and meters for the new (or returning) customers; and (2) the start of billing and collections.
- Post-regularization focuses on helping customers to adapt to paying

their electricity bills regularly and reducing their consumption through more efficient electricity use.

- Evaluation entails post-project financial analyses and any post-project surveys to assess customers' satisfaction (or problems) with the project. These can inform future utility actions to improve program results or its replication or scaling-up elsewhere in the utility's service territory.
- Scale-up is the most important and desired outcome and the true measure of the success of the regularization initiative, when management agrees to invest substantial sums for replication throughout similar areas in its service territories.

Challenges

Early attempts to electrify slums, whether in Latin America, Asia or Africa, initially yielded increased collections and reduced losses, only to have these results deteriorate after a short period. Many low-income neighborhoods or slums, particularly in countries where 'electrification' rates are high, such as in Latin America with its 98 percent electrification of urban areas, are littered with poles, cables and meters that are no longer being maintained by the utility, and instead have become the distribution backbone for illegal tapping and theft. The abandonment of earlier efforts to 'regularize' slum customers reflects the extreme challenges faced by utilities in implementing sustainable programs.

The major threats to sustainability vary with the specific conditions in the targeted slum community. But, in many cases, utilities face a common, overarching set of challenges. These include a 'culture of non-payment', limited ability to pay, technological 'arms race', and conflicting government and regulatory incentives and requirements, and are described briefly below.

'Culture of non-payment'
Utility companies often refer to a 'culture of non-payment' to explain their failures to serve low-income customers sustainably. They feel that there is an ingrained unwillingness of customers to pay for service. However, often their non-payment is due to distrust of the utility, prior misdirected government 'social' policy allowing unlimited free electricity to the poor, and a perception that the electricity company – often a private company with foreign capital or ownership – is making large profits at the poor's expense while providing poor quality of service. Past negligence by the company, often previously owned and operated by the government, in collections or disconnections of service for non-payment, fuels illegal consumers' beliefs

that non-payment will not lead to disconnection of service. The challenge to companies then is to understand consumers' motivations for non-payment better and to use that understanding to their mutual advantage.

Limited ability to pay
By virtue of their low-incomes, slum customers will be limited in their ability to pay connection fees that are very large in proportion to their budgets and in the amount of electricity they can purchase, or may find it difficult to amass the funds needed to pay a lump-sum bill once a month. In 'regularizing' illegal consumers, utilities typically assess customers' 'ability to pay', particularly if they have enjoyed 'free electricity' prior to regularization and own and operate a large number of old, high-consuming appliances or a small business within their home. Some utilities estimate 'affordability' to be about 5 percent (or less) of income and, in an effort to prevent bad debt, design regularization programs so as to enable customers to meet this level.

Technological 'arms race'
Local middlemen enable low-income consumers to get service through illegal tapping of lines or bypassing or tampering with meters. The prospect of getting 'free' service has motivated these middlemen to find creative ways to overcome utilities' efforts to deter theft. This has led to a costly technological 'arms race' in which utilities are relying on increasingly more sophisticated anti-theft solutions. In turn, neighborhood theft enablers seek new and sometimes dangerous ways to circumvent them.

Conflicting government and regulatory incentives and requirements
In some countries, such as South Africa, Brazil, and India, utilities have time-bound mandates for providing universal service yet face regulatory challenges in achieving them. Regulatory authorities may not recognize the problems and extra costs of serving informal areas plagued by electricity theft and/or non-payment, nor the very poor technical conditions of any existing distribution system. Other such barriers may include inflexibility in new operational and technical approaches that a utility may take to address the unique conditions in slum areas and effectively regularize an area, and restrictions on the type of investments that can be recovered through the tariff.

Utilities can face complex tenure issues when trying to regularize informal low-income communities. For example, low-income consumers may have informal property rights that lack official recognition, or may be squatting and not have any legal rights to occupy the property. These conditions may persist for decades and, despite any informal arrangements being understood within the community, may not be sufficient to meet legal requirements for service provision. This usually requires regulatory approval. There must be an appropriate local and national policy and regulatory framework in place to allow for special measures to regularize low-income customers, possibly including financial incentives.

Additional governmental hurdles include political interference in utilities' efforts to enforce collection of payments for service from low-income voters. Government officials may informally prohibit the cutting of 'essential' services for non-payment or hinder prosecution in the cases of proven theft. Regularization of customers and collection of payment for service requires, in some countries, strong political will, particularly where expected improvements in the quality of service do not materialize and consumers refuse to pay for service. This chapter does not cover these political challenges as they cannot be directly addressed through a regularization program (although they must be factored into the financial viability and feasibility assessments prior to regularization of service) but, instead, require changes in political leadership and will.

NEW RELATIONSHIPS WITH THE COMMUNITY AND CUSTOMER

Typically, when a utility decides that it is necessary to regularize an area, it has not been much involved in the community for some time. The most critical component of a regularization program is the establishment of a new relationship between the customer and the utility, particularly crafting a 'value proposition' that is acceptable to the community, prospective customers and the company. This is key to breaking the prior community–company impasse and replacing it with a relationship in which each party values and trusts the other. This typically starts at the highest levels, with intensive dialogue among the electricity supplier, community leaders, local government officials and any other major stakeholders about the reasons why the company wants to regularize the community, community concerns about how and when the regularization might take place and, most importantly, to jointly develop the value proposition. Open communication should continue throughout the regularization program and beyond to resolve issues that may arise, keep track of progress and prevent misunderstandings about such issues as meter reading, consumption and bill payment, as well as to dispel any rumors circulating in the community about what the company is doing and why. Building a relationship between the utility and individual customers requires time and resources and contributes to lengthy lead times in implementing a regularization program. Technical fixes (discussed later) are almost always necessary but are insufficient on their own to overcome entrenched attitudes and habits of consumers used to 'free' electricity. Moreover, outreach efforts must be continued beyond regularization as slum residents are often transient and new customers must be familiarized with the utility, its services and expectations of regular payment.

In some cases, such as in Colombia, the new relationship and the utilities' and communities' respective responsibilities were explicitly defined up-front in 'social contracts'. With assistance from the regulator, the Colombian utility, ElectroCosta, developed these agreements which stipulated that the utility would fulfill its promise of safe, reliable, affordable and high-quality service and, in turn, the customers in the community would pay their electricity bills. These were signed in 82 percent of the municipalities served by the utility and, in combination with technological and social measures, resulted in a drop of overall company losses from 32 percent to 18 percent over six years.

In extreme cases, where the utility's reputation is so poor that its acceptance in the community would be highly unlikely, new companies have been established to present a different face to the customer and serve as an interface between the utility and the customer. For example, in post-apartheid Cape Town, the Phambali Nombane Energy (PN Energy) – meaning 'Forward with Electricity' – was started in 1994 as a pilot project by a joint venture between Eskom, Electricité de France (EDF) and East Midlands Electricity of the UK[1] and continues to operate today. This company was established to test a new scheme for providing electricity to the Khayelitsha township (slum) on the outskirts of Cape Town. The Khayelitsha township had a track record of non-payment and theft of power from the municipality, which had provided poor-quality service. In addition to using technical innovations, such as a prepayment metering system, the company fostered stronger links with the community through the establishment of community-based customer service centers of the distribution company, which were built and staffed by locals, as well as locating vendors of prepaid electricity at convenient locations within the community. From 1994 to 2003, 60 000 connections were made and reductions in non-payment from 70 percent in 1994 to 5 percent in 1998 were achieved. PN Energy continues to exist today and its approach to electrification has been replicated elsewhere in South Africa by Eskom and municipalities (although not necessarily establishing a separate entity).

Rather than establish a new company to interface with the community, some utilities may establish mini-networks that are maintained and managed by local community representatives. The community representatives work as trusted intermediaries between the utility and the slum community. For example, in Morocco, after taking over the Casablanca electricity distribution system in 1997 and trying to eliminate theft amounting to 1.4 million euros through disconnections, LYDEC designed a model of 'temporary electrification', targeting approximately 130 *bidonvilles* ('slum' in French) in 2004. LYDEC convinced the municipality to let it operate in informal areas that by government policy would be either upgraded or eliminated. It did so by locating transformers and master meters at the perimeter of the slums or in easily accessible areas within the slums so that they could be quickly removed on short notice. The slum residents own the distribution network after the master meter. Restrictions on the load served were also applied as the municipality did not want significant growth in these areas (Massé et al., 2005).

Under this scheme (the technical aspects of its 'temporary' nature are described in more detail below), LYDEC works with local representatives designated by the community, each of whom is responsible for a 'secondary network' which supplies around 20 households. In exchange for payment by community members, the representative manages the installation and maintenance of the network and is responsible for collecting from the households their share of the bill (as measured by the collective meter for the network) based on their individual household meter reading. If the bill is not paid in full, the service is disconnected for all families on the circuit.

The electrification program results were impressive: approximately 93 percent of the communities were electrified, the number of businesses increased by 17 percent after electrification, and 3500 jobs were created (including the 1250 community representatives). Payments were on the order of 96 percent of billing and the project payback was around one year.[2] The cost to LYDEC for the representatives is offset by the reduced costs of billing and collections. There were some complaints from the representatives about difficulties with collections and others about insufficient remuneration for the effort involved. Some residents and businesses wanted to have their own meters, bypassing the collective aspect of the scheme.

Utilities' reliance on community members, who are trusted by both the utility and the community, to interact with individual households on their behalf has become an effective practice in a number of countries. One of the best-documented and most effective 'community agent' programs has been that of Companhia de Electricidade da Bahia (COELBA), the utility that serves Salvador, Brazil, a city with a high proportion of low-income customers (in the order of 60 percent of customers). 'Community agents' are hired from the community itself and include unemployed youth and women who have strong communication skills and are highly familiar with households' energy consumption patterns. COELBA generally works through a trusted local NGO to recruit, train and manage the agents, further reinforcing the community relationship.

As intermediaries between the company and the community, the agents allow COELBA to introduce program activities to the community in the vernacular of the inhabitants via trusted neighbors. The agents work with households to educate consumers on how to make efficient use of electricity, reduce their bills and take complaints from consumers. COELBA credits these community agents with the community's high acceptance of its regularization program objectives and activities, and has attributed an average 13 percent reduction in household consumption to the education and outreach efforts of the agents.

In addition to utilizing individuals from the community, utilities have relied on local NGOs to enhance their access and acceptance within slum communities. In some countries, this approach has been used in pilot programs but then eliminated once familiarity and trust have grown between the utility and community and the utility feels that it can provide full services without the aid of an intermediary. This was the case in Ahmedabad, India, where the utility, Ahmedabad Electricity Company (AEC), 'internalized' the communication, outreach and intermediary roles that had initially been assumed by the two NGOs, Saath and the Self-Employed Women's Association (SEWA) (in the initial USAID-supported pilot project effort). These NGOs believe that their role in the pilot led to a change in the utility mindset and resulted in a subsequent expansion of the slum electrification activities by AEC. In Georgia, Energy Services Consumers' Associations (ESCAs) were developed, with USAID assistance, and existed for a period of time to help build confidence between the utility, Telasi, and the consumers by mediating disputes between them, and monitoring utility decisions and performance and sharing this information with consumers.

To build a positive image of the utility in the local community and, in some cases, improve the affordability of service for consumers, utilities have developed a number of initiatives to contribute to improving the slum community's welfare. These have included the construction of schools, sports arenas and community centers; the development of credit schemes; and the creation of jobs and income-earning opportunities. As described earlier, jobs have been created as a direct result of the regularization program. An additional example is the case of Bangladesh, where the utility, the Dhaka Electricity Service Company (DESCO), hired slum dwellers in Dhaka to assemble the prepayment meters used. Given COELBA's high proportion of very poor neighborhoods in its service territory, it has augmented its community actions over time and worked to provide job- and income-creating opportunities. For example, it provides credit on households' utility bills for recycled waste brought into recycling facilities as well as supporting community businesses, such as a cooperative bakery. These actions not only improve the company's image within the community but they also bring funds into the community, extending residents' budgets for electricity and other necessities. Similarly, a pilot electrification project in Angola developed a Community Electrification Revolving Fund (CERF) in part to gain community support for the project. In this scheme, part of the money collected from electricity bill payments post-regularization goes back into the fund to provide capital to expand access to new project areas.[3]

Some companies have launched new services to maintain the momentum gained in initial regularization campaigns. An ambitious and highly successful credit program for appliance and services for low-income customers was developed by Codensa, the distribution company serving Bogotá, Colombia. Created in 2002, Codensa Hogar (*hogar* means home or family in Spanish) provides credit to its low-income customers, many of whom did not previously have access to credit, for goods such as appliances and services. This program that bundles services of high value to customers provides a new source of revenue to Codensa but also helps low-income customers establish a credit rating, which in turn allows them to transition to traditional lenders for other credit needs. Customers can also use Codensa Hogar to pay electricity bills if they temporarily run short of funds, a common problem with BOP consumers. The program works in partnership with appliance and other vendors to open up new market segments for them. In 2007, the program had lent over US$230 million. BOP customers turned out to have excellent credit performance (as good as or better than the average) and slightly less than half were able to make the transition to conventional credit as a result. About 60 percent were able to gain access to a second line of credit. Overall appreciation of Codensa as a result of this program increased significantly.[4]

One last but very important change in the relationship between the distribution company and the customer relates to the widely established practice that defines utility service as stopping at the meter. In other words, anything within the home or business, whether it is electrical in nature such as the internal wiring or related to consumption, such as the size, condition or inefficiency of the electricity-consuming appliances within a home, is considered the customer's business and not the company's. Yet, the regularization programs that seem to work best have modified this practice dramatically in these two particular areas: electrical safety and improved energy efficiency. The following section delves into the reasons and ways that companies have modified the customer–utility relationship in order to make bills affordable as well as safe which requires taking action within the home.

DESIGNING SERVICE PROVISION FOR SLUM CONSUMERS

As noted, companies face considerable challenges in serving low-income and possibly skeptical consumers. To overcome these, the company tailors the design of the service provision program to the community's physical layout and its technical and socio-economic situation. It must make its service not only safe and reliable, but also more affordable and possibly more controllable for the consumer. As described below, measures might include improving household electrical safety, providing assistance to households to reduce their electricity consumption, and in some cases modifying payment mechanisms to make payment more controllable.

Household Electric Safety Measures

Regularization programs in Brazil and South Africa have pioneered ways to ensure that the internal electrical systems in BOP residences and appliances are safe to hook up to the grid. They are motivated in part by the fact that community goodwill might be lost if accidents occur post-regularization as a result of unsafe internal wiring. Consumer advocates may even bring lawsuits against the companies in such cases. These unsafe conditions occur more in slum neighborhoods than elsewhere, since formally permitted structures are usually required to meet certain electrical safety standards.

Fires and accidents related to faulty wiring or appliances are very prevalent within slums, and a great concern to the communities as a whole. Thus, in Brazil it is now common practice to inspect the homes prior to regularization and provide assistance to those whose wiring is so poor that it poses a liability to the company and a great risk to the residents. The programs in Brazil have usually comprised the replacement of all faulty wiring and fuse boxes. Given the poor structural condition of the residences and the difficulty and high cost of rewiring within concrete block walls, the most prevalent solution is to encase all of the wiring in electrical conduit. In the case of the USAID/AES-Eletropaulo/International Copper Association (ICA) Slum Electrification and Loss Reduction (SELR) Brazil project in São Paulo, the program went even further and replaced the existing electric showers with ones that would not trip the ground-fault interrupt circuit-breaker installed for the new shower circuit.

Companies also perform electrical safety audits during the regularization stage and point out unsafe situations that need to be fixed to the owner or occupant of the residence. Rewiring is one of the more costly components of the Brazil model program. Therefore in other countries, particularly those where the households have simpler electrical requirements, so-called 'ready boards' are employed. These are a single unit that contains the circuit-breakers and a number of plugs that allow the resident to plug in several appliances and/or lights. Their main advantage is the ease of installation and the relatively low price. They are less advantageous in situations where the appliances and/or lights are relatively long distances from the ready board, requiring the stringing of extension cords which in themselves can become a hazard. Ready boards are now widely used in African regularization and electrification of BOP customers. It should be noted that post-regularization polling in Brazil found that recipients of rewiring were in general more satisfied with the regularization process than those who did not get it. Even those who did not receive rewiring cited it as a benefit of the program because of the improved safety that it had afforded to the community.

Affordability: Efficiency Measures to Reduce Consumption

In cities where low-income consumers have illegal connections and are paying little or nothing for electricity service, there is no incentive for consumers to use electricity rationally. Consumption levels can be very high (as high as 250 kWh or more per month), as many household appliances are old and poorly maintained, particularly in Latin America where used appliances are readily and cheaply available, and consumers do not efficiently manage their electricity consumption. In these cases, regularization can easily lead to high levels of bad debt as consumers cannot afford to pay for their consumption, even at subsidized tariff rates. However, this situation is not common to all slums as, in many cases, consumers are being charged – sometimes much more than if they had legal service – by neighbors or electricians for their illegal connection and service and appliance ownership may be limited due to the high levels of poverty in the slum. For example, in Mumbai and Delhi, India, many slum households only had one or two lights and a fan.

Studies conducted by COELBA indicate that unaffordable levels of energy consumption are caused by levels of appliance ownership that are disproportionate to the owners' income levels (almost all Brazilian slum households have a refrigerator and many have an electric shower), poor internal wiring, refrigerators that are in bad condition, and housing with no natural ventilation or lighting. Reducing consumption by low-income

customers to affordable levels is a critical regularization program component for increasing collections, reducing bad debt and sustaining program
results over the medium to long term. Many Brazilian utilities have utilized the 1 percent Energy Efficiency Fund described above to incorporate
efficiency measures into their regularization programs.

The SELR program in São Paulo, Brazil showed that significant energy
savings can be achieved through implementation of a range of efficiency
measures, which enhanced the affordability of service for households.
Prior to the regularization program, energy consumption was about 250
kWh per household, which would not be affordable for most households
even if they were charged the low-income tariff. Household consumption
dropped to 192 kWh in response to households being metered and billed
for the first time (the 'regularization effect') and then dropped to 151 kWh
after efficiency measures were implemented. Replacement of traditional
incandescent lightbulbs with high-efficiency compact fluorescent lightbulbs (CFLs) and swapping old refrigerators with efficient refrigerators
contributed the highest energy savings. Per household, replacement of
about three lightbulbs with CFLs achieved average monthly savings of 17
kWh or $65 over a year, and refrigerator replacement resulted in 48 kWh
in monthly savings or $73 over a year. Rewiring and replacement of elec-
tric showers also yielded, respectively, monthly savings of 11 kWh (or $17
each year) and 18 kWh (or $27 each year). In addition, inefficient exterior
lightbulbs that were installed by individual households were removed and
replaced with more efficient public lighting.[5]

Reductions in energy consumption from the implementation of efficiency measures can improve the affordability of service by both moving
households into a lower tariff block and reducing household bills to within
5 percent of their average income (this is considered an affordable level
for most households).[6] For example, in the Eletropaulo target area in São
Paulo, only 40 percent of the households were in the lower tariff blocks
(0–100 kWh/month and 101–150 kWh/month) prior to receiving a new
refrigerator, whereas after refrigerator replacement about 60 percent were
in these lower consumption blocks, which enabled them to receive the low-
income tariff. In one slum community, where COELBA rewired households,
installed windows and provided refrigerators, average monthly household
consumption dropped from $17 in August 2006 to $5 in June 2007, which
made electricity service affordable for the majority of households.

Controllability of Consumption

Other distribution companies have tried new technical approaches to
payment for electricity that help low-income customers to stay within

their means while enjoying the benefits of electricity service. Prepayment electricity meters operate in the same manner as prepaid cellular telephones which have revolutionized access to telephony by poor consumers unable to afford landlines and monthly service. As consumers purchase in advance only what they can afford at the moment, there is no risk to the distribution company of them falling into arrears, and likewise no need to maintain service crews ready to disconnect customers for non-payment.

Prepayment systems are technologically somewhat different from conventional systems in that there is normally an intermediary vendor who sells electricity units as needed. The system can be relatively low-tech (with a vending machine or a merchant set up to sell the units to the consumer), or it can be set up to vend kWh via cellphones or even the Internet. Prepayment systems for low-income consumers tend to be on the lower-tech side, but they are evolving, particularly where cellphone service is practically universal such as is found in most urban areas. The systems are set up to be relatively fail-safe with identification numbers linked to the prepayment meters associated with the physical address of the customer. The company is then able to track all consumption and match it to sales (usually prepaid by the vendor) in order to identify irregularities that might indicate theft or malfunctions that need to be inspected.

While prepayment systems are in use throughout the world, they could be said to be sweeping Africa, particularly for low-income consumers. Eskom (and its spinoff PN Energy described earlier) pioneered the low-income prepayment system which has been picked up by numerous other countries in Africa such as Rwanda, Cote d'Ivoire and Nigeria. Liberia is converting its reconstructed war-torn distribution system to prepayment, and the Kenya Power & Light Company (KPLC) in Kenya is also moving away from a conventional system to prepayment in its slums (after trying load limiters). Likewise in Latin America, interest in prepayment systems is picking up. Empresas Publicas of Medellin, Colombia has adopted a full-fledged prepayment system in its slums after a successful pilot project. Argentina has gone one step further in its Meter Administrator program, and combined its delivery of 'social' electricity benefits via electronic meters in poor households via a 'drip' system that spreads the free electricity out over a month and allows customers to 'top up' whenever they wish to with prepayment purchases. For low-income customers not eligible for social benefits, a fixed invoice for the set amount of electricity to be dripped into the residence (with topping-up by prepayment possible if desired) is another choice.

Being relatively new and requiring electronic internal workings (instead of mechanical dials and gears), prepayment meters provide benefits to the consumer that increase their acceptance of prepayment systems. The

primary benefit is a digital readout that can warn of impending deple-
tion of units as well as provide real-time information about the electricity consumption rate. The meters can even be programmed to allow for
a few kWh to remain for use while the customer purchases more units
(much like the reserve tank in a car). The digital readout feature allows
for another benefit to the company. The digital readout and data input
keyboard can be split from the meter and located within the residence
where it is convenient to the customer, while the 'meter' connecting the
residence to the grid can be located high on poles in plain sight outside
the residence. Potential for theft is diminished as bypassing the meter has
to occur high on the pole. It should be noted that there may be consumer
protection and tariff issues to resolve, related to moving from a conventional payment system with a monthly bill to one involving vendors and,
potentially, a single price for all kWh purchased under a prepayment
system.

Companies using prepayment find that, in general, consumption drops
as customers take control of their consumption (for example, Argentina
reported an overall 37 percent drop in consumption with its system). The
lower per-household revenues resulting are offset by the lower costs in the
areas of billing, collections and disconnections that are required with conventional systems, as well as reduced losses from theft of power (as long
as companies maintain a good data management system). It should be
noted, however, that the initial cost for prepayment meters and the management systems needed to operate them are substantially more expensive
than conventional meters. Thus, in determining which approach to take
in serving the BOP, the company has to weigh the benefits relative to the
costs carefully. It is often the case that the avoided costs of billing, collections and disconnection are not readily quantified, particularly on a per-
customer basis, which can make the basis of the business decision difficult
to evaluate and the higher initial costs hard to justify to management and
regulators.

TECHNOLOGICAL ADVANCES

Non-technical losses in BOP neighborhoods generally derive from either
theft or non-payment or a combination of both. Distribution companies
have been testing various technological approaches to reducing theft,
listed in Table 7.1. Typical theft situations occur when someone taps into
the low-voltage distribution grid, bypasses the meter (so that the meter is
not reading any consumption), and/or tampers with the meter so that it
malfunctions. The methods used may be as rudimentary as driving a nail

Table 7.1   Technological solutions for electricity distribution at the BOP

	Distribution system level	Customer level
Anti-theft technologies	Twisted cable in LV system MV/LV configuration Macro-metering and energy balancing Elevated meters in enclosed tamper-alarmed boxes	Coaxial service drop Tamper-resistant/ tamper-proof meters Elevated/exposed meters Load limiters Electronic meters
Collections improvement technologies		Prepayment meters Collective meters and submetering

attached to the house wiring into the low-voltage (LV) distribution line, or disconnecting the wires into and out of the meter and reattaching a bypassing wire.

Companies generally acknowledge that no one technology or even combination of technologies, no matter how sophisticated, can be relied upon to eliminate all theft. This is why a combination of technologies, techniques and program elements (that is, soft and hard) almost always makes up the overall approach to the BOP. Nevertheless, technological advances can help reduce theft dramatically. Technological innovations can be grouped into three main areas: distribution system upgrades (stopping 'flying connections'); customer-level upgrades (stopping meter bypass, or reducing the amount that could be stolen or might not be paid for if the customer goes into arrears); and improvement of collections via prepayment or collective meters. Table 7.1 lays out the range of options that are being used in each of these areas.

The use of advanced cable designs and configurations makes it much more difficult and risky to tap directly into the low-voltage distribution system. Elevated, tamper-alarmed enclosures for meters are much harder to access and can shut down the supply of electricity if tampering is attempted. Macro-metering and energy-balancing techniques help the company to identify specific 'hot-spots' of potential illegal activity for later investigation.

At the customer level, tamper-resistant meters (for example, the meter is enclosed in plastic that must be broken to bypass the meter) are placed in easily observed and sometimes less accessible locations. These meters can be rigged to shut down – and send a Global Positioning System (GPS) signal to the company – when tampering occurs. The coaxial service drop (from the LV system to the meter) uses cable that cannot be tapped because it short-circuits (stopping the flow of electricity).

Electronic meters can be used in a variety of ways. To reduce theft, they can be used to shut down electricity service remotely when access to an area is risky (as may be the case in some more violence-prone BOP neighborhoods). To reduce bad debt, electronic meters can be programmed to cut off a non-paying customer when a set level of consumption is exceeded, that is, limiting the customer's usage but not cutting off essential power supply to a business in the slum (dubbed 'social' cutting by AES Eletropaulo). Other new metering options allow for the prepayment options described earlier.

The degree of sophistication in the technologies required reflects local conditions of non-payment as well as geographic or cultural challenges. For example, LYDEC's relatively simple technological approach may be successful because of the orderly layout of the slum households and the social cohesiveness of the slum communities In Ahmedabad, India the technological solution of easily accessed but tamper-alarmed meters was sufficient to minimize theft in BOP areas. Contrast this with the situation in Rio de Janeiro, where practically all efforts of Light have failed because of the rampant lawlessness and graft that accompany the poverty found there. Ampla, which also serves parts of the state of Rio de Janeiro, encounters the same culture and has for this reason developed and implemented what is probably the most effective (but costly) theft prevention system used in BOP communities with significant success (for example, theft reduced to less than one-third the original level). Given the system's costliness, the company has also concentrated on developing macro-metering and energy-balancing techniques that help it to pinpoint the areas that need its anti-theft configuration the most.

Technological advances can also help in speeding up the pre-regularization process. In Angola, a pilot electrification project (in part supported by USAID) is under way to provide electricity to the under-served areas of Luanda. The project began with a tripartite partnership between the communities, the municipalities and the electricity company, EDEL. The community residents and the municipalities developed a geographic information system (GIS) database and map of the areas that were to be regularized. Mapping, using satellite imagery, geo-referencing, GIS and GPS surveying of the satellite imagery was completed within a matter of months, was probably more accurate than could have otherwise been produced, and had the added advantage of actively tapping local knowledge.

REGULATORY AND GOVERNMENT INITIATIVES

A country's overarching policies on citizens' access to electricity service can drive and shape regularization programs. Government policies that mandate service for all are often translated into time-bound universal service requirements in utilities' concessionaire contracts, which can spur utilities to find effective ways to regularize their low-income customers. In support of government policy, the regulator plays a key role in developing the specific rules and guidelines for service provision that can impact the design and implementation of regularization programs. For example, the regulator can set a limit on the amount of losses that can be recovered through the tariff, which may in turn accelerate regularization efforts to reduce losses in slum areas. The regulator can provide fiscal incentives through the establishment of special funds for use in low-income areas and the development of subsidy programs for low-income consumers, including waiver of connection fees, billing schemes and subsidized tariffs. The regulator can also be flexible in allowing for new technical measures to be used in slum areas, such as special meters and anti-theft cables, as well as permitting new equipment standards that may be lower than typically used but are more cost-effective and appropriate to slum conditions. Regulatory treatment of complex tenure issues can either hinder or facilitate the treatment of low-income customers, as described below.

Overcoming Tenure Barriers

Where slum dwellers do not have legal land tenure, regulators have permitted electrification where certain criteria are met. For example, in Ahmedabad, India the electricity utility, AEC, was able to provide service to slum communities that had received a 'no-Objection Certificate (NOC)' from the local government, which effectively ceded tenure to the slum dwellers. Obtaining such a certificate is relatively straightforward if the land is owned by the state but otherwise can be difficult to acquire. Private sector land required going through the legal process to establish abandonment by the private owner or buying out the owner.

As noted earlier, in Morocco, municipal approval to electrify legally some slum neighborhoods could only be obtained if the distribution company was able to pull its infrastructure out of an area within 24 hours. Electrification would then not hinder any decisions by the municipality or private owner to upgrade the slum to formal status. This resulted in an infrastructure network design where transformers and master meters are located at the perimeter of the slums or in easily accessible areas within the slums. In Manila, Philippines a less successful initiative was undertaken to circumvent tenure problems and an inability to gain legal right of way for electricity supply infrastructure in the slum area. Right of way on land with disputed ownership is particularly difficult to obtain. The utility solved these problems by limiting its service to the perimeter of the slums and erecting walls of individual meters there. The households ran distribution lines, sometimes quite long ones, from the meter to their home. Unfortunately, these long distribution lines invited illegal tapping by others and subsequently ran up high bills for the metered households, and eventual disconnection when they were unable to pay them.

In other countries, regulations may allow for service provision if the land has been occupied for a specified length of time. In Brazil, any private land that had been occupied for more than five years is legally treated as abandoned, and the electricity company could ignore land tenure issues for most slums although it still needs to work with the municipality before going ahead. Likewise, in Cape Town, South Africa the electricity company would ignore tenure only if the municipality would give permission to go ahead or if the area had been occupied for more than five years, as this period indicated a stable enough situation for the company to risk its investment in the area. In 2004, approximately 20 percent of the slums still remained excluded from electric service because of imminent resettlement plans.

Experimenting through Pilot Projects

Effective regularization programs have frequently begun as small pilots from which lessons are distilled for use in a larger-scale roll-out. This requires regulatory support for trials of new billing schemes and/or technical approaches that may be scaled up, if proven successful. In some countries, the regulator has proactively encouraged new schemes to fulfill national policies for expanding electricity coverage and reducing losses. For example, in support of a new Law 812 of 2003 – National Development Plan for 2002–06, the Colombian regulatory body allowed new billing schemes for low-income areas such as community billing and flexible billing periods. In São Paulo, Brazil the regulator approved a billing cap of 150 kWh per month for low-income consumers for a minimum of three months or until all consumers in the slum community had been regularized, whichever was longer. This would help customers make the transition to paying for their service and, as they were informed about what their actual consumption was and what they would have paid for it, would educate them on the extent to which they would need to reduce their consumption once their bill was uncapped.

Regulatory approval is typically required for testing new technologies or allowing lower performance standards than what would normally be required. Typical service standards required by regulators may not always be appropriate for developing cost-effective programs that meet the needs of slum consumers. For example, where household consumption is low and theft is high, utilities may want to put limitations on the service provided. In New Delhi, slum consumers can have the choice of regular metered service, or a maximum 2 amp service and 500 watt connection (which would allow for two bulbs and one fan) but a lower connection fee and a low flat monthly rate.

Utilities' pilot programs often test new equipment that can better address the unique problems in the slum community. Regulators must first be satisfied with the proposed use of the equipment and its quality. In Brazil, the regulatory agency's concerns regarding the accuracy and mode of use of electronic meters with remote reading and disconnection capability had to be resolved before the utility, Ampla, was permitted to utilize them in their pilot program. In Argentina the regulator had to be persuaded of the benefits of the new metering technology, the Meter Administrator (described above), and that the utility and consumers' interests would be protected per the existing laws and regulations. It is important to anticipate and deal with regulator approvals prior to beginning a test program.

Defraying the Costs of Regularization Programs for the Utility and Consumer

Where there is a strong national policy promoting the expansion of access to low-income customers, regulators have supported mechanisms for defraying the costs of service expansion for the utility and the consumer. For the utility, this may include the establishment of special funds, sourced from utility revenues, cross-subsidies or public funds, to help defray the costs of infrastructure upgrades. In Colombia, the government created a number of funds to expand access in both rural areas and the 'subnormal' urban neighborhoods. In the late 1990s, the Brazilian government created an 'electricity-industry-wide' fund to be split evenly for research and development (R&D) and energy efficiency (EE) improvements. Utilities' concessionaire contracts contain provisions to access this fund, which amounts to 1 percent of the utility's net revenue for use in their own territory (0.5 percent for R&D and 0.5 percent for EE). Even more recently, ANEEL has added the requirement that one-half of the set-aside for EE (that is, 0.25 percent) be used for low-income households. Annual cycles of planning, application and approval by ANEEL govern each year's allowable activities and expenditures. Recently, slum electrification initiatives (for example, reconnection and metering) became eligible to use the EE fund as they enabled customers to understand and monitor their own energy consumption. In addition, expenditures on energy-saving appliances within slum households were also eligible if they achieved a maximum cost–benefit ratio of 0.8. This indicator considers the estimated annual savings accruing over the annual cost of the project.

For the slum household, connection fees might be waived and 'social tariffs' or subsidies for low-income customers for some or all of their usage provided. The regulator must also approve any special tariffs to be piloted. In Venezuela, a pilot program using prepayment meters was thwarted because Electricidad de Caracas could not obtain regulatory approval to include a special prepayment tariff, even for a limited duration to test consumer acceptance. Regulators may permit the connection fee to be waived or for it to be paid over time through the electricity bill. Lifeline tariffs are commonly used to enhance the affordability of service, but if these are not well targeted they may not reach the neediest, or may be enjoyed by those that do not need them.

Countries' efforts to streamline and better target subsidies can impact the roll-out of regularization programs. In Brazil, ANEEL began to tighten the eligibility procedures for the low-income tariff (LIT) by requiring that consumers be registered in government low-income programs such as Bolsa Família[7] as proof of their low-income status. This would eliminate the low-income self-declaration process for eligibility now used for electricity consumers in the 80 to 200 kWh per month consumption range. Using registration in government social programs would eliminate some non-poor from the LIT rolls (for example, those with vacation homes and single occupancies). At the same time, inclusion would improve for very large low-income families that use more than 220kWh and are now excluded from the LIT.[8] Although ANEEL temporarily halted this initiative as a result of pressure from utilities that would be impacted by this change (the amount of subsidy they receive from ANEEL is dependent on consumption by customers that are eligible for the LIT), it is very likely that they will return to this issue again as the government continues to seek ways to streamline the Brazilian social safety net and more effectively administer subsidies.

IMPLICATIONS FOR SUSTAINABLE SOLUTIONS

There is ample evidence that electricity suppliers are finding ways to turn the corner on converting BOP electricity consumers into good paying customers and are scaling up their initial (pilot) programs as a result, possibly with 'tweaks' to improve on the original design. It is safe to say that none of them approached the task without trepidation, given the usually dire conditions that they encounter when attempting to enter this market. Certainly, none found it possible to overlay the conventional service design on BOP communities successfully. A change in the paradigm for electricity distribution and special efforts was necessary to tap the BOP electricity market sustainably in a financially viable way, particularly in the areas that are identified in this chapter: that is, strong focus on community engagement, creating good customer payment performance where there was none and eliminating the theft which was the norm prior to starting their efforts through effective theft reduction techniques. Such a change in paradigm perforce requires government and regulator 'buy-in' and possibly support to remove barriers encountered.

There is no single model that fits all situations. So much depends on the local conditions, the regulatory framework and even the fabric of the societies that exist in these neighborhoods. Indeed many companies found that a sustained, iterative process with continued injection of added value was needed to lock in benefits over the long term. Assessment of what it will take to penetrate the market should be thorough and take into account not only the special conditions that will be encountered, but also the opportunities to improve the baseline conditions. Especially important in this regard is improving the company's image within the community, so that it becomes – and remains – a trusted service provider instead of a threat.

There are numerous facets to be considered in the design of the strategy to succeed in this market. One of the foremost is estimation of the cost of upgrading service to safe and reliable levels in a way that deters theft. In the toughest markets, highly sophisticated technological solutions may be needed. However, the question will arise as to whether the cost is worth the small revenues to be expected from BOP consumers. Where financial analyses of the results of such efforts have been revealed (and there are too few examples available, unfortunately), the answer is that the return on investment is favorable and that financial results can also be improved by targeting the most sophisticated technological solutions to the toughest areas. Fortunately, in many areas of the world, theft in BOP communities can probably be deterred by much simpler and less costly technologies and techniques. Needless to say, whichever the case, one of the most important upgrades has to occur within the company itself, where a culture of good management needs to be instilled so that theft monitoring and detection can bear fruit for the company's bottom line and not just the pockets of officials subject to the temptations of graft.

Returns can degrade rapidly if good payment performance cannot be maintained over the long term. Therefore, the focus on affordability and control of consumption becomes paramount. Again, solutions need to be tailored to the situation. In Brazil and the rest of Latin America, the relatively high level of appliance ownership almost necessitates efforts to help customers with more efficient lighting and appliances to reduce consumption to affordable levels, particularly when new customers are getting used to paying for their electricity on a consumption basis. Elsewhere, it may be more appropriate to introduce prepayment options that allow the customer to control consumption by purchasing in advance just what can be afforded. While no financial analyses were available showing the comparative costs and benefits of prepayment versus conventional metering, those companies that have utilized prepayment find it to best serve their own and the customers' needs, and plan to continue and most likely expand their efforts to convert to prepayment.

As electricity provision is a highly regulated market, many details of service provision and how the company earns its return must be examined to understand financial viability fully. Likewise, such details might be a sticking point between the regulator and the company if the regulator is not fully behind the effort. This is particularly important when tariff and/ or subsidy issues arise or when scaling up from pilot project to service area-wide programs are being proposed. Furthermore, providing service in BOP neighborhoods can pit municipal goals for slum upgrading against electricity service provision to the existing community. Coordination among all of the stakeholders in these communities will be essential – in planning and in rolling out the programs.

An open and cooperative relationship with the regulator and other government officials will help to ensure that they are fully aware of how conditions might be changing and what the company is doing to accommodate them. As regulators try to reduce subsidies by making them more effective in reaching only those customers who truly need them, the company will need to anticipate this trend and prepare for a time when BOP customers become truly 'regular' customers. Helping them to move into this category is another function that can improve the company's image while improving the overall economic situation in slums. Social responsibility programs, such as transitional credit schemes or job creation or economic development schemes, can go a long way to achieve this.

Finally, it should be noted that a long-term, multipronged effort will be required to meet what should be considered a permanent challenge. Slum communities have a seemingly renewable supply of new inhabitants, and slums are growing and starting up in new locations on a daily basis. Likewise, thieves continuously find new ways to steal, whether it is electricity or copper wire. Experience has shown that a continued presence in the slum, through either community agents or local offices, can help maintain program results through ongoing negotiations with households on their bills, familiarizing new residents with becoming a regular customer and thwarting any new efforts to tap lines.

NOTES

*   This article is a work of the US Agency for International Development (USAID) and therefore is not protected by copyright and is in the public domain. It may be reproduced, published or otherwise used without obtaining the authors' or publisher's permission as long as proper attribution to USAID is provided.
1. East Midlands was bought out in 2000.
2. Djerrari, Fouad, Chief Operating Officer, LYDEC. Statement made at workshop: meeting the Energy Needs of the Urban Poor, Salvador de Bahia, 12–14 September 2005.
3. Melikian, 'Utility–Municipality–Community Collaboration in Angola for Electricity Distribution Improvement', presentation at workshop, 'Improving Electricity Service for the Urban Poor', 4–6 December 2007.
4. Proceedings of the workshop, 'Improving Electricity Service for the Urban Poor', 4–6 December 2007.
5. The savings from public lighting upgrades in the pilot area were calculated to be US$19 258 per month. This cannot be reported on a per-customer basis because the number of households having exterior lights removed when public lighting was installed was not tallied.
6. COELBA has done analysis of payment performance versus proportion of income represented by the electricity bill in its slum electrification program in Salvador, Bahia and derived the 5 percent figure. Subsequent analysis indicates that this number might even be too high.
7. Initiated in 2003, Bolsa Família is a conditional income transfer program for qualified low-income families. It reaches about 11 million families.
8. Source: CanalEnergia.com, August 2007.

8. Delivering utility services to the poor using output-based aid approaches

Patricia Veevers-Carter and Cathy Russell

CONTEXT FOR OUTPUT-BASED AID

Improving access to basic infrastructure and social services for poor people around the world is critical to improving their health, environment and opportunities for development. In recent decades both donors and developing country governments have put major efforts into achieving this goal, but the challenges are great. Despite progress since 1990, around 884 million individuals lack access to safe drinking water and 2.5 billion individuals lack access to basic sanitation (WHO/UNICEF, 2008). Nearly 75 percent of sub-Saharan Africans and 50 percent of South Asians, or 1.25 billion people, still do not have access to electricity. In South Asia and sub-Saharan Africa, less than 50 percent of births are attended by skilled health staff (World Bank, 2008).

One of the challenges in increasing access to basic infrastructure and social services is the gap between what it costs to deliver a desired level of service, and what can be funded through user charges. Subsidies have often played a role in funding this gap because of, for example, limited ability to pay by the poor; the 'public-good' characteristics of the service, which make it difficult to collect user charges; and positive economic externalities of a service, so that the benefits of one individual's consumption are felt much more widely in society, as in the case of health care and sanitation. However, given concerns about aid effectiveness and fiscal viability, it is critical to ensure that donor or government resources are achieving the desired results and that the projects being funded increase productivity and are financially sustainable (that is, services with tariffs that cover at least operation and maintenance costs). Improving the delivery of public services can also help governments to increase their credibility and thus to attract more financing, from both private companies and international donors. Output-based aid (OBA) is one approach that can be used to improve the delivery of basic services to the poor by contracting out their provision and linking subsidy funding to the actual delivery of services, or 'outputs'.

In this context the purpose of this chapter is to:

- Present the key characteristics of OBA, including core concepts and an example of a typical OBA structure.
- Summarize experience with OBA approaches to date, including the role of the Global Partnership on Output-Based Aid (GPOBA), OBA piloting through GPOBA, and an overview of GPOBA's utilities portfolio with an example of a project in Uganda.
- Analyze key lessons and challenges in OBA.
- Explain how OBA can help target services to people at the base of the pyramid.
- Illustrate how OBA works through a case study on an OBA project in Colombia involving a national gas utility.
- Discuss how to mainstream OBA approaches in development finance.[1]

WHAT IS OBA?

Output-based aid is a results-based financing mechanism that is being used to increase access to basic services for the poor in developing countries and improve the delivery of services that exhibit positive externalities, such as reductions in CO_2 and improvements in health. OBA is used in cases where people at the base of the pyramid are being excluded from basic services because they cannot afford to pay the full cost of user fees such as connection fees. OBA is one of a spectrum of results-based financing instruments that includes provider payment incentives, conditional cash transfers, and the like. It is part of a broader donor effort to ensure that aid is well spent and that the benefits go to the poor.

The OBA concept was introduced in the World Bank Group (WBG) in 2002 through the Private Sector Development Strategy, and more formally in January 2003. At that time, the Global Partnership on Output-Based Aid (GPOBA)[2] was launched as a World Bank-administered donor-funded pilot program to test the approach with a view to mainstreaming OBA within the World Bank as well as with other development partners.

OBA ties the disbursement of public funding in the form of subsidies to the achievement of clearly specified results that directly support improved access to basic services. Basic services include improved water supply, energy access, health care, education, communications services and transportation. Subsidies are defined as public funding used to fill the gap between the total cost of providing a service to a user, and the user fees charged for that service. Policy concerns such as improving basic living conditions for the poor or reducing disease may justify the use of subsidies.

In the case of OBA, 'outputs' are defined as closely to the desired outcome or impact as is contractually feasible. For example, an output might be the installation of a functioning household connection to the electricity network. In some cases, an output might also include a specified period of electricity delivery demonstrated through billing and collection records. The intended outcome of such an output-based scheme would be to improve the basic living conditions of the poor household by reducing indoor household pollution, increasing opportunities for education through better lighting or through information passed through radio and television, and the like. The intended development impact could include, for example, a reduction in morbidity or increased lifetime earnings.

Neither performance arrangements nor subsidies are new. Performance contracts have been implemented for several decades, using both public and private operators. However, outputs in OBA schemes are generally more narrowly defined than benchmarks in traditional performance arrangements, which in some cases may be more input-oriented. Subsidies have also existed in the infrastructure and social service sectors. OBA refines the targeting of subsidies by bringing them together with performance-based arrangements through the explicitly linking of the disbursement of subsidies to the achievement of agreed outputs. Figure 8.1 provides a simple contrast of a traditional input-based approach to an output-based approach.

Another way of looking at how OBA differs from input-based approaches is to analyze the contracting spectrum often seen in infrastructure and social service delivery. Since the 1990s, schemes that harness private financing to deliver infrastructure services have expanded considerably. Under traditional procurement, private infrastructure services are contracted at the 'input' end of the spectrum: the government purchases specific 'inputs' and uses them to build assets and provide services itself. Under OBA schemes, services are contracted to a third-party provider, and that contract or other official arrangement is the mechanism through which the output-based disbursement criteria are established.

Contracting 'closer to the input end' (for example, the construction of water treatment plants) does not guarantee that the inputs the government purchases actually lead to the outcomes (for example, a reduction in waterborne diseases) or impacts (for example, decreased morbidity) that the government actually wants. Because outcomes and impacts are a combined product of: (1) what the provider can influence; and (2) other factors

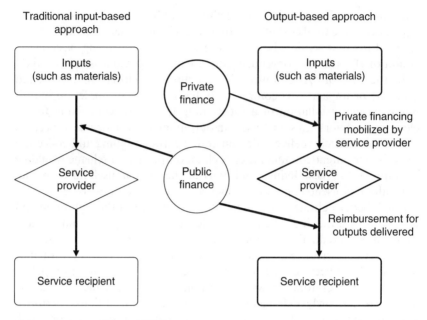

Traditional input-based approach

Output-based approach

Source: Brook and Petrie (2001).

Figure 8.1   Contrast of a traditional input-based approach to an output-based approach

outside the service provider's control, either governments seeking to pay on outcomes and impacts will not find a willing, credible service provider or the provider will charge a substantial premium for making its receipt of payment contingent on factors that it cannot control. Nevertheless, governments can contract for an output related as closely as possible to the desired development outcome or impact, while leaving performance risk still largely under the service provider's control. This is the rationale behind output-based aid.

OBA CORE CONCEPTS

When OBA was launched in the WBG in 2002–03, certain criteria and benchmarks were postulated against which the success of the approach could be judged. Namely, because of the link between pre-identified outputs and *ex post* payment ('subsidies'), the following advantages of OBA over traditional approaches were assumed:

- Increasing transparency through the explicit targeting of subsidies, tying these subsidies to defined outputs.
- Increasing accountability by shifting performance risk to service providers by paying them after they have delivered an agreed output.
- Encouraging innovation and efficiency by leaving the service 'solutions' partly up to the service provider.
- Increasing engagement of private sector capital and expertise, and sustainability of public funding, by encouraging the private sector to serve customers (usually the poor) that they might otherwise disregard, through the linkage of ongoing subsides to sustainable service.
- Enhancing monitoring of results, since payments are made against agreed outputs.
- Increasing sustainability of public funding through the use of one-off subsidies and by linking ongoing subsidies to sustainable service.

This section examines each of these five 'core concepts' and explains the ways in which they distinguish OBA from traditional, more input-based approaches to aid.[3]

Targeting of Subsidies

A key distinction of OBA interventions – by contrast with some other forms of publicly funded subsidy – is the explicit recognition of why the subsidy is being provided, who it is being provided to and by whom, and what is being subsidized in terms of both the activity and the financial sums involved.

Historically, implicit rather than explicit subsidies have often been involved in infrastructure service delivery in both developed and developing countries. Such implicit subsidies are frequently hidden – for example, bundled into a concessional loan so that it is not possible to determine the degree of subsidy – and it may not always be clear who the ultimate beneficiary is. These implicit subsidy approaches are not well targeted and are often inefficient. Better-off, mainly urban customers tend to benefit from such subsidies, while poorer people are left with no service at all. Subsidized infrastructure services may be priced well below both what customers are able to pay and what they are willing to pay. Using scarce public resources in this way is also likely to detract from other uses to which subsidies might be put.

Conversely, in an OBA scheme, the end-users are the direct beneficiaries of the subsidy and the subsidy is reimbursed for an agreed portion of the costs incurred to provide a service. This explicit recognition and identification of subsidy flows ensures transparency, reduces the scope for corruption, and helps to reduce the economic distortions that subsidies are prone to introduce. (See the section below on 'Targeting Services to the Poor'.)

OBA schemes normally apply performance-based subsidies in three ways: one-off subsidies such as connection subsidies, transitional tariff subsidies that taper off as user contributions increase, or ongoing subsidies. The subsidy design chosen will depend on factors such as the sustainability of the funding source, the capacity for administering the subsidy scheme, the type of service to be subsidized, and the extent to which the service provider is willing and able to be paid over time.

For utility services, most OBA schemes in water, energy and telecommunications rely on one-off subsidies enabling initial access, partly because OBA is targeted to the poor, and the poor are usually not connected to network services in the first place so often cannot benefit from ongoing or transitional tariff subsidies. A one-off OBA subsidy may be used, for example, to help connect a poor household to the water or electricity network, or to reduce a community's contribution for provision of payphones or Internet points of presence.

Ongoing output-based subsidies in the utility sectors are seen more often in countries with higher rates of access. For example, in Chile an income-based targeting scheme channels an ongoing output-based subsidy through service providers to poor urban households for a lifeline (minimum acceptable) amount of water consumed.

Accountability

The second key distinction of the OBA approach is that payment to service providers is performance-based, strongly linked to the delivery of outputs – that is, specified services – by the providers. This payment on outputs transfers performance and finance risks to the service provider. As such, the service is largely self-funded by the provider, with reimbursement occurring mostly on verification of successful delivery. This contrasts with other approaches in which inputs are prefunded by donors or governments and in which the transfer of performance risk to the service provider is commensurately less. The OBA approach has the advantage of maintaining pressure on the service provider to deliver the prespecified outputs. Clear delineation of outputs also increases the accountability of donors and governments.

The difference between payment under traditional schemes and under OBA projects can be illustrated by examples from the health and energy sectors. In a traditional energy scheme, payment could be for the delivery of transmission lines, while in an OBA energy project, payment could be for working connections made or actual electricity delivered, or both.

Similarly, in a traditional health scheme public funding could be disbursed for the building of a hospital or for the procuring of special medical equipment, whereas in an OBA health scheme, payments to service providers could depend on delivery of well-child visits or the administering of vaccinations. For instance, in Uganda, GPOBA is funding a voucher scheme to support medical services for safe childbirth deliveries and the treatment of sexually transmitted diseases. Disbursements are made to preselected service providers based on a fee for services, performed on a fixed per-item basis, and reflect actual costs. Service providers are reimbursed after service delivery, and are at risk of not being reimbursed if services do not meet set standards.

Innovation and Efficiency

A well-designed OBA scheme should lead to lower costs – depending on the efficiency of the service provider, and to opportunities and incentives for the service provider to innovate as provided by the terms of the contract. Where there is competition for new services to be offered with the support of the subsidy, private sector creativity is solicited as the providers compete by offering the most cost-effective solutions. Efficiency can be achieved both through competition for new services and through benchmarking leading to value for money.

Both the emphasis on improving efficiency and the focus on reaching the poorest households can encourage innovation in OBA schemes. Poor families often live in remote rural areas, where grid access is difficult or impossible, or in informal settlements, where unclear land tenure may be an obstacle to providing service. The search for ways to reach these families can result in increased subsidy efficiency and more affordable services. In Uganda, for instance, a competitive bidding process to provide water supply resulted in an average efficiency gain of 20 percent in ten towns. OBA can also contribute to positive externalities such as energy efficiency. In a rural electrification project in Ethiopia, each targeted household will receive not only an electricity connection but also two compact fluorescent lamps that will reduce their electricity consumption by 55 percent and make their bills more affordable.

Using Incentives to Serve the Poor

OBA may be used as a tool to implement public–private partnership (PPP) for service delivery to the poor: better-designed subsidy mechanisms that are explicitly channeled through the service provider with credible payment and monitoring systems can attract and mobilize the private sector. For example, in a rural electrification concession in Senegal requiring a minimum number of connections 20 km beyond the grid, the winning bidder proposed to more than double the required minimum – from 8500 to 21 800 – by providing $9.6 million in private financing, that is, 60 percent of total financing, compared to the 20 percent minimum private financing requirement under the tender. However, OBA is not only a tool for PPPs. OBA also works well for public sector companies that operate on a commercial basis and hence are subject to the same incentives to increase efficiency as private sector companies are.

The subsidy incentive in an OBA scheme creates a 'win–win' situation for the end-user and the service provider. It makes the connection cost affordable for the end-user; it allows the service provider to recover the costs of providing the service; and it incentivizes the service provider to provide financing for 'green field' or expansions, leveraging the subsidy. OBA can help bring services to areas that would not otherwise be commercially viable and can thus be an effective way to address gaps in service coverage for poor customers.

Output Verification and Monitoring

A distinguishing feature of OBA schemes is the requirement that subsidies be paid within a performance regime in which payments are strongly linked to service outputs, the main form of performance risk transfer to the provider of services. This makes monitoring of outputs (or results) easier and more precise in an OBA scheme, as the subsidy payment reimburses the service provider only after verification of service. Each OBA scheme has a payment schedule which specifies the percentage of the subsidy that will be disbursed after the pre-agreed outputs have been delivered. The outputs have to be verified by an independent verification agent before disbursement can take place, which helps increase transparency and ensure that public funding is used for the intended purpose and not wasted.

In Vietnam, for example, a project to provide safe drinking water for 75 locally managed, village-based piped water schemes disburses 80 percent of the subsidy on verification of connection and 20 percent after six months of satisfactory service. The subsidy payment is triggered by quarterly monitoring reports that document the number of connections made, the total number of beneficiary households, the uptake ratio of beneficiary households in each eligible area, the average monthly consumption per beneficiary household, the average expenditure on service by beneficiary households, and the collection ratio for water bills and of connection fees.

Sustainability

One objective of the OBA approach should be to find a sustainable solution that benefits all the parties: the government, the users and the service provider. Key factors in the sustainability of the scheme include affordability for users and cost recovery for service providers. A sustainable funding source is also important. Where it is possible to pay a one-time subsidy – for example, to establish a service connection for a customer who can then afford the ongoing service costs – the degree of sustainability is likely to be high, as there will be no need for future public funding after the one-off payment upon connection has been made. Many OBA schemes have focused on developing these more sustainable approaches. For example, in the rural electrification project in Ethiopia mentioned above, 50 percent of the subsidy is paid after a working electricity connection is made, and the remaining 50 percent is only paid after three successful billing cycles in order to ensure sustainability of the electricity provided to poor households.

Whatever the type of subsidy used, government commitment is a key factor in the sustainability of a project. Tariffs must cover cost of operations and maintenance and there must be clearly defined regulatory process and adjustment mechanisms, adequate tariff setting and adjusting policies, and agreed procedures for dispute resolution.

EXAMPLE OF A TYPICAL OBA STRUCTURE

A typical OBA structure usually involves a municipality or other authority which has a service contract or other form of legal agreement with a service provider (see Figure 8.2). The service provider serves a certain geographical area in which there are poor communities not currently connected to the service. Under the OBA scheme, the service provider is responsible for prefinancing and delivering the outputs (connections installed, services delivered) to the poor communities. An independent verification agent (IVA) such as an auditing or technical firm verifies the outputs and reports to the Subsidy Fund, which may be GPOBA or an OBA facility managed by the government, as in the case of a GPOBA-supported water project in Honduras. Once the Subsidy Fund is satisfied that the services have been delivered, typically as evidenced by three to six months of collected bills, it provides the subsidy, either directly to the service provider or through a financial intermediary. As noted above, the subsidy payments are linked to specific outputs or milestones and are only made once these outputs have been delivered to the satisfaction of the IVA and the Subsidy Fund.

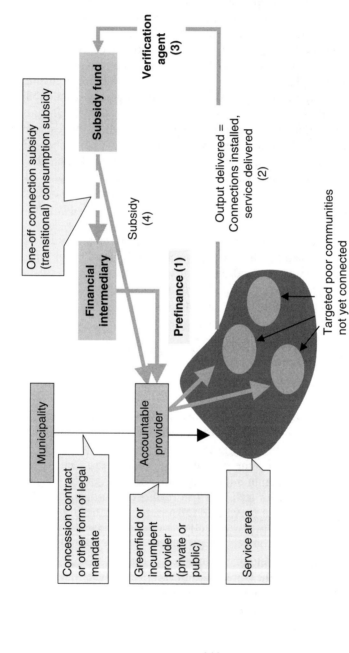

Source: GPOBA.

Figure 8.2 A typical OBA structure

The flow of funding and accountability varies from project to project due to sector and country differences and factors such as whether the service provider is new or an incumbent, and the degree to which the provider has access to the finance they need to prefinance the project. The diagram for the Colombia natural gas project (see Figure 8.3 in the case study below) provides an example of the funding and accountability flows in a subsidy scheme involving an incumbent provider with adequate access to finance.[4]

OBA EXPERIENCE TO DATE

The first OBA pilots in the World Bank Group were launched in the 1990s in Latin America, mainly in the information and communication technology (ICT) and roads sectors. They include output-based contracts for payphones in Peru, road maintenance in Argentina and water services in Chile. Other early OBA schemes include primary health care in Romania and schools in the United Kingdom (Brook and Smith, 2001). With the establishment of GPOBA, the development and documentation of OBA schemes has become more systematic. This section explains GPOBA's role and experience so far, gives an overview of GPOBA's portfolio of projects involving utilities, and presents an example of a project in Uganda involving a water utility.

Role of GPOBA

As mentioned above, GPOBA was launched in January 2003 as a World Bank-administered donor-funded pilot program to test the OBA approach with a view to mainstreaming it in the World Bank as well as with other development partners. The program's donors include the UK's Department for International Development (DFID), the Australian Agency for International Development (AusAID), the Dutch Ministry of Foreign Affairs (DGIS), the International Finance Corporation (IFC), and the Swedish International Development Cooperation Agency (Sida). As of 30 June 2009, donor funding for GPOBA including contributions and pledges totaled $238.7 million.

In fiscal year 2008, DFID commissioned an independent mid-term review of GPOBA, carried out by Ernst & Young. The review was generally positive, noting increased knowledge and use of OBA in the World Bank, careful targeting of OBA projects to the poor, successful piloting of new and innovative approaches to OBA, and significant private sector involvement in OBA schemes. As a result of this review, GPOBA developed a Vision Statement setting out the program's goals for the period 2008–13. GPOBA will focus on mainstreaming OBA with development partners (including governments of developing countries, international financial institutions and bilateral donors), with mainstreaming defined as OBA being used on a regular basis in project design. GPOBA will remain a multidonor global program housed in the WBG and will act primarily as a center of OBA expertise by 2013. This vision provides the framework for GPOBA's activities going forward.

Documenting OBA Schemes

An important part of GPOBA's role is to document projects using OBA approaches, whether these are funded by GPOBA or by other organizations. This involves identifying OBA schemes, collecting and compiling data, monitoring and evaluating project implementation, and analyzing the emerging challenges and lessons learned. The focus of this activity is primarily on OBA schemes that target the poor in developing countries and the results are disseminated through GPOBA's publications and reports.[5]

In fiscal year 2009, GPOBA and the World Bank's International Development Association – International Finance Corporation (IDA/IFC) Secretariat conducted a joint review of OBA in six sectors (Mumssen et al., 2010). According to the review, there were approximately 32 OBA projects at the time of the 'official launch' of OBA in the WBG in 2002–03 for a total funding amount of US$1.5 billion.[6] About 131 OBA projects with a total subsidy value of about US$3.5 billion (excluding US$2.8 billion in subsidy funding provided by recipient governments) have been identified in the WBG by 2010. Of these projects, 34 have closed, 78 are under implementation and for the most part delivering outputs, and 19 are in design stage. Another 66 OBA schemes have been identified outside the WBG – mostly in the ICT, transport (mainly roads) and energy sectors.[7]

The piloting phase of OBA has provided a wide array of lessons and in many cases has been a success. The 131 OBA projects that have been implemented or are under way in the WBG are expected to reach at least 61 million beneficiaries worldwide.[8] The first WBG OBA pilots were launched in the ICT and roads sectors in the 1990s in Latin America. These pilots were replicated and scaled-up first in that region, and eventually lessons learned were transferred from middle-income to low-income countries. It could be reasonably claimed that OBA has become 'mainstreamed' as one of the mechanisms used to expand access in these two sectors in many parts of the world – and in fact many non-WBG OBA projects identified are in ICT and roads. In the health and off-grid energy sectors, OBA has become an important results-based financing instrument enabling improved access for the poor, and OBA schemes are increasingly found outside the WBG as well. OBA is still at pilot stage in the water, education and grid-based energy sectors, although lessons for scale-up in some cases are now starting to become available.

OBA Piloting through GPOBA

In addition to documenting OBA approaches, GPOBA provides grant funding for technical assistance and subsidy schemes in the energy, health, ICT, and water and sanitation sectors in countries in East Asia and the Pacific, Central and Eastern Europe, Latin America and the Caribbean, the Middle East and North Africa, South Asia and sub-Saharan Africa. As of 15 November 2009, GPOBA had signed 28 grant agreements for OBA subsidy schemes for a total of US$109.3 million, expected to benefit an estimated 5.8 million people in 22 countries. GPOBA focuses its operations on the poorer countries and all but three of the grant agreements signed in fiscal years 2008 and 2009 are in IDA countries, with almost 50 percent of the funding going to sub-Saharan Africa.[9]

GPOBA projects involve different types of service provider, including not only public utilities but also private firms, non-governmental organizations (NGOs) and community-based organizations. A rural water project in India, for instance, is using a community-based PPP model involving an Indian foundation and an international water technology provider. At the other end of the spectrum, an electricity project in Ghana is subsidizing installations of off-grid solar photovoltaic systems for people in rural areas using a 'dealer model' which promotes free market entry and competition between rival firms. In each case, GPOBA's aim is to find a reliable and motivated service provider (private or public) and a solution that is adapted to the local context.

GPOBA Utilities Portfolio

Of GPOBA's 28 signed grant agreements, 16 involve utilities, representing US$59.3 million in subsidy funding (see Table 8.1). Nine of the projects involving utilities are in the water and sanitation sector (which represents 62 percent of funding), four are in the energy sector, and three are in the ICT sector. A breakdown by region shows that five of the 16 projects are in sub-Saharan Africa, which represents 46 percent of funding, and six are in East Asia (18 percent of funding); the other projects are in Latin America (two), South Asia (one), Europe (one) and North Africa (one). These projects include, for example:

Private utilities and poverty alleviation

Table 8.1   GPOBA projects involving utilities

Project	Sector	Region	Grant (US$ million)	Beneficiaries	Subsidy efficiency per capita (US$)
Armenia Heating and Gas	Energy	ECA	3.1	18 676	165.99
Colombia Natural Gas*	Energy	LAC	4.9	204 852	23.82
Mongolia Telecom	Telecom	EAP	0.3	22 315	11.62
Morocco Water and Sanitation	W&S	MNA	7.0	56 000	125.00
Honduras Water	Water	LAC	4.4	240 000	18.50
Senegal Sanitation	Sanitation	AFR	5.8	135 900	42.41
Manila Water	Water	EAP	1.1	35 250	29.79
Jakarta Water	Water	EAP	2.6	55 824	46.09
Uganda NWSC Water	Water	AFR	2.5	409 050	6.18
Mozambique Water	Water	AFR	6.0	468 000	12.82
Cameroon Urban Water	Water	AFR	5.3	240 000	21.88
Ethiopia Rural Electrification	Energy	AFR	8.0	1 142 857	7.00
Cambodia Telecom	Telecom	EAP	2.5	261 000	9.58
Surabaya Water	Water	EAP	2.4	77 500	31.06
Indonesia Telecom	Telecom	EAP	1.9	758 210	2.46
India Mumbai Slum Electrification	Energy	SAR	1.7	104 000	15.87
Total			59.3	4 229 434	14.01

Note: * The actual grant amount at signing was US$5.1 million, but the total disbursed at project closing was US$4.88 million, so the latter amount has been used to calculate the subsidy efficiency.

Source: GPOBA.

- Uganda: a scheme to connect an estimated 400 000 poor people to water services through a combination of new yard tap connections and public water points; involves the National Water & Sewerage Corporation (see Box 8.1).
- The Philippines: a scheme to provide affordable piped potable water to poor households in Manila; implemented by the Manila Water Company, Inc.
- Ethiopia: a project to expand access to electricity to 228 571 poor households in rural areas; grant recipient is the public sector Ethiopian Electric Power Corporation (EEPCo).
- Armenia: a project to improve access to gas and heat supply for an estimated 10 000 poor urban households (4600 through GPOBA funds, the rest through World Bank funds); involves the country's privatized gas company, HaiRusGasArd.

As these examples suggest, most OBA schemes involving utilities in the water, energy and ICT sectors rely on one-off subsidies enabling initial access. This is partly because the poor are usually not connected to network services in the first instance and so could not benefit from ongoing or transitional tariff subsidies.

PROJECT RESULTS

Of the $59.3 million in GPOBA subsidy funding for projects involving utilities, $10.1 million has been disbursed based on verified outputs as of 1 November 2009, benefiting over 311 000 people. These figures reflect the fact that many of the projects have only recently been signed and that it takes an average of 12 months for outputs to be delivered and the first OBA payments made (see section on 'Project Implementation' below). By completion, the 16 GPOBA-funded projects involving utilities are expected to provide around 4 million people with access to essential services. Two projects which were among the first to be signed by GPOBA have completed their activities:

- The Colombia Natural Gas Distribution for Low-income Families in the Caribbean Coast project closed on 31 July 2008, having achieved its goal of connecting poor households in underserved areas to Colombia's natural gas distribution network (see the case study below).
- The Mongolia OBA Pilot Project of Universal Access Strategy closed on 30 September 2008, having delivered two types of output – a public

BOX 8.1   OUTPUT-BASED AID IN UGANDA:
WORKING WITH A PUBLIC UTILITY

The Uganda NWSC Water project is an example of how GPOBA
is working with utilities to bring services to the poor. The
grant recipient is the National Water and Sewerage Corporation
(NWSC), a public utility responsible for water supply and sewerage services in Uganda's large urban centers. NWSC is an
'autonomous public corporation' 100 percent owned by the government of Uganda, with a reputation as one of the most efficient
public water utilities in sub-Saharan Africa. The central government, represented by both the Ministry of Water and the Ministry
of Finance, maintains a performance contract with NWSC. In
turn, NWSC has developed a set of delegated management area
contracts through which it monitors performance in its various
urban centers. Through these performance contracts, NWSC
management and staff have clear incentives to perform efficiently
– and in many ways emulate a private corporation.

NWSC has a mission to serve the poor and currently (2010)
serves about half of the poorest residents of Greater Kampala.
But NWSC does not have strong financial incentives to build new
connections for the growing number of poor residents, without
external funding. Firstly, many of these consumers cannot afford
the connection fee for household yard taps, so they are best
served through public water points (PWPs) which do not involve
connection charges and which charge the 'social' tariff which only
covers operation and maintenance costs. Secondly, the amount
of water consumed per capita by the poor is very low. Thirdly,
poor people's payment behavior, which is less consistent than
that of wealthier customers, means additional operating and overhead costs for NWSC.

To achieve its social aims while maintaining its financial stand-
ing and efficiency, NWSC applied to GPOBA to help connect
Kampala's poorest residents to the water supply network. In
February 2008, the two parties signed a grant agreement for
US$2.5 million. With the GPOBA grant and NWSC co-financing,
the NWSC will connect an estimated 400 000 poor people living
in the slums to piped water supply through over 19 000 new yard
taps and over 800 PWPs. The project will target the poorest
households, that is, those with an income of less than U Sh 80 000

(US$48) per month. The total new investment (over a four-year period) is about US$4 million. GPOBA is contributing a fixed subsidy to the connection cost so that poor households can afford access. All of the connections will be prefinanced by NWSC, which will receive GPOBA reimbursement only after the outputs have been independently verified.

NWSC has noted that the OBA scheme poses an additional challenge for project roll-out compared to other donor schemes undertaken, since the OBA scheme is 'demand-driven' and requires that poor communities apply for connections and thus must understand the benefits, payment terms, and so on. This has resulted in NWSC thinking more strategically about pro-poor payment schemes, such as moving from billing monthly to billing twice a month, as more frequent billing can increase poor households' ability to pay their bills.

access telephone network for the herder community and a wireless network for the *soum* (district) – to poor households in remote areas of Mongolia, benefiting a total of 22 315 people. The competitive bidding process in this project resulted in substantial savings which were reallocated to an additional tender, allowing more people to be served than originally estimated (Dymond et al., 2008).

KEY LESSONS AND CHALLENGES IN OBA

The concept of OBA – payment upon results – is simple, but designing and implementing OBA schemes can be complex, as the experience in projects involving utilities and other types of service provider is beginning to show. Viable OBA schemes require reliable and motivated service providers; tariffs that cover at least operation and maintenance costs; and an effective method for targeting the subsidies to the poor. Moreover, OBA projects, like most projects in the infrastructure sectors, can benefit from clearly defined rules of engagement and a sound regulatory environment.

GPOBA's *Annual Report 2007* (GPOBA, 2007) identified some initial lessons and challenges of OBA projects, including the need to design and apply OBA schemes flexibly, according to the local context, the importance of building the capacity of local implementers (be they private or public), and the challenge of providing the right incentives in OBA schemes involving public service providers (GPOBA, 2007). During fiscal year 2008, GPOBA began supervising its first projects, which deepened its understanding of OBA schemes and helped to identify additional success factors. More lessons were compiled as part of the review of OBA conducted in fiscal year 2009 (Mumssen et al., 2010), which analyzed the performance of the OBA portfolio against the six criteria or 'core concepts' outlined above. This section presents some key issues. The issue of targeting services to the poor, which is particularly important for the base of the pyramid, is the focus of the following section.

Project Implementation

Based on the OBA schemes it has funded so far, GPOBA estimates that it takes on average 12 months after grant signing for outputs to be delivered and the first OBA payments to be made, and another two to three years for full disbursement. Projects that build on existing pilots or work with entities that already provide the service to be subsidized are usually able to deliver outputs in less than 12 months, but greenfield projects tend to take longer. This is due to a variety of factors (which may or may not be unique to OBA). Many projects use competitive bidding to select the service provider. Monitoring and output verification systems can take time to set up. Project uptake may involve awareness-raising among beneficiaries. Institutional factors, such as a change of responsible ministry, can cause delays in some projects.

Furthermore, projects involving small-scale service providers or community organizations can require extensive capacity-building. Capacity limitations are most obvious in regards to transaction design and implementation, output monitoring and verification implementation, and demand management. Targeted training, hiring of independent verification agents, involvement of NGOs, and private administrators to manage universal access funds are all part of solutions being implemented to mitigate capacity constraints. Given that OBA is about reaching the poor and underserved, GPOBA considers it worthwhile investing time and effort in these activities.

Mobilizing Other Sources of Finance

Experience so far shows that OBA does leverage private funding. As of 30 June 2009, for 28 grant agreements signed for a total of $111 million in GPOBA grant funding, an additional $290 million had been mobilized from other sources such as user contributions ($37 million) and private sector investment ($123.60 million), as well as co-financing from governments and other donors. For every dollar in GPOBA funding, almost

$2.60 has been contributed by other sources (not taking into account demonstration effects, which can also help mobilize additional funding). In addition to this, GPOBA funding has resulted in additional funds raised either for scaling-up (such as IDA funding of $5.4 million for the Mongolia telecommunications project) or to conduct additional pilots (such as the European Union funding of approximately $2.2 million for a project in Kenya that combines microfinance and OBA for small water schemes).

Because OBA projects target the poor, who often are charged social tariffs or who consume small amounts, the possibilities of mobilizing additional funding are limited compared to non-OBA schemes which do not target the poor. Nevertheless, OBA schemes have shown that with relatively small amounts of subsidy they can mobilize private sector expertise to serve customer segments that the private sector might otherwise not serve. Ultimately, the effective use of private sector participation depends on the enabling environment – for example, the depth and quality of experience with PPP contracts, regulation and access to finance.

One clear lesson to have emerged is that for network and utility services, mobilizing private finance is linked to tariff reform: ultimately, the service provider must be able to recoup its costs through the tariff. If the aim is to have a smaller amount of subsidy with more of the investment recovered through private financing, the tariff would need to be able to absorb these costs. Given affordability constraints on the tariff, this implies that in order for the private sector to recover its investment the contract would have to be for a longer period than is currently being used.

Incentives for Efficiency, Quality and Innovation

Some evidence indicates that output-based payments have led to improvements in operational efficiency and the delivery of innovative (often pro-poor) access to service solutions. Moreover, OBA has demonstrated efficiency gains through competition in most sectors when competitive pressures have been applied in the selection of the OBA service provider (although competitive tendering processes can take time). The focus on outputs rather than inputs should lead to innovations that translate into future efficiency gains, as has been seen in ICT and to some extent in roads.

Competitive bidding can lead to increased efficiency – usually expressed as a decrease in unit costs. The Mongolia telecommunications project offers an example of a competitive bidding process that produced efficiency gains and innovation. Furthermore, quality standards need to be carefully defined and penalties established for not achieving them, especially since a degree of freedom is allowed under an output-based approach. This is one of the key challenges in 'getting it right' with an OBA design:

not micro-managing and monitoring inputs, but still ensuring value for money.

The Manila Water Company (MWC) project in the Philippines offers an example of how quality standards are used in an OBA project. The output for this scheme is sustainable access to modern water services, as evidenced by working connections to the MWC network and three months of satisfactory service provision. To ensure that MWC has delivered these outputs, the independent verification agent must confirm the following four outputs on a representative sample of beneficiary households: (1) installed water meter; (2) 24-hour water supply (beneficiary confirmation); (3) water pressure of at least 5 psi (pounds per square inch) (from MWC operational records); and (4) water bill delivered, demonstrating consumption and service delivery (confirmed by beneficiary and MWC billing records).

Access to Finance

Compared to similar input-based schemes, OBA shifts the performance risk to service providers by paying providers only after delivery of verifiable access and service. However, the degree of performance risk shifted depends on the ability of the service provider to 'prefinance' investments and services until output-based payments are disbursed. This is a big challenge for projects involving smaller service providers and public sector utilities. It implies that the service provider must either fund the proposed outputs through its own financial resources or seek external funding, for example through local commercial banks. This is sometimes difficult, as local banks and other financial institutions may have little or no experience in lending to sectors such as infrastructure development or health. Furthermore, many infrastructure projects, even small-scale ones, require loans with longer tenures than many banks are used to giving. The financial crisis is likely to exacerbate these problems.

GPOBA is exploring innovative financing solutions to ease access to finance and make these projects work, including:

- Making some payments for intermediate outputs or project roll-out milestones. This can ease project fund flow constraints until the prescribed output is achieved and thus reduce the amount and tenure of prefinancing required.
- Phased-in roll-out of outputs linked to a revolving loan facility which is replenished by the subsidy payment once the first phase of outputs has been delivered.
- Working with local banks to extend loans to service providers with

little or no credit rating by using the grant agreements as a form of security for the loans.
● Working with funding and guarantee agencies.

An example is the Extension of Water and Sanitation Services in Low-Income Areas of Honduras project. Under this scheme, local banks have been prepared to extend loans to service providers with little or no credit ratings, based on the security that if the service provider achieves the pre-agreed outputs, payments will be made by GPOBA. This allows the service providers to create a relationship with local banks, which could lead to future lending.

Enabling Environment

As with most PPP arrangements, in order for OBA schemes to be sustainable and of scale, there should be basic elements of an environment that supports the development, monitoring and adjustment of contracts, which is often demonstrated by a successful track record of private sector participation. Relatively transparent legal or regulatory arrangements, for example for tariff setting and adjustment, would be among such enabling factors, and ultimately aim to reduce perceived risk to providers and to some extent the cost to final users.

Increasing Sustainability

It is too early to analyze whether OBA schemes have provided long-term sustainable solutions. No evidence to date (2010) suggests that schemes involving OBA subsidies are less sustainable than their input-based counterparts. In fact, the design of OBA schemes (for example, greater degree of demand risk shifted to service providers given the link between outputs and uptake, which in turn incentivizes efforts at stakeholder participation and education through community organizations, non-governmental organizations, and so on) can enhance longer-term sustainability.

Competing Interests

Ultimately, all else being equal, service providers will opt for input-based schemes because they transfer less risk to the provider. But donors and governments should want the contrary, that is, to transfer risk to the providers to hold them accountable (as long as providers are equipped to take on that risk). If OBA is to be the mechanism chosen for a given intervention, donor–government coordination is required.

As suggested above, OBA provides a good platform for targeting infra-structure and social services subsidies. The focus on subsidies for access is inherently pro-poor: the poorest segments of the population, that is, those at the base of the pyramid, often cannot afford initial access (for example, cost of connection) and therefore often do not benefit from subsidies for ongoing service provision. Furthermore, if outputs are explicitly defined, targeting can be made more precise. The process of output verification can also provide an additional check on the targeting of subsidies and is helping to provide early evidence that OBA schemes are reaching the poor. The following section looks at targeting in more detail.

TARGETING SERVICES TO THE POOR[10]

If OBA is to be an effective means of serving people at the base of the pyramid, special attention needs to be given to targeting OBA subsidies to the poorest households. Good targeting practices can both help reduce the need for subsidies and ensure that they reach the intended beneficiaries.

Although the need for targeting is generally acknowledged, subsidies have not always been effectively targeted to reach the poorest, a failure that can be attributed to various factors:

- Policy makers may have incentives to cater to more politically influential groups first at the expense of the poor.
- There is a gap in understanding as to how services can be provided so that they are most useful and accessible to the poor.
- Targeting on the basis of income can involve sophisticated and often costly data systems that allow for collection and storage of income data on the poor.
- Low social tariffs that do not fully cover the cost of maintaining the system and providing service present a disincentive for utilities to serve the poor. This can even be the case where cross-subsidies are meant to allow the utility to cover the shortfall, as income from cross-subsidies is not tied to service delivery to the poor.
- The poor are not always aware that they are entitled to service.
- Sometimes subsidies are depleted by middle-class households who provide false information or bribe officials to obtain subsidized services to which they are not entitled.

For utility services, additional factors come into play. In some poor countries large swaths of the population, including even the better-off, may not be connected. Where this is so, politicians and service providers may see greater gains in serving the better-off customers first – even though the services may be subsidized through utility tariffs that are inefficiently low, leading to wasteful use of public resources. The notion that the poor cannot afford to pay sustainable tariffs may be another factor. Yet many interventions, as well as studies and surveys, have shown that a large share of poor people are willing and able to pay sustainable tariffs – and usually already spend much more on alternative services such as water from water vendors or batteries for power supply.

Where Do Subsidies Go?

The fairness and effectiveness of subsidy targeting is commonly evaluated by the extent of coverage of the target group and the 'leakage' to non-target groups (also known as errors of exclusion or inclusion). Experience in many countries suggests that projects in infrastructure and to some extent in social services have failed to target subsidies effectively to the poor and vulnerable. Many have lacked an explicit targeting mechanism for subsidies and any efficiency gains achieved were purely incidental.

In the water and energy sectors, subsidies are most commonly channeled through the tariff so that users do not pay the full cost – sometimes not even the running costs – of the service. A 2005 study on tariff subsidies for water and electricity services found that these subsidies are invariably regressive, benefiting the non-poor more than the poor (Komives et al., 2005). This is due largely to one of two reasons: the poor are not connected to the system in the first place; or there are only minimal differences in consumption patterns between the rich and the poor, so that quantity-based subsidy schemes such as increasing block tariffs actually lead to considerable leakage. The study argues that alternative forms of targeting – such as connection subsidies that support initial access rather than consumption – would be more effective in reaching the poor. Most OBA utility schemes involve one-off subsidies enabling initial access.

Sharpening Traditional Forms of Targeting

The key characteristics of OBA described in this chapter – such as output specification and verification, payment only on delivery of outputs, and demand management incentives – all allow OBA to reach the poor more effectively by using some of the traditional methods of targeting, such as geographic, self-selection and means-tested targeting.

Geographic targeting is usually the easiest way to reach the intended beneficiaries. It is useful in areas in which intended beneficiaries are concentrated and few people outside the target group live. For projects in such areas, excluding unintended beneficiaries can be costlier than including them. For instance, the Uganda water project described in Box 8.1 is focusing on slum areas of Kampala where most households are very poor and excluding the few non-poor households would be too costly. An analysis of GPOBA projects shows that most use geographic targeting and more than half use it as the only targeting mechanism. Many GPOBA projects are pilot projects in very poor countries and their small size makes geographic targeting relatively easy.

Self-selection targeting involves designing projects so that outputs chosen by poorer beneficiaries receive a higher share of subsidies. Subsidies can be targeted progressively by providing higher subsidies for more basic services – for example, smaller solar home systems, as in a rural electrification project in Bolivia; or by subsidizing services less attractive to the rich – such as public water points, as in the Uganda project.

Self-selection targeting can also be achieved by introducing a service to an unserved area and starting a subsidy scheme only after some time. Households that can afford to connect immediately will do so, as long as the benefits of service during the time lag will outweigh the cost. With this approach, self-selection can be used even for homogeneous outputs such as electricity connections, as is being attempted in the IDA/GPOBA-supported rural electrification project in Ethiopia.

Means-tested targeting is used in several OBA schemes mainly in middle-income countries. Means testing involves measuring a beneficiary's wealth to assess whether a subsidy is warranted. Such schemes require more advanced administrative systems, as in the case of an urban water project in Chile. For this reason, OBA schemes that rely on means testing usually piggyback on broader welfare programs that identify poor households for a variety of public services. This is being done in the GPOBA-supported Armenia Heat and Gas project, for example. A related approach used by some OBA projects is proxy means testing, in which easily observable characteristics such as possession of indicative assets, for example a dwelling of a certain size, are used as a proxy for income.

Community-based targeting relies on collaboration with the local community or its representatives to help identify the community members most in need of the service. Community involvement can increase ownership and reduce the risk of targeting criteria being rejected by the population in the service area. But community-based targeting may have drawbacks, such as the risk of being hijacked by special interests. Moreover, this form of targeting can be costly and time-consuming, as evidenced by an OBA water project in Cambodia.

In sum, targeting can result in improved equity, effectiveness and efficiency (including sustainability) in the use of funds, although the costs of targeting must always be weighed against its potential benefits. Many existing targeting strategies for channeling subsidies for basic service provision to the poor have not reached those most in need. OBA, while no panacea, is a promising mechanism for enhancing the effectiveness of schemes for targeting subsidies to the poor.

In order to give a more concrete illustration of how OBA schemes involving utilities work and the lessons learned through their implementation, the next section presents a case study of a natural gas project in Colombia.

CASE STUDY: CONNECTING COLOMBIA'S POOR TO NATURAL GAS SERVICE[11]

Background

Throughout the 1980s and into the 1990s armed conflicts between various guerrilla factions, government forces and private land owners hampered the development of Colombia. Encouragingly, recent reforms enabled 1.4 million people to move out of poverty between 2000 and 2004. While these figures are heartening, substantial work remains to be done – over 50 percent of Colombia's entire population still lives below the poverty line. High levels of unsatisfied needs and poverty in the Caribbean coastal area are particularly troubling.

According to recent estimates, Colombia's major gas fields hold 4.2 trillion cubic feet of reserves. During the early 1990s government developed an initiative focused on increasing the number of households to benefit from gas service connections. This project successfully reached more than 17 million people, or about 40 percent of Colombia's total population, 85 percent of whom belong to one of the country's two poorest economic strata. Despite these efforts, many low-income families still rely on dangerous and less efficient energy sources for their daily lives due to the high costs of switching to gas (over US$370 per household). This problem is particularly acute in Colombia's Caribbean coastal area where one-time connection fees often amount to more than 220 percent of a poor family's annual income. In contrast, monthly natural gas service bills are relatively affordable – especially when considering the money saved from not purchasing other fuels, such as liquefied petroleum gas (LPG), wood, kerosene, and so on.

How GPOBA Brings Natural Gas to Colombia's Poor

The situation in Colombia, where families cannot afford connection fees but are able to pay monthly gas service bills, allows for the one-time use of output-based subsidies. An earlier small-scale program involving funds from the Dutch government tested this concept and demonstrated the effectiveness of subsidized connections at delivering gas services to poor households. GPOBA's grant built upon this earlier success and applied new connection subsidies on a much larger scale. The public donor funding made available by GPOBA enabled Promigas, Colombia's largest gas transmission and distribution holding company, to connect 35 000 families to the nation's natural gas distribution network and provide them with a gas stove. Fundación Promigas, a social work foundation established by Promigas, helped to implement this OBA project along with Promigas's regional distribution companies which provided the resources, household financing and technical know-how needed to make the new connections. Fundación Promigas oversaw this work and ensured that the new connections had been properly made. GPOBA provided subsidy financing and project oversight to ensure that Colombia's poor received the maximum benefit from each dollar spent.

Selecting Eligible Households

Colombia's Public Utilities Services Law, through the National Planning Department, provides ranking criteria that classify households into one of six socio-economic strata. This system, known as the Estratificación Socio-Económica (or ESE), has helped target social programs toward the country's most needy areas since the mid-1960s. Families who received GPOBA subsidies had to belong to one of Colombia's two poorest strata as classified by the ESE. Because of this precise targeting, GPOBA funds directly impacted poor beneficiaries. Additionally, the subsidy would only be paid if the new connections resulted in ongoing service.

Implementation Arrangements

GPOBA's grant of US$141 for each eligible household was designed to cover approximately 38 percent of new connection costs, which totaled US$370. Regional distribution companies provided additional assistance through customer financing plans over six years for the remaining cost per connection (US$229). GPOBA engineered its subsidy amount to make each connection economically feasible while still requiring individual families to make a substantial financial contribution toward the new service. Choosing the appropriate level of subsidy helped GPOBA funds reach more families and encouraged ownership through meaningful household involvement.

Functional Steps to New Service

This project followed four steps to bring service to new households (see Figure 8.3):

1. Fundación Promigas directed regional distribution companies to make new natural gas connections at each qualifying household.
2. After making the specified connections and commencing new gas service, regional distribution companies documented that new connections met quality standards and that households had successfully paid three months of billing.
3. Fundación Promigas (through an independent agent) reviewed each connection and performed random technical audits to ensure that project criteria were met.
4. GPOBA reviewed Fundación Promigas's output verifications and disbursed funds into a designated account which then compensated the regional distribution companies that made each new service connection.

Making Sure that Good Work is Done Well

This project's output-based approach ensured that money spent delivered tangible benefits to those in need. GPOBA made funding contingent on three primary criteria:

1. Proof that each newly connected household belonged to one of Colombia's two poorest economic strata.
2. Certification and inspection of new connections – each new connection had to be able to support a natural gas stove, which was provided to poor families as well (at no additional cost).
3. Proof that newly connected households had obtained (and paid for) service for at least three months.

Fundación Promigas, on an annual basis, evaluated the impact of this project and monitored average household consumption, savings and satisfaction related to new in-home connections. Additionally, Fundación Promigas retained the services of independent auditors and technical consultants to audit project expenditures and to inspect randomly the quality of new connections.

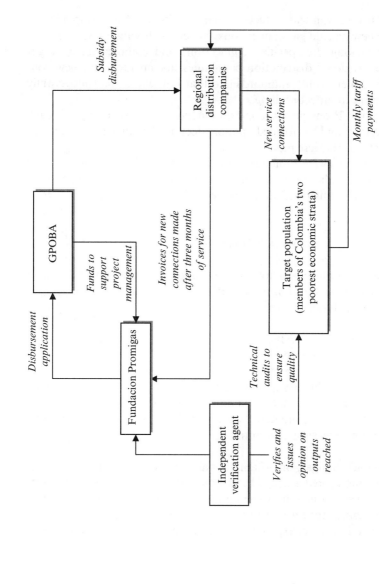

Source: Mandri-Perrott and Patella (2007).

Figure 8.3   Colombia natural gas project flow diagram

Results and Lessons Learned

At closing on 31 July 2008, the project had achieved its goal of connecting poor households in underserved areas to Colombia's natural gas distribution network, having installed natural gas connections and gas stoves, and provided at least three months' billed service, for a total of 35 000 poor households. Because the design of this project clearly targeted poor populations and delayed payment until measurable outputs were realized, each GPOBA-sponsored connection represents an efficient and effective use of funds. Moreover, because families made their own significant contributions to the new service, ownership of the project's accomplishments remains at the local level.

As a result of switching to natural gas for cooking purposes, subsidized families will save approximately 50 percent of one month's income per year. They will also forgo the dangers associated with using other fuels in the home: a preliminary study by Promigas, based on a sample of 10 000 beneficiary households, suggests that the change from biofuels to natural gas has led to a decrease of almost 80 percent in the incidence of respiratory infections in the targeted areas. Additionally, this project's successful design will provide regional Colombian gas distribution companies with an example to replicate throughout the country.

This project has served as a pilot program to demonstrate an arrangement that could be used to scale-up the rate at which poor households can access piped natural gas. By using an output-based approach, GPOBA's subsidy transferred performance risks to privately held regional distribution companies and provided incentives for quality work and timely project completion. GPOBA's effort in Colombia is an example of how output-based aid increases accountability and leverages the strengths of private firms, to produce tangible results.

MAINSTREAMING OBA

As this chapter has sought to demonstrate, OBA is increasingly being used as a tool to improve access to basic services for the poor in developing countries. As the review of OBA conducted by GPOBA and the IDA/IFC Secretariat has shown, the number and value of OBA projects has increased significantly since the launch of OBA in the WBG in 2002–03. And OBA projects are delivering results: of the 131 OBA projects identified in the WBG, data were retrieved about the expected number of beneficiaries for 89 projects, showing a total of 61 million planned beneficiaries. For the 36 projects for which actual beneficiaries have already been verified, so far 17.4 million people have benefited. The 13 closed projects for which information is available have reached 12.5 million people, 16 percent more than planned.

Nevertheless, the percentage of the OBA portfolio as compared to overall World Bank activities remains small. About 3.2 percent of the World Bank project portfolio in the transport, ICT, health, water and sanitation, energy and education sectors approved between fiscal years 2000 and 2009 used an OBA approach. ICT was the sector using OBA most commonly, with 12.5 percent of its portfolio using OBA, followed by health (8 percent) and transport (4.2 percent). This would suggest that, although OBA is gaining ground and recognition, there is still some way to go in terms of scaling-up so that real strides can be made toward improving access to basic services for the poor.

The reasons for OBA's predominance in some sectors, as well as its origination in Latin America in the 1990s, are to a large extent related to sector and country circumstances. More specifically, in order for an OBA approach to be viable, service providers must be able to take on performance risk, and in particular, 'prefinance' investments until subsidies are disbursed based on output verification. Although there are several cases of OBA with public sector providers, private sector operators traditionally are better structured to respond to performance-based incentives and are usually better able to prefinance outputs. Thus there appears to be a correlation with the prevalence of OBA and the sector and regional experience with PPP. This would imply that OBA will take stronger root where contractual and regulatory practices have traditionally been more supportive of the private sector taking risks. At the same time, OBA can be an important mechanism through which efficiency gains from sector reform are shared with users through improved access, and thereby can help underscore the benefits of PPP.

The WBG and other development partners have a role to play in enhancing the effectiveness of OBA schemes to improve the reach of basic services to the poor. For example, the World Bank and IFC could work together to provide financial solutions to help mitigate the access-to-finance constraint by encouraging banks to improve lending conditions to service providers, both for prefinancing of outputs and for longer-term project finance project. The WBG and its partners can also provide capacity-building and technical assistance (for example, for transaction support, tariff design and subsidy policy, monitoring and evaluation).

Donor coordination is also important for mainstreaming OBA. Donors need to work closely with client countries to understand better how performance-based arrangements such as OBA could best work in their specific context, and to ensure harmonization of aid. Similarly, donor funding and discipline are key to secure and sustain sources of funding for OBA. The WBG is well placed to transfer lessons from country to country and between sectors – for example, between universal access and service funds in ICT, road maintenance funds and rural electrification funds. This could help OBA practitioners across sectors and regions to benefit from the lessons learned over the past decade (2001–10), while tailoring them to specific contexts.

Finally, GPOBA is stepping up its efforts to facilitate sharing of experiences and best practice in OBA, and to provide the development partners with the practical knowledge they need to assess when OBA is suitable and to design and implement OBA schemes. This is in line with GPOBA's strategy to evolve from providing subsidy funding to acting primarily as a center of OBA expertise by 2013. This includes activities such as training events for staff of the WBG, the regional development banks and other development agencies; creation of online resources and an e-learning course on OBA; and development of a diagnostic tool which provides guidance to project teams on issues such as project design and relevant characteristics of an enabling environment for OBA schemes.

CONCLUSION

This chapter has demonstrated that OBA, with its use of explicit performance-based subsidies targeted to the poorest households, can be an appropriate and powerful tool for improving the delivery of basic infrastructure services to people at the base of the pyramid. Of the 28 subsidy schemes supported by GPOBA until 2010, 16 projects involve utilities as the service provider. As of November 2009, these schemes have disbursed US$10.1 million based on verified outputs, benefiting over 311 000 people; by completion they are expected to provide an estimated 4 million people with access to essential services such as water and sanitation, telecommunications and energy. The GPOBA-supported natural gas project in Colombia is a vivid illustration of how OBA can be used to provide safer and more environmentally friendly energy services to poor households that would not have been served by the natural gas utility without the GPOBA subsidy.

Although OBA schemes can be challenging, and many OBA projects are still in the pilot stage, the OBA approach has shown its potential to foster public–private partnerships, encourage innovation and efficiency, and make service providers more accountable to their customers and to the government and donors. Most importantly, OBA can help ensure that the poorest households have access to essential services at an affordable price and thus a chance for a better future.

NOTES

1. The authors acknowledge their debt to Mumssen et al. (2010) for much of the analysis presented in this chapter.
2. For more information on GPOBA, visit http://www.gpoba.org.
3. This section draws on GPOBA (2005) and Mumssen et al. (2010), among others. Many of the project examples were gathered as part of GPOBA's Knowledge & Learning Program for WBG staff and development partners.
4. Other examples of the flow of accountability and funds in OBA projects can be found in GPOBA's OBApproaches series, available at http://www.gpoba.org/gpoba/pub/12.
5. See: http://www.gpoba.org/gpoba/publications.
6. At the time of the Private Sector Development Strategy and the creation of GPOBA, only 22 OBA projects of a total value about US$100 million were identified, but further research has identified 11 more projects and substantially more OBA funding.
7. GPOBA continues to identify OBA projects within and outside of the Bank; the figures here reflect projects identified up to 30 September 2009.
8. Data on the number of beneficiaries is not readily available for public access ICT and transport projects. Beneficiary information is particularly limited in the case of the transport sector (available in only two of the 23 World Bank implemented projects) due to the difficulty in identifying the number of beneficiaries for non-exclusive road projects.
9. For a more detailed overview of GPOBA-funded activities, see GPOBA (2008).
10. This section is based on Mumssen et al. (2008).
11. This case study is based on Mandri-Perrott and Patella (2007).

9. A utility's perspective on assisting BOP communities: the AES Corporation's experience

Scarlett Álvarez and Francisco Morandi

AES Corporation is a Fortune 500 US-based global power company. Through a diverse portfolio of thermal and renewable fuel sources, AES safely provides affordable and sustainable energy in 29 countries. Its workforce of 25 000 people is committed to operational excellence and meeting the world's changing power needs. In the more than 25 years it has been in business, AES has contributed to the development process of several countries by generating and distributing power. The company has been at the forefront of world changes and trends, demonstrating a commitment to the welfare and quality of life of local communities.

AES began operations in Latin America in 1993, and by 2009 had a presence in seven countries (Argentina, Brazil, Chile, Colombia, El Salvador, Dominican Republic and Panama), an installed capacity of 11 345 MW, approximately 9600 employees, and served more than 8.5 million customers across the region. AES has developed relations with local communities in accordance with its overall vision of social commitment, which means aligning its efforts with the particular realities of each community, sharing responsibilities and seeking comprehensive solutions.

Latin America and the Caribbean's diversity of climates, cultures and social classes, in addition to the different types of AES businesses (generation, distribution and utilities) in the region, has motivated the company to create a variety of social programs tailored to specific local needs. One such program was designed in 2003 to help the large segment of the region's population that can be considered low-income, or 'poor'.

The low-income segment in Latin America, with a per capita income of US$1.3 to $8.6 a day, represents more than 70 percent of the population and constitutes the socio-economic base of the pyramid (BOP) in the region (Hammond et al., 2007). Within this segment, those with an income of US$2 or less a day – 25 percent of the total population – are considered to be living in poverty. According to the United Nations Development

Programme, energy is essential to poverty reduction efforts since it affects all aspects of development – social, economic and environmental – including livelihoods, access to water, agricultural productivity, health, population levels and education.[1]

The population of Latin American and the Caribbean in 2008 was estimated at 565.29 million people. In 2005 the region was estimated to have electricity consumption per capita of 1745 kWh having grown 10 percent since 2000.[2] The industrial sector (which comprises electricity) is an important generator of value-added in these economies, ranking as the second-largest contributor to regional industrial gross domestic product (GDP) in 2008 (32 percent) after the service sector (62 percent).[3]

AES aims to provide power services to low-income sectors, bringing to these communities the benefits of formal and safe electric service, thereby contributing to improvement in the quality of life and social inclusion. The development of BOP programs by AES calls for adapting the electric service value chain to the needs of customers and consumers who make up the extensive BOP market.

AES's experience has shown that BOP assistance requires the allocation of human and financial resources to study viable needs and solutions in order to create new approaches and solutions. It also requires management and technological innovations that include the involvement of communities.

DEVELOPING BOP INITIATIVES

AES was prompted to enter the BOP market by the growth of that segment of consumers and the impact they were having on the business, which forced the company to acknowledge this market niche. Because of its field experiences, the approach that AES has taken in its BOP programs has greatly affected these communities by providing a formal and safe electrical service while also helping to improve the overall quality of life and social inclusion of the residents through capacity-building and community organization. The service provided by AES must ensure security, quality and efficiency at a minimum cost.

AES first began to work with the BOP in 2003 in Venezuela, where AES was the majority shareholder of La Electricidad de Caracas (AES-EDC).[4] AES-EDC was the only electricity provider to the metropolitan area of the capital city, Caracas. More than half of the city's population lived in barrios (shantytowns) where illegal connections to the electricity grid were widespread.

The growth of poor areas in Caracas meant an increase in the construction of precarious dwellings in zones with difficult access and without the benefits of the basic public services. This situation resulted in, among other things, lack of security (due to poor lighting); an increase in illegal connections to obtain electrical service, which created additional problems, including hazardous conditions; and poor quality of service. For the company, the illegal connections meant a significant rise in non-technical losses of energy (caused by illegal connections), which resulted in financial loss and damaged the electrical network, affecting service to the company's legal customers.[5] For 2000, for example, the electricity losses were estimated at 12 percent of the energy the company produced;[6] this amount increased to 18 percent by 2004. In 2005, non-technical losses (mainly theft) amounted to a revenue loss of approximately US$35 million for AES-EDC.

During the company's initial efforts to reduce non-technical losses, and following standard technical and business procedures without the development of joint social programs, the company began to search for the causes of this problem and discovered that the communities perceived it as a stranger, devoid of interest in their needs. The company adjusted its overall strategy, attempting to approach the residents directly and better understand their needs. AES-EDC engaged the low-income communities of Caracas's barrios in order to convert illegal consumers of electricity into paying customers by improving the relationship between the company and the residents, improving service quality and introducing innovative distribution practices.

In 2003, AES-EDC launched the Barrio Eléctrico (Electric Barrio) initiative to turn illegal consumers of electricity into customers. This pilot program was developed with 300 families in the barrio of La Morán. After an initial phase of study and contact with the community, AES-EDC decided to implement, by 2004, an electricity prepayment system, similar to the one used by cellphone companies. By means of the initiative, the company aimed to:

- reduce non-technical losses attributed to electricity theft, thereby improving the company's financial situation;
- convert illegally connected consumers into regular customers;
- increase the reliability and security of the electricity service;
- improve the quality of life of the concession-area neighborhoods.

Implementing this pilot program entailed the execution of several non-traditional steps within the commercial and distribution scheme of the company:

- It became necessary to establish a close relationship with the residents of the barrio and their leaders and organizers.

- To convince communities to pay for power services instead of stealing them, it was necessary to provide uninterrupted service that would not require residents to spend money on continuous repairs of household appliances that broke down because of the poor quality of service obtained illegally. Besides the safety risk, illegal connections entailed average annual expenses per household of approximately US$100 in electric appliance repairs, plus illegal reconnections cost between US$10 and US$20. In comparison, a social tariff amounted to US$0.75 per month, or US$9 per year.
- The conversion process involved relaxing the usual requirements for becoming a customer, given that barrio residents did not have property titles for their dwellings and failed to meet the common requirements for requesting a contract with the power company.

The entire process, including social workers who were specially hired by the company, also educated La Morán barrio residents about the efficient use of power, the safety of their electrical facilities, and the proper use of electrical meters and their components.

This pilot initiative enabled AES-EDC managers and field workers to understand the following:

- It was possible to conceive of barrio residents as potential company customers.
- In this market it was necessary to modify the traditional view under which the company operated its commercial and distribution processes.
- Low-income customers could not be understood and served in the same way as the middle-class customers the company was used to dealing with.
- Establishing a closer relationship and links between the company and communities was key to achieving good results.
- Internally, it was necessary to integrate different departments and various levels of company management.
- It was necessary to provide a comprehensive solution for this type of customer, beyond simply providing power service.

BOP EXPERIENCES IN VENEZUELA

Integrating the lessons from the pilot experience with prepaid meters in Caracas, the AES-EDC Barrio Eléctrico program evolved into a new phase by mid-2005. By 2006 the program was established as part of the company's strategy, involving 12 percent of the annual company budget. The new version of Barrio Eléctrico addressed these main issues:

- neighborhoods and/or residential areas with illegal connections;
- misinformation about the efficient use of energy and the safety of electrical installations;
- lack of citizens' security arising from deficiencies in the public lighting system;
- insufficient capacities and skills for self-management in dealing with community needs and problems.

The new Barrio Eléctrico was a comprehensive program with a formal methodology and a series of subprograms that fit the various needs of the communities and the company:

- Electric round tables. This mechanism for participation and negotiation allowed the company and community members to diagnose electrical problems and elaborated a draft project and a full project. Accompanying every round table were educational programs on the safe and efficient use of energy and on the benefits of having formal and affordable electric service.
- New public lighting system. Besides traditional public lighting the company designed a special public lighting model for barrios where geography or other conditions made it is impossible to set traditional posts.
- Installation of prepaid meters. A pilot program based on individual prepaid meters was implemented, including instruction on using the meters. This initiative allowed self-management of energy consumption since each house.
- Installation of collective meters. Collective meters connecting a maximum of 25 houses to the same meter allowed the community organization to learn about the efficient use of energy and to acquire legal recognition as a community. Communities made internal agreements to pay the consumption registered on the meters.
- Creation of Coopeléctricas (Electrical Cooperatives). This pilot project organized, through community involvement, the commercial processes needed to offer good-quality electric service. The project also created jobs in the communities.
- Establishment of authorized community commercial agents. Collection agencies, authorized by the company and managed by community members, increased bill collection and established a closer rapport with customers in the community.

- Training of community leaders. This program was intended to foster local leadership within communities and give the leaders tools for participating in diagnosing the problems of their communities. The program also strengthened the capabilities of natural leaders to take initiative and represent the interests of their community in other arenas. Participants were selected through the Electric Round Tables Program where company's employees interacted with different people from the communities. In the process, they detected potential leaders, that is, people who stood out because of their organizational skills or influence among other community members.

The methodology of Barrio Eléctrico, now conceived as an umbrella program encompassing the various initiatives aimed at the BOP population segment, included the goal of improving the quality of life in communities, by providing organizational skills for creating effective interacting with the company. The focus was on co-developing solutions to solve electric power service problems in served communities, based on the assumptions that communities can learn how to solve their own problems themselves and can remain active, organized, and receptive to the advantages and benefits of formal electric service.

In addition, the methodology systematized the activities to be performed within each of the Barrio Eléctrico's initiatives, and it established result indicators and means of verification. This allowed the monitoring and measuring of the impact of executed components of the program. For example, the information for the electric round tables and the community leader training program is summarized in Table 9.1.

These programs showed significant results for both the company and the communities:

- The number of the formal electric service users increased by 110 000 households (460 000 people).
- Non-technical losses were diminished from 17.72 percent in 2005 to 14.89 percent in 2006.
- 176 electric round tables were established.
- 233 collective meters were installed, benefiting more than 11 000 people.
- two Coopeléctricas were established in conjunction with AES-EDC; 8139 clients were incorporated into the Coopeléctricas (six-month pilot project).
- 22 authorized community commercial agents were opened attending approximately 10 000 clients monthly and collecting an average of 33 million bolivars monthly (US$15 349).

Table 9.1   *Summary of methodology and results for Barrio Eléctrico's electric round table and community leader training programs*

Program	Activities	Accomplishment indicators	Means of verification
Electric round tables	• Promotion of round tables • Installation of round tables • Preparation of the company's draft projects • Preparation of project plans • Implementation of projects	• Number of electric round tables installed in served communities • Number of draft projects prepared for the electric round tables	• Review of status of round tables installed and progress in the process through the commercial management system • Review and monitoring of draft projects and completed projects • On-site inspections to confirm progress
Training of community leaders	• Hiring of partner non-governmental organization • Promotion of lectures and courses in communities • Selection and registration of participants • Design of evaluation instruments • Delivery of lectures and courses • Processing of evaluation results	• Number and type of training courses/workshops for community leaders • Number of community leaders trained, number of communities, and number of institutions involved	• Evaluation of workshops planned versus workshops offered

- 257 community leaders were trained in 16 communities and 12 institutions.

BOP EXPERIENCES IN BRAZIL

Another country where AES has launched BOP initiatives is Brazil. As in Venezuela, the impetus for the Brazil program was the growing number of illegal power connections in the distribution grids.

In 2004, AES Eletropaulo (AES-ELP) began a program with the objectives of regularizing clandestine connections and buildings occupied by squatters, providing meters in low-income collective households (*cortiços*), assisting clients deprived of electricity for lack of payment, and incorporating barrios with full but illegal service as formally served areas.

As in Venezuela, turning illegal consumers into customers was a challenge that demanded a paradigm shift within the company and a cultural change in the communities. In this mutual process, both the company and the communities recognized their mistakes in the previous approach.

In addition, beginning in 2006, AES-ELP began a pilot program in Paraisópolis, one of the barrios in the area the company serves, in order to test initiatives, techniques, and alternative solutions that might be replicated elsewhere, such as the installation of a special anti-theft cable and more powerful transformers. The development of the AES-ELP strategy was based on four pillars:

- special attention to community relationships, with the support of social workers;
- education;
- implementation of energy-efficiency measures;
- a customized commercial policy that included a transition payment period for new customers.

One of the most important things AES has learned is that establishing close relationships with low-income communities and listening to their specific needs is a critical part of the process. For this stage of the process, four teams of social workers – 20 in total – were put in place. Education, culture and safety were also elements incorporated into the regularization project. With regard to education, for example, 50 reading rooms were set up in schools and associations in needy communities; people from the community were selected and given professional qualifications to become residential electricians and to have an income-generation activity, teachers were trained to address issues involving the safe and rational use of electric power in their classrooms; and the Eletropaulo in the Community project benefited more than 150 000 people per year with events related to leisure, food guidance, sex education and community services. Annually, about 30 Eletropaulo in the Community events were carried out in municipal schools in São Paulo and state schools in the outlying concession-area municipalities.

As for safety, in 2006, for example, the Youth Building Citizenship project was developed in partnership with the military police of São Paulo. In this project, 20 youths – aged 14 to 17 years – from the outskirts area were trained to act as agents who instructed low-income families about the proper and safe use of electric power.

Energy efficiency measures included the replacement of refrigerators in poor condition with more efficient devices, replacement of incandescent lamps with compact fluorescent ones, refurbishing of internal electric installations in households, and installation of outdoor lighting in alleyways adjacent the households. Paraisópolis was also the site for testing something new: solar panels installed on houses. The system enabled solar heating of water for showers, allowing for substantial savings because electric water heaters are a major energy expense in households.

The success of the project and all the lessons learned made AES-ELP decide to implement the same actions in all the *favelas* where the company is working in the regularization of illegal connections. After the pilot program more than 450 *favelas* have benefited from the BOP approach: regularization of illegal connections, new technologies, community agents, lectures in *favelas* and schools, energy efficiency actions (such as the replacement of bulbs and refrigerators) and special commercial policies. By the end of 2009 AES-ELP was able to regularize more than 355 500 illegal connections in 903 slums improving the quality of life of more than 1.4 million people with the benefits of having a safe and reliable electricity service.

In addition to these actions developed by AES-ELP, a new community improvement project is being carried out by AES Sul, a distribution company in Rio Grande do Sul State in Brazil.[7] The AES Sul in the Community program began as an initiative to reduce illegal electricity connections in the city of Canoas. The project grew to attend to the needs of the underprivileged population of the Guajuviras neighborhood in the Porto Alegre metropolitan area. This program has several specific objectives:

- training families to use electricity safely and efficiently;
- providing adults with training courses so that they can generate income;

- creating a community center to teach basic vocational courses to adults, to provide computer services and training for adults and children, and to serve as a common space for community development.

The project started with contacts with community members, the neighborhood's community association and the local authorities of Canoas. Several meetings took place to increase awareness about the problems of illegal connections to the electricity network, including its dangers and environmental issues. Theatrical plays also helped in this effort, as well as lectures and household visitations.

The AES Sul in the Community program evolved into the establishment of a community center, which was built during the course of activities and inaugurated in 2007. In addition to educating families about the efficient and safe use of electric power, the center has designed work training programs, including courses on dressmaking for women and electrical installation for men. Income-generating opportunities are being provided at the center, whose short-term goal is to become self-sustaining and to continue to improve service provision to the impoverished community of Guajuviras.

As a result of this AES Sul program, more than 3000 households were added to the legal electricity network. Kits for connecting to the network, as well as economical light bulbs, were distributed; diverse meetings and technical training courses were held; and more than 60 theatrical plays were presented.

NEW EXPERIENCES

The experiences of AES in its programs for communities at the bottom of the pyramid in Venezuela and Brazil are now being reviewed and implemented in other countries where AES has distribution companies, such as Cameroon and El Salvador.

Energizing Cameroon

In Cameroon, the public image of AES-SONEL and the company's relations with local communities were not very good.[8] In some cases, frustrated and upset communities had even blocked roadways to protest their lack of electrical power. Consequently, AES-SONEL decided to establish a sustainable development project aimed at communities, and in late 2007 and early 2008 it began conceiving and developing a strategy with the following objectives:

- Contributing to the improvement of the living standards of communities.
- Keeping up with innovation in the area of sustainable development, equitable business, microfinancing and the provision of electricity access to the underprivileged.
- Developing company–community partnerships in customer care activities (meter reading and billing).
- Involving community partners in asset protection actions (vandalism prevention, tree pruning).
- Obtaining the sustainable support of communities, opinion leaders and administrative authorities.
- Contributing to improving the company's profits.
- Contributing to the well-being of communities by implementing value-added and/or revenue-generating community projects.

The approach that was developed began with an exchange of knowledge and experiences of other AES companies that had already developed initiatives aimed at the BOP market. AES-SONEL then began taking the following steps:

- Identifying potential communities in collaboration with operating managers (density, population, type of habitat, distribution efficiency, and so on).
- Selecting pilot communities.
- Partnering with communities to develop appropriate, significant, interesting, cost-effective and value-added projects.
- Sensitizing adults, youths and children about safety and respecting AES-SONEL assets.
- Maintaining close working partnerships with the communities identified.
- Sharing successful experiences.

In 2008, AES-SONEL developed a number of activities:

- Creating a project to standardize connections, reintegrate discharged customers and convert illegal consumers into customers. This program included meetings with leaders, sensitization campaigns on safety and energy saving, and campaigns on the advantages of an individual connection. The outcome was improvement in safety conditions, better quality of life and an improvement in billing and recovery rates.
- Partnering with communities in meter reading, distribution and

pruning activities. This program's main objective was to create revenue-generating activities for the communities while simultaneously attaining business objectives. Also, the program attempted to create a sense of belonging by instilling a desire in customers to help protect equipment.

- Organizing youths into common initiative groups and granting them plots for low-level agriculture to guarantee cleanliness along the power transmission line and thereby improve service by reducing accidents related to tall vegetation.
- Initiating other diverse community actions such as distributing one-month supplies of breakfast packs to children, furnishing cots and mattresses to health care centers, and creating revenue-generating activities for street children.

All of the actions taken in Cameroon have yielded results. Thanks to the close relationship with the communities involved, the company's image significantly improved and communities were no longer hostile toward the company. In one community alone, 700 new connections were made according to standards, which increased safety; and in another community all residents who did not have power service agreed to become customers of the company after they were approached and received safety talks. In addition, a health center and two schools were connected to the power grid.

While the ultimate goals are the same, the challenges and realities of this country differ from the countries of Latin America where AES is present. One of the main challenges was to work with the leaders of hostile tribal communities, because for years companies had earned a bad reputation among them. Additionally, the country's situation represents a level of greater complexity: in Cameroon just over half the population (57 percent) live in urban areas (in the Latin American countries the average is 77 percent);[9] the population is composed of a variety of ethnic groups, each of which has its own leaders and dialects. Access to electricity in the country is not widespread and the population without access to electricity in Cameroon (13.4 million)[10] is greater than the sum of the whole population without access to this service within the seven Latin American countries where AES is present (10.4 million).[11]

Increasing Access to Electricity in Central America

For AES in El Salvador (AES-ES), experiences in the BOP market are still new and at the most basic level, with the company seeking to bring electric power to low-income sectors by appropriately adapting its value chain.[12] AES-ES's relationship with low-income communities is exemplified in three programs sponsored by the national government: rural electrification, connection discounts for the country's poorest families, and connection discounts for social-interest dwellings.

Rural electrification contributes to the initiative to bring electrical power to 100 percent of the country by extending it to rural areas and the country's poorest areas. AES-ES takes part in public biddings and finances part of the projects it is awarded. Any individual or corporation, either privately or publicly owned, can request a project, which is then submitted to a public auction and any operator of power grids that wishes to make those projects a reality in its coverage areas may participate. Once the bid is awarded, technical information for the project is gathered jointly by the government, the company and the project requesters. The share and economic contribution of each of the three parties in project development are subsequently established.

Additional to this project, sponsored by the national government, AES-ES signed an agreement with a development organization called Fomilienio in 2009 to build 1385 km of power lines in the northern zone of the country.[13] By the end of the year the first phase of the project was completed, executing 74 projects and installing more than 115 kilometers of new power lines.

As a complement to this project, AES's volunteers provided educational lectures in those communities that had electricity for the first time. The information provided to customers included: processes for the connection of the service, invoice data, closest pay centers to clients' area, efficient use of energy, subsidies and safety.

In the second national government program, a reduction in the cost of connection is offered to poor families who lack service, along with financing for the discounted cost of the connection. The distribution company offers a discount between 50 percent and 75 percent and assumes the financing of the remaining connection cost for eight months, at no interest, for preselected and government-classified families living under conditions of severe or extreme poverty.

In the same manner, discounts help provide electric power access to families who own social interest housing units, which are part of projects that, according to the law, qualify as social interest dwellings.[14] For this program a preferential pricing system was designed and applied to the cost of electric service connection, based on the number of housing units requesting connection (Table 9.2). Both discount programs were executed until the end of 2008.

Between 2006 and 2009, AES-ES was awarded and executed more than 140 rural electrification projects, which benefited more than 26 000 people in diverse municipalities who now enjoy power service. In conjunction

Table 9.2   Example scheme for discounting service connection costs, based on the number of social-interest dwellings requesting connection

Number of housing units simultaneously requesting connection	Reduction in cost of home connection (%)
0 to 5	5
6 to 15	7
16 to 30	10
More than 30	12

with these projects, both programs of AES-ES connection discounts between 2006 and 2009 benefited more than 100 000 people.

As these initiatives demonstrate, although AES-ES adapted part of its operations to add low-income customers to its value chain, neither the company nor the communities reaped any additional benefits. That explains why in 2009, based on the experiences of AES-EDC and AES-ELP, the company studied the possibility of establishing projects with the communities. Company representatives met with officials from universities and different institutions that could become potential allies in implementing programs, such as the Salvadoran Foundation for Economic and Social Development and the Secretariat for Family Affairs. An initial idea was to to provide training in agricultural production. So far this has not begun because it is too costly for the company given the distance and dispersion of the communities. A win-win proposition for communities and company did not exist.

LESSONS LEARNED

Through its experiences with the BOP-targeted initiatives it conducted in Venezuela, Brazil, Cameroon, and El Salvador, AES has learned a number of lessons, which have permitted a continuous improvement of those programs. Low-income sectors can be viewed as potential customers, and to convert them to customers, changes in traditional company processes are necessary. The design and development of every element aimed toward the BOP must begin with approaching and creating relations with communities. The participation of social workers may add a great deal of value at this stage. Furthermore, information and opinions from the employees in the field are vital, because the employees are part of the communities and confront the conditions in the barrios on a daily basis. As part of this early process, it is also key to identify community leaders. Improving community ties involves understanding the concerns, expectations, family dynamics and budget, social and commercial networks, and other factors, and then adapting programs to each case. For instance, the initiative of community commercial agents came after AES-EDC understood that for residents of certain communities it was more costly to go to a bank or the closest payment facility than to pay their energy bill through a local agent.

To achieve success in these programs and thereby to support the major-ity of the population (that is, the BOP population), the integration and participation of several company departments – such as distribution, commercialization and social responsibility – are necessary, as well as the involvement of senior managers to ensure appropriate company support for the initiatives. It is important to relax company processes and adapt them to the needs of communities. AES understood that residents of barrios and other low-income sectors had been forced to set up illegal power connections simply because the company did not approach them with the necessary tools to provide the service. In many cases residents of these communities were willing to pay to receive an increase in the quality and reliability of their power service.

The application of innovative ideas and new technologies can play an important role in the solution of providing energy to the BOP segment. For example: the prepaid meters, an idea that had never been imple-mented before in Venezuela; and all the new technologies introduced in the projects in Brazil such as the antitheft cables.

A key part of the process is the selection of the appropriate partners, such as governments, organizations, other businesses and individuals. Each type of partner has its own strengths, and experience and knowledge can be tapped through a strategic alliance to ensure the best outcome for the project objective. AES-EDC, for example, used this approach to gain support and specialized knowledge and experience. For the training of community leaders, a non-governmental organization provided the themes for lessons and teachers, and the authorized community commer-cial agents were administrated the businesses. In addition, a central part of AES-SONEL's new strategy is to develop a constructive partnership with communities, political leaders, administrative and traditional authorities, associations and the civil society in general. Some of the partners with whom alliances have been established are the Association for the Rights of Cameroonian Students, several youth associations, the Ministry of Agriculture, health care centers and community readers, among others. In Brazil, AES-ELP developed the pilot program in Paraisópolis through a Global Development Alliance partnership with the International Copper Association and the United States Agency for International Development (USAID); all worked together to ensure a coordinated approach to project design and implementation, and a responsibility matrix tracked the project's components, responsibilities and funding. The integration of communities as strategic partners in the process is also important. For example, the Coopeléctricas, as well as the authorized community commercial agents, were project elements that empowered small entrepreneurs and provided benefits and comfort to the residents of the communities by having services closer to their homes.

Prior education of residents is necessary during the implementation and development of power connection programs. Because residents previously did not have to pay for electricity, community campaigns are important for educating consumers about the importance of understanding and paying their electricity bill and implementing efficiency measures to reduce consumption and costs.

Creating and tracking progress indicators for each program is an important part of the company's strategy, as is developing an integrated data system between all areas involved in such programs. Also, all programs strive to be replicable across a region such as Latin America, with adaptations to the specific needs and environmental regulations of each country. A key aspect for replicability is the transfer of knowledge between the different companies. Although needs may be similar, technical, operational, economics, social and environmental aspects may differ from one company to other. These factors determine the actions and processes the companies change or retain for implementing the initiatives. At the same time, customized commercial policies, such as those developed by AES-ELP, are important for retaining customers.

In sum the above lessons show that it is necessary to provide a comprehensive solution that goes beyond the supply of power services and also creates social, environmental and economic value in the community.

CONCLUSION

Providing tools and opportunities to the communities AES serves is a contribution the company brings to the equation, through which it can bring improvements in the quality of life for residents, generating social inclusion. The importance of businesses like AES is that the services they provide contribute to the development of BOP communities. Access to energy has a direct relationship with poverty, human health and the environment, and better access to energy services is essential for making improvements in these areas.

The AES business model for BOP programs is financially viable because the programs not only help the company reduce non-technical losses, but also result in an educated and empowered community that contributes to the preservation of electrical installations, improvements in safety conditions and more efficient energy use. There are some non-financial benefits for the company as well, such as increased customer satisfaction; fewer accidents related to faulty electrical installations; the improvement, development and empowerment of communities; and enhanced relations with communities. Besides bringing the general benefits of formal electric service to communities, AES's initiatives have had further social benefits, such as reducing dangerous conditions in areas that lacked street lighting. Also, in the cases of AES-EDC and AES-ELP, barrio residents who previously had no access to the banking system became eligible, because a utility bill with their name and address was accepted as documentation for opening a bank account.

In the future, AES plans to dedicate its efforts to consolidating these lessons in the businesses highlighted in this chapter. Doing so will enable the company to continue to attend to this important sector of the population and to develop a sustainable platform that can be replicated in other countries to serve customers better around the globe, as well as create new opportunities for solutions in BOP communities that will be profitable for all of the stakeholders.

NOTES

1. United Nations Development Programme, http://www.undp.org/energy/.
2. World Bank, World Development Indicators, http://ddp-ext.worldbank.org/ext/dd preports/ViewSharedReport?&CF=&REPORT_ID=9147&REQUEST_TYPE=VIEW ADVANCED.
3. World Bank, World Development Indicators.
4. AES acquired La Electricidad de Caracas in 2000. The largest private electric company of Venezuela, it was an integrated utility with more than 1 million customers and a generation capacity of over 2600 MW. In June 2007, after the Venezuelan government decided to nationalize the country's entire electricity sector, AES sold its assets in the country.
5. Non-technical losses account for the difference between energy produced that theoretically can be billed and the proportion of energy consumption that is actually billed. These losses stem mainly from electricity fraud (clandestine connections or tampering with meters), as well as theft and vandalism to electrical installations and wiring.
6. Energy losses are equal to the difference between electricity input and output as a result of an energy transfer between two points and can be classified as technical and non-technical losses.
7. AES-Sul is a utility that distributes electricity to more than 1 million customers in the state of Rio Grande do Sul, in southern Brazil. It has been owned and operated by AES since 1997.
8. In 2001, AES acquired AES-SONEL, which provides power to Cameroon. An integrated utility, AES-SONEL both generates power and distributes it to more than 571 000 customers in the country.

9. United States Department of Defense, CIA Factbook (https://www.cia.gov/library/ publications/the-world-factbook/fields/2212.html?countryName=Cameroon&country Code=cm&regionCode=af&#cm).
10. According to the International Energy Agency (IEA), the electrification rate in Cameroon is near 30 percent of the country; while in the other countries where AES has a presence in Latin America, on average this rate is about 93 percnet; http://www.iea. org/weo/database_electricity/electricity_access_database.htm.
11. IEA.
12. AES has been present in El Salvador since 1999 and currently (2010) owns four power distribution companies in El Salvador, which serve a little over 1 million customers, or nearly 80 percent of the national market.
13. Fomilenio or 'Millennium Fund' is an entity created in El Salvador to manage and monitor the funds coming from the Millennium Challenge Corporation (an independent US foreign aid agency that is helping to lead the fight against global poverty).
14. Social interest is construed by the El Salvador Deputy Housing Minister's Office as pertaining to particular residential projects intended for low-income households. The construction of the projects must be conceived under minimum city planning standards, that allow future improvements in the infrastructure and require the use of low-cost construction materials and systems, as well as both community effort and government assistance; and, in accordance with the law, the projects must have been qualified as social-interest projects. The value of said housing units, including the land, may not exceed US$10 000.

10. One step toward citizenship: the Slum Electrification and Loss Reduction pilot project in São Paulo, Brazil

Ivar Pettersson

Urban concentration in Brazil continues to increase more rapidly than the budgets for public services. In this context, providing electricity to low-income urban communities poses great challenges. At the same time, access to reliable and affordable electricity is central to stimulating economic growth and social development in excluded neighborhoods and slums. Thus, a key question for electricity distribution companies in Brazil and other developing countries today is: how can we best meet the electricity demands of the growing urban population at the base of the pyramid (BOP)?

Historically, utility companies have learned to expect low or negative returns in providing services to low-income people. Company managers have little knowledge about the attempts of low-income communities to overcome problems associated with living in slums, such as lack of land tenure, poor infrastructure and crime. Companies do not understand slum residents' sense of being excluded from society, and their imperative to survive even if it entails connecting illegally to the electricity distribution network. Poor enforcement of regulations, difficulties in providing access to services and infrastructure, and the complexity of the technical and administrative solutions required to contend with theft and fraud in services can all increase a company's challenge in serving the base of the pyramid.

This chapter showcases the experience of AES Eletropaulo and its business strategy for supplying public utility services to BOP communities on a financially sustainable basis. To address the needs of these communities, the company had to develop commercial policies, technologies and relationships compatible with the reality of the poor in urban slums. A pilot project, carried out in São Paulo, took into account the specific needs of the low-income sectors in the slums of that city and lends itself to potential replication in other BOP areas and by other companies.

PARTNERSHIP MODEL

To supply the slums with electricity on a legal basis, AES Eletropaulo developed a Slum Electrification and Loss Reduction (SELR) pilot initiative in the São Paulo slum of Paraisópolis in 2005, in partnership with the International Copper Association, the United States Agency for International Development (USAID), and two smaller partners, Nexans and Itaipu Transformadores. The objective of the pilot project was to develop a sustainable service model for AES Eletropaulo and other distribution companies to service the BOP. The project was to serve as a controlled test, particularly of external elements that were not under company control.

AES Eletropaulo

AES Eletropaulo distributes electricity to 5.7 million customers in the 24 municipalities that make up Greater São Paulo, including the city of São Paulo itself. The concession area – 4526 square kilometers – constitutes the largest conurbation in South America and one of the largest in the world, with approximately 18 million inhabitants. It also enjoys the highest per capita income in Brazil and a large concentration of the country's economic activity. As a result, AES Eletropaulo is the largest electricity distribution company in Latin America in terms of both revenue and the amount of energy distributed. The company directly employs about 4200 people. Its fixed assets include 133 distribution transformer stations with a total transformation capacity of 12.8 megavolt-amperes; 42 300 kilometers of distribution lines (39 500 km overhead and 2800 km underground); 1700 kilometers of subtransmission lines (operating at 138 kV and 88 kV); and 1.1 million poles carrying the overhead and subtransmission lines.

AES Eletropaulo is committed to social and environmental sustainability in addition to financial profitability. In 2008 and 2009 it was among the top 35 companies in Bovespa's Corporate Sustainability Index (ISE), which is based on criteria of economic efficiency, environmental balance, social justice and corporate governance.[1]

AES Eletropaulo's Program for Regularizing Electrical Installations was developed within this context. While its primary focus was to reduce theft from the electricity grid in all the slums in the areas served by the company (approximately 2000 slums), it also provided a major benefit for the consumer that could be described as a 'passport to citizenship'. With an electricity bill in hand that contained a legitimate address, people from low-income communities covered by the program had sufficient documentation for receiving a number of benefits, such as access to bank accounts and credit. Having a formal address and a bill statement also created a greater sense of social inclusion.

Other Partners in the Pilot Project

Founded in 1989, International Copper Association Ltd (ICA) is the world's leading organization for the promotion of the use of copper. ICA increases awareness and usage of copper by communicating the unique attributes of this element through funding of international initiatives and promotional activities and by supporting scientific and technological research for the development of new copper applications. The association has 38 members, representing most of the copper producers including wire and cable manufacturers around the world, and its programs and initiatives are executed in more than 50 countries. In Brazil, ICA is represented by the Brazilian Institute of Copper (Procobre), a non-profit organization that develops local programs together with the main companies in the industry. Part of ICA's mission to promote the use of copper is to find sustainable solutions for the electrification of low-income communities, incorporating the safe and efficient use of wires, cables and electrical equipment.

The United States Agency for International Development (USAID) is an independent institution maintained by the US government. USAID's mission in Brazil is to support Brazilian efforts for sustainable development. Since 2003, USAID has pursued an electrification program intended to help governments, utilities and other partners develop legal, reliable and sustainable access to electricity services.

Headquartered in Paris, Nexans produces cables and cabling systems in more than 90 plants on five continents. In the Paraisópolis pilot project, all wires and cables were specifically produced and financed by Nexans Brasil SA.

Located in Itápolis, in the state of São Paulo, Itaipu Transformadores has been one of the main manufacturers of transformers in Brazil for more than three decades. In the Paraisópolis pilot project, the company assumed responsibility for everything from the conceptual design to the manufacture of highly efficient transformers, in partnership with the Federal University of Itajubá, in the state of Minas Gerais.

PLANNING FOR THE PILOT PROJECT

AES Eletropaulo has had significant experience in developing programs to incorporate illegally connected residents formally as customers in its distribution network, a process called regularization. Prior to the Paraisópolis SELR pilot, AES Eletropaulo had already regularized more than 150 000 low-income customers, developing its own methodology and looking for the best and most efficient solutions to regularize another 300 000 households in its concession area. However, these programs had uneven levels of success, and the company had not conducted a critical analysis of its efforts in order to pinpoint the key elements to achieving sustainability in supplying electricity to low-income sectors. The new approach developed for the Paraisópolis pilot project led the company to discover internal and external enablers for effectively serving low-income consumers who were illegally connected.

At the start, all of the partners recognized that project deployment should be financially viable for the distribution company, and that the success of the venture would rely on both the willingness and the ability of consumers to formalize their connection and pay for their consumption of electricity. Another important element for success was the regulatory context of the pilot. In this sense, Brazil proved to be a particularly favorable area for the pilot, because of the progressive attitude of the regulator, the National Agency for Electric Power (Agência Nacional de Energia Elétrica, or ANEEL), in promoting solutions for the legalization of electricity services in low-income communities.

A memorandum of understanding established three main objectives for the pilot project: to test alternative solutions for the legal supply of electric energy in a sustainable manner at an affordable price, to achieve improved energy efficiency, and to meet the needs of the low-income population in the city of São Paulo. The pilot's specific aims were as follows:

- To test and evaluate technical solutions that would prevent energy theft (using, for example, coaxial cables in secondary power distribution networks, as well as remote metering and reading) and improve the efficiency of the network (using highly efficient transformers, among other measures).
- To improve the affordability of electricity service for low-income consumers through efficiency enhancements in homes and businesses.
- To assess the economic, financial and social impacts of the pilot.

The solutions developed within the pilot were to be documented for subsequent publication and dissemination for large-scale use by AES in its regional and global programs, as well as among other electricity distribution companies at the national and international levels.

Intended to ensure the greatest flexibility in developing solutions, the program's main components were these:

- Assessment framework: created with the aid of a database to measure the socio-economic and financial impacts of the program.
- Actions to educate, communicate and raise awareness: engaging community members in the electrification program and educating consumers in energy-efficient practices.
- Technological development: improving the distribution system, including the installation of meters and new antitheft technologies, and installing public lighting upgrades to replace inefficient light bulbs and improve safety in low-income communities.
- Energy efficiency measures: helping regularized customers manage the efficient use of electric power in their homes and businesses by implementing two types of measures:
  - actions inside customers' homes, such as replacing incandescent light bulbs and highly inefficient refrigerators and revamping the electric wiring;
  - actions for local businesses, including brief audit visits to provide business owners with guidelines to improve energy efficiency and lower energy expenditures, and to make them more aware of the impact that paying for electricity can have on their business.
- Financial analysis in the post-pilot phase: calculating the results of the solutions adopted for regularization.
- Assessment of the pilot project's socio-economic impacts: carrying out a survey to assess customers' changes in attitudes, knowledge about electricity use, ability to pay for the services and satisfaction with the services provided, and to detect changes within the community as a result of the program's activities.
- Dissemination of pilot results: developing a case study and conducting an international workshop with participants from 23 countries from Latin America, Asia and Africa.

THE PARAISÓPOLIS *FAVELA*

Paraisópolis (literally 'Paradise Town') is the second-largest *favela* (slum) in São Paulo and the fourth-largest in Latin America. It covers an 84-hectare area surrounded by the medium- and high-income households of one of São Paulo's most exclusive residential areas, Morumbi. In fact, like many slums, Paraisópolis emerged as families migrated from northern and north-eastern Brazil, attracted by household jobs in the surrounding residences. As is the case in most slums, the community is informally constructed and lacks many services, despite the special attention provided by the municipal administration through its so-called reurbanization program. The topography of Paraisópolis is challenging when it comes to providing services; the area is extremely uneven, with brooks and ravines carved out by rainfall run-off, although it does contain a relatively flat plateau in its center. In addition, haphazard settlement patterns and the gradual addition of upper floors to the slum's dwellings have resulted in narrow streets and alleys, at times resembling tunnels, without any planning for minimum distances between buildings, including space for the electrical network.

A survey conducted by the São Paulo Municipal Secretariat of Housing (Secretaria da Habitação e Desenvolvimento Urbano, or SEHAB) found Paraisópolis to be growing vigorously. The 2000 census recorded 45 154 inhabitants, and by 2005 this figure had risen to 55 590, implying an annual growth rate of more than 4 percent. The survey also found that around 75 percent of the slum's households consisted of families of three to four people, with family monthly incomes ranging from one to three minimum wages (US$200 to US$600), which meant that they were very poor relative to other neighborhoods in São Paulo. A subsequent survey commissioned from the research institute Instituto Brasileiro de Opinião Pública e Estatistica (IBOPE) as part of the pilot provided additional information about the community, based on a sample of 400 heads of households within the pilot area:

- 12 percent of households had a monthly household income of one minimum wage or less.
- 31 percent of respondents held informal jobs.
- 36 percent of respondents lived in houses with two or fewer rooms.
- 67 percent of households were headed by women, of whom 57 percent were 39 years of age or older and 22 percent were older than 50.
- 40 percent of respondents had left school after only four years of schooling, 8 percent had no formal schooling, and only 2 percent were college graduates.

Door-to-door visits by agents hired as part of the pilot further revealed that only 3 percent of the houses were wood shacks and the remainder were made of bricks and mortar, attesting to a certain 'maturation' of the slum. Electrical appliances were widely used, chiefly refrigerators, irons and TV sets. More than half of the respondents owned refrigerators that were in good condition, having been bought within the previous five years, and nearly 40 percent of those interviewed intended to buy a new refrigerator within the next two years. More than 80 percent of the households had electric showers, a very common type of water heater in Brazil, with an average voltage of 5800 W.

Paraisópolis's central area has paved streets where commercial enterprises of various types of services are found. The area's stores catered at first to the needs of the community's residents, isolated as they were in the middle of a high-income area. Subsequently, however, the availability of 'free' electricity attracted other business owners who could supply products to other commercial establishments in the Morumbi area at a lower cost. The central shopping area had become highly attractive to large stores, opening points of sale within the *favela* to take advantage of the growing local economy. By diminishing illegal connections among businesses it became clear that AES Eletropaulo contributed to diminish unfair competition.

With regard to community organization, the research related to the pilot revealed that around 80 non-governmental organizations were active in Paraisópolis and its surroundings, making this one of the *favelas* with the greatest presence of social assistance organizations. The main areas of activity of these organizations reflected the greatest needs of this population – namely, health and education.

INITIAL STRATEGIES FOR IMPLEMENTING THE PILOT PROJECT

The pilot project covered two neighboring areas within Paraisópolis (Antonico and Centro), comprising 4365 households and businesses, almost all of which were illegal consumers of energy from AES Eletropaulo. Since the goal of the pilot, if successful, was to extend legal connections to the entire area of concession of AES Eletropaulo and then to disseminate the program to other distribution companies and stakeholders, key performance indicators were established at the outset to assess and document results during the entire length of the pilot. Performance indicators were classified into three categories:

- financial viability for the company;
- affordability and acceptability for the customer;
- societal and community acceptance.

These categories were described in detail, and indicators were associated with each one of them. The initial planning of the pilot was developed on the basis of these indicators and the definition of the investments required for pilot implementation, with an associated schedule of activities to be carried out.

The next step in implementing the pilot involved contacting the leaders of the community and the companies operating in the area, to learn about the dynamics specific to the community and its organizational structure and to identify the agents who could be placed in charge of subsequent project-related actions. All project-related actions relied on the participation of community leaders. 'We cannot turn Paraisópolis into a regular neighborhood without electrical energy. We do want regularization,' said community leader José Rolim da Silva when the pilot was launched.

On 27 September 2006, around 100 people participated in the ceremony marking the launching of the pilot. Held on the premises of a local community organization, the ceremony was attended by Clifford Sobel, the US Ambassador to Brazil, and David Wolfe, the American Consul in São Paulo, as well as representatives from USAID, ICA, AES Eletropaulo and the municipality of São Paulo.

An extensive information campaign publicized the pilot in newspapers, on radio and television, and within the community, cars with loudspeakers explained that the service line (including the standard connection-related materials – box, grounding and fuses) and the connection labor would be free of charge. Information about how to register in the Low-Income Social Tariff Program, which involved a 50 percent discount over regular electricity rates and was mandated for all utilities by the regulatory agency ANEEL, was also widely publicized. In addition, a major educational effort about the safe use of energy was begun at this point and continued throughout the entire regularization period.

Customer regularization was also encouraged by making people aware of the benefits derived through regularization. Having an address as evidenced by electric bills issued in one's name enabled people in low-income communities to establish legal residence, opening opportunities for greater access to services such as bank accounts and loans.

AES Eletropaulo joined efforts with other public utilities providers to facilitate and encourage regularization. Specifically, AES Eletropaulo coordinated with Sabesp (Companhia de Saneamento Básico do Estado de São Paulo), which provides water and sanitation services in São Paulo, and with the Housing and Urban Development Corporation of the São Paulo state government (Companhia de Desenvolvimento Habitacional e Urbano, or CDHU), which was working with SEHAB in the slum reurbanization program.

Prior to the launch of the pilot, hardly any households paid for electricity. Thus there was little concern about managing consumption efficiently;

a situation that led, for example, to the extensive use of obsolete and defective electrical appliances. Consequently, the consumption of electricity was extremely high (around 250 kWh per month per household). This situation made it harder for customers to participate in the Low-Income Social Tariff Program, which was based on a household's consumption level, and made it very costly for households to regularize their connection, because they would suddenly be faced with high electricity bills each month. To address this challenge, one of the first actions of the pilot project was to define a transition phase, which lasted from the beginning of the pilot up to the regularization of the whole *favela*. During this time, the monthly bill for each customer was capped at the amount payable for 150 kWh, even for customers who consumed more than 150 kWh. During the transition, residents were also informed about their actual consumption, so that they could start lowering their consumption by learning to use electricity more efficiently.

AWARENESS-RAISING EFFORTS

The actions that promoted awareness of both the cost and the safety of electrical energy use were the main tools for reaching the pilot's goals, and they unquestionably contributed to the success of the project. The most important element for promoting awareness was a program of visits to the households and businesses in the area by 'community agents' hired by AES Eletropaulo for this purpose.

Initially, community agents conducted more than 5000 visits (sometimes they had to visit one household on more than one occasion), obtaining information from 3092 people. During these initial contacts, in addition to providing guidelines about the efficient use of electricity, the agents presented information about the regularization process, an element that proved to be essential for both transparency in the process and a positive reception of the process by the clients. The community agents provided the following information during their home visits:

- How to register for the Low-Income Social Tariff Program.
- Features of the pilot project:
  - free formal connection to the distribution network;
  - temporary cap on billed amount during the pilot's implementation, set at the cost of 150 kWh.
- Explanation of the metering process and the electric bill.
- How to manage electricity consumption to lower bills:
  - how to calculate consumption;

Table 10.1   Awareness of pilot project among visited households

Information conveyed to residents during community agent visit	Residents responding yes (%)
Learned about the first energy bill	92
Received guidelines as to how to save energy	70
Learned about the installation of the meter for energy consumption	98
Knew about the pilot project	87

Source: AES/IBOPE.

- appliances' consumption of electricity;
- tips for saving energy.

After the connection to the new energy network was made and the illegal connection was removed, the agents paid more than 8000 follow-up visits to the households. In these visits, guidelines about electrical appliances and their impact on the energy bill were provided. According to subsequent research commissioned by IBOPE, after the visits program a large proportion of slum residents knew about the pilot project and were familiar with information related to it (Table 10.1).

In addition to individual visits, on weekends AES Eletropaulo organized events in public spaces, which were heavily attended by the residents during all phases of the project. In total, 12 events were held, in which 45 percent of the households in the pilot area participated. Another outreach and education effort targeted the younger residents, in order to reduce risks of electrical accidents. The pilot project's partners prepared a presentation tailored to this audience, which was then disseminated through 13 lectures delivered at eight schools within Paraisópolis and attended by a total of 3501 children and 146 educators.

NEW ELECTRICITY DISTRIBUTION TECHNOLOGY

The pilot used state-of the-art technologies, with both safety and loss reduction as major project goals. On the safety side, the project deployed several technologies to meet its objective of ensuring that the primary and secondary distribution networks were adequate to supply energy reliably and safely to the community:

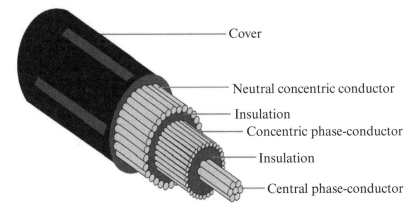

Cover

Neutral concentric conductor

Insulation

Concentric phase-conductor

Insulation

Central phase-conductor

Source: AES Eletropaulo.

Figure 10.1   *Biconcentric cable section*

- Spacer cable. Chiefly in sites where no minimum distance was required for the facade of buildings to connect to the primary distribution network of 13.2 kV, spacer cable was used to ensure safety.[2]
- Multiplexed network (twisted cables). In the secondary distribution lines (127/220 V), twisted cables were installed to increase reliability and safety.
- Biconcentric cables. Widely used by AES Eletropaulo, these are copper cables with one core covered by two concentric layers. The core and the first copper layer are used as concentric phase conductors, whereas the outside layer serves as a neutral conductor. Insulation on the copper and outside layer phases is made of XLPE – cross-linked polyethylene (Figure 10.1). These cables make energy theft more difficult because attempts to drill through them result in short circuits that stop the flow of energy. These cables were connected to a connection box, located at the pole and interconnected to the secondary distribution line (Figure 10.2).
- High-efficiency transformers. Efficient transformers, properly designed and located, were used to achieve reductions in energy losses, service interruptions and repair times in emergency situations. These transformers reduced load losses by 26 percent, equivalent to energy savings of 2 MWh per year (the electricity consumption of an average Paraisópolis household for eight months) per 100 kVA of transformer capacity. As a result, the payback for the efficient transformers installed as part of the pilot was 1.42 years.

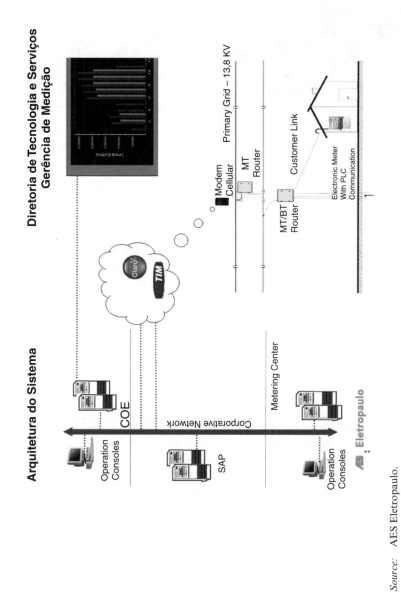

Source: AES Eletropaulo.

Figure 10.2   Metering systems with mobile telephony

218

INTERNAL MEASURES TO IMPROVE EFFICIENCY

The high density of housing, the irregularity of occupation,[3] and the cultural habits of the population were factors that contributed to high energy consumption in Paraisópolis homes. Controlling the consumption of electricity thus became a key factor in the success of the pilot, so that electricity bill amounts would be affordable for families to remain as formal customers and not revert to theft or fraud. This reasoning led AES Eletropaulo to encourage the adoption of the following efficiency improvement measures that would reduce consumption to a level compatible with the economic conditions of the slum's population.

Replacement of Incandescent Light Bulbs with Compact Fluorescent Ones

During the door-to-door visits conducted after the service entrance equipment had been installed by the utility company free of charge, three incandescent lightbulbs were replaced by three compact fluorescent lightbulbs of 20 W each on average, in each household. The removed incandescent bulbs were sent back to AES Eletropaulo for disposal and recycling. In total, 9588 lightbulbs were replaced in the pilot project area, yielding savings of 165 497 kWh per month for the area. Public lighting points were also installed in narrow streets, where residents had kept lights on continuously outside their houses, sometimes 24 hours a day, to ensure the safety of passers-by. The aggregate monthly savings resulting from these replacements in small alleys and narrow streets amounted to 19 258 kWh.

Replacement of Old Refrigerators

Rather than merely keeping food from spoiling, refrigerators in Paraisópolis are a survival item for a population residing in small spaces with little ventilation and where high temperatures are predominant throughout the year. In Paraisópolis, 30 percent of the population had at least one refrigerator that had been in use for more than five years. A total of 2598 assessments of refrigerator energy efficiency and physical condition were conducted in the course of 6525 visits to households participating in the pilot. After the visits, a database related to refrigerator manufacturing and operation was compiled, including brand, model, age, condition of exterior paint, state of the rubber seal, and analysis of efficiency during operation. About 30 percent of the audited refrigerators (727 refrigerators) showed unsatisfactory performance that increased household electricity consumption by approximately 35 percent. These were replaced with new, more efficient units. A survey conducted by IBOPE indicated a high degree

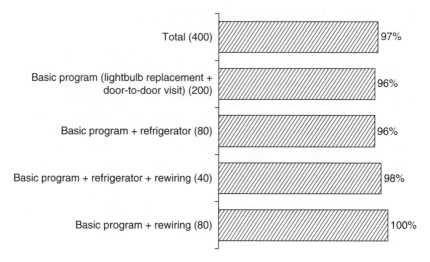

Source: AES Eletropaulo.

Figure 10.3   *Level of residents' satisfaction with the pilot project (% of respondents answering 'good' or 'very good'; numbers of respondents are in parentheses)*

of satisfaction among the population regarding the whole process and type of benefit (Figures 10.3–10.6).

In addition to leading to high customer satisfaction levels, the exchange of refrigerators yielded total savings of about 23 856 kWh per month, or 10 percent of the total savings obtained by the pilot project. The improved efficiency in energy use was widely recognized by the population and was also acknowledged during the opinion survey, as indicated in numbers of respondents who intended to buy a new refrigerator within the two next years (Figure 10.7). The survey indicated that more than 85 percent of the population knew that the old refrigerators consumed more energy. Thus, it is easy to understand why residents were willing to adhere to a financing plan to replace their refrigerators or other energy-inefficient appliances.

Safe and Adequate Electrical Wiring

Based on the positive experience of Procobre elsewhere in Brazil through its Casa Segura ('Safe House') program, the pilot program conducted 2433 audits in 5515 visits to households in the selected area. A total of 1406 households had electrical wiring in bad condition, representing 58

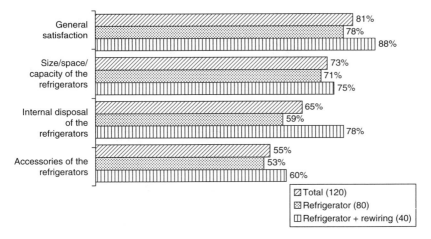

Source: AES Eletropaulo.

Figure 10.4 *Level of participants' satisfaction with the new refrigerator (% of respondents answering 'good' or 'very good' considering the quality of the refrigerators; numbers of respondents are in parentheses)*

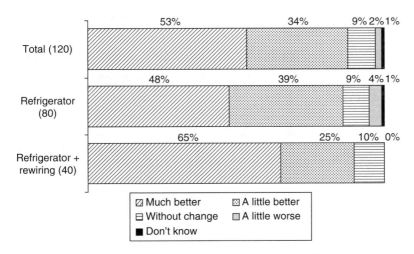

Source: AES Eletropaulo.

Figure 10.5 *Participants' perceived quality-of-life improvement with the new refrigerator (% of respondents giving a particular answer; numbers of respondents in parentheses)*

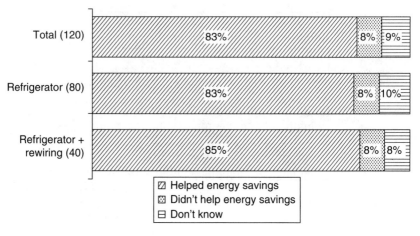

Source: AES Eletropaulo.

*Figure 10.6   Participants' perceived savings with the new refrigerator
(% of respondents giving a particular answer; numbers of
respondents are in parentheses)*

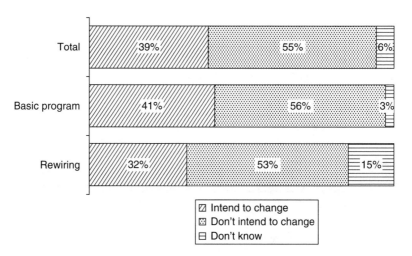

Source: AES Eletropaulo.

*Figure 10.7   Participants' intention to buy a new refrigerator in the next
two years (% of respondents giving a particular answer)*

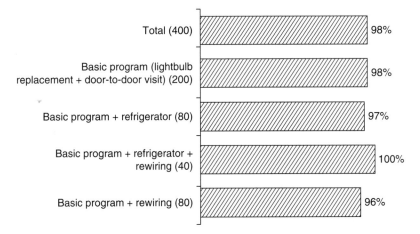

Source: AES Eletropaulo.

Figure 10.8 *Level of participants' satisfaction with the rewiring initiative (% of respondents answering 'good' or 'very good'; numbers of respondents are in parentheses)*

percent of the households audited. Overloaded wires, badly distributed circuits and the total absence of a protection system made these houses unsafe. The dwellings that were in the worst shape were rewired to comply with Brazilian electrical norm NBR 5410. Badly made splices, intense use of 'Benjamins' (multiple sockets or outlets with several connections), and peeling and overheated conductors were eliminated in these 496 homes in which the electrical wiring was redone during the pilot project. Adequately dimensioned cables, plus balanced and protected circuits, made the new electrical installations in these dwellings safe. In particular, installation of circuit-breakers and the replacement of the electric shower water heaters with ones with a shielded resistance design ensured that residents would be protected against electric shock. During the audits, residents reported more than 20 cases of small accidents they had experienced that involved faulty electric wiring and fixtures.

Internal electrical rewiring and the replacement of water heaters not only complied with Brazilian standards and brought comfort to the residents but also contributed to monthly savings of 13 289 kWh. According to the IBOPE opinion survey, this was the pilot project measure that most pleased the population (Figures 10.8 and 10.9).

The residents' perceived improvements in their quality of life after the completion of the pilot project are illustrated in Figures 10.10–10.13.

Source: AES Eletropaulo.

*Figure 10.9   Level of participants' satisfaction with the services performed
            (% of respondents answering 'good' or 'very good'; numbers
            of respondents are in parentheses)*

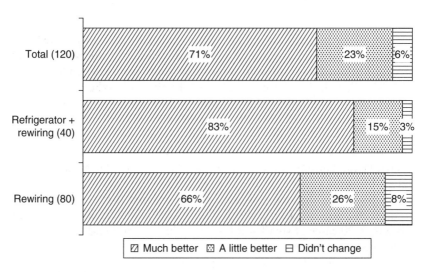

Source: AES Eletropaulo.

*Figure 10.10   Participants' perceived improvements in quality of life
            after completion of the pilot project (% of respondents
            giving a particular answer; numbers of respondents are in
            parentheses)*

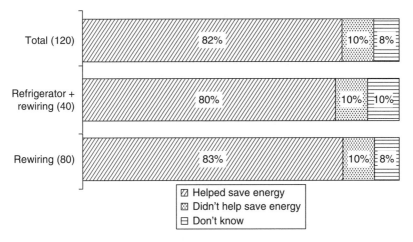

Source: AES Eletropaulo.

Figure 10.11   Participants' perceived energy savings after rewiring and improving fixtures (% of respondents giving a particular answer; numbers of respondents are in parentheses)

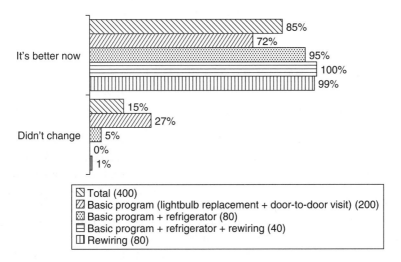

Source: AES Eletropaulo.

Figure 10.12   Participants' perceived safety after internal rewiring (% of respondents giving a particular answer; numbers of respondents are in parentheses)

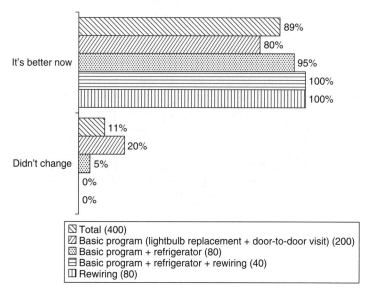

Source: AES Eletropaulo.

Figure 10.13 All area residents' perceived safety after internal rewiring (% of respondents giving a particular answer; numbers of respondents are in parentheses)

FINANCIAL RESULTS

In addition to project assessment by performance indicators, a financial assessment based on present value of investments and revenues was performed, as this was the parameter chosen as the main tool for the analysis of financial viability. A second assessment was conducted to check the sustainability of the project in the medium term (ten years). This assessment was important because some behavioral changes may occur over time, such as those provoked by the economic impact consumers experience after regularization, which generally are not perceived until some time after pilot implementation. Other changes, such as the increase of the bad debt rate, or a decrease in the reduction in efficiency gains due to replacement of lightbulbs or refrigerators, may also occur.

Financial sustainability depends essentially on two factors: the company's capacity to make a business case for the project, so that it may serve as an example of service for low-income clients; and affordability of electricity to consumers and their satisfaction with the services provided.

To determine whether the Paraisópolis pilot project could be considered sustainable for the company, a feasibility analysis of a case was conducted, the so-called real process. The analysis was developed so as to reflect real results of the pilot. The pilot's results were analyzed, considering two possible different scenarios for the future: an optimistic one and a pessimistic one. Sensitivity analyses were conducted to determine the impact of not developing the initiatives. Global results were then compared with key performance indicators for the company, the consumer and the society as a whole.

To assess project sustainability from the consumer perspective, consumption measurements were made at the client, billing and revenue levels for the company under the conditions of regularization and use of anti-theft technology, and of the energy-efficiency measures and default rates. Next, project sustainability was analyzed from a societal perspective, verifying chiefly the effects of subsidies received by the company to reduce losses in its activities relative to its other clients. For this analysis, data were collected during the pilot project to be used as indicators, such as the cost of distribution system upgrades in the project area, the number of lightbulbs and inefficient refrigerators replaced, the socio-economic conditions of the families receiving the benefits, and the accumulated energy savings as a result of the replacement of equipment by high-efficiency units. The calculations related to actions conducted within the project scope are summarized in Table 10.2, and the major monthly energy savings obtained with the energy efficiency enhancements are given in Table 10.3.

At the household level, educational actions and the regularization process by themselves yielded an average initial consumption reduction from 250 kWh to 192 kWh per household every month. After the energy-efficiency improvement measures, consumption was reduced to an average of 151 kWh per client within the project area (Figure 10.14). The rate of non-payment also decreased from 98 percent before the pilot to 32 percent during the first 11 months of the project.

Per regularized client, the average investment by the company and its partners was 800 Brazilian reias; the average annual revenue, 260 reias; and the average monthly energy saved, 99 kWh. Details of the company's overall investments and results are summarized in Table 10.4. In a pessimistic analysis, allowing for an increase in bad debts due to economic factors and assuming the bad debt rate going from 32 percent to 50 percent, payback would be achieved in 1.60 years. On the other hand, the optimistic perspective says that if a default level of 12 percent is reached after the first year – which is the actual average obtained by AES Eletropaulo's General Regularization Program in other communities in São Paulo – payback would be achieved in 1.25 years, taking into account

Table 10.2   Results of pilot project actions

Action	Number installed or completed
Primary distribution grid upgraded	2.98 km
Secondary distribution system upgraded	5.4 km
Transformers replaced (conventional; efficient)	6; 12
Service entrance and posts installed	3890
Electronic remote-reading meters installed	435
Pre- and post-regularization door-to-door visits by community agents	8594
Community and school events	25 events with 4906 attendees
Inefficient incandescent lightbulbs replaced with efficient compact fluorescent bulbs	9588
Refrigerator assessments completed	2598
Inefficient refrigerators replaced with PROCEL A-rated ones as needed	497
Wiring safety assessments completed	2433
Rewiring of unsafe internal wiring and fixtures, and replacement of electric showers	496
Replacement of individual outside lights with public lighting	505 (472 in alleys; 33 in main streets)
Commercial audits and recommendations made	70

Source: AES Eletropaulo.

Table 10.3   Major energy savings obtained with pilot project's energy efficiency enhancements

Enhancement	Energy savings (KWh/month)
Public lighting	19258
Household compact fluorescent lightbulbs	165497
Refrigerators	23856
Rewiring	5456
Showers	8928
Efficient transformers	4361
Total	227356

Source: AES Eletropaulo.

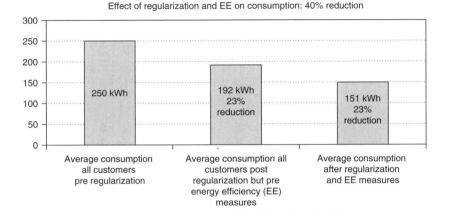

Source: AES Eletropaulo.

Figure 10.14   Summary of average energy consumption reduction for all consumers due to deployment of pilot project measures

the cost of energy saved (99 kWh/month) not included in the average annual revenues as well as the low-income subsidy.

The opinion survey conducted after the project's completion points to a very high rate of approval and satisfaction by this population: an average of 62 percent of the people were 'delighted' (that is, the total of respondents giving the two highest ratings, 9 and 10, on a ten-point scale). It was surprising to see the positive strength of opinion, expressed in unprompted comments by people of all segments that no more accidents had occurred after the illegal wiring was removed. Additionally, the population's satisfaction with the improved quality of electrical energy at the end of the project was clear (Figures 10.15 and 10.16). In the households where rewiring was done, energy problems practically disappeared. There was a clear perception of improved quality of life among the households where rewiring was done or refrigerators exchanged, along with a perception of improved savings after such initiatives. All of this led to overall project approval ratings between 83 percent and 98 percent. The reasons for approval most frequently mentioned by respondents were these:

- No more fire risk due to short circuits or overload.
- Having a proof of address, which provided a series of benefits.
- Safe installations, without the risk of burning-out electrical appliances.
- No more outages.

Table 10.4 Financial analysis of the Paraisópolis pilot project

Investments			Revenues							
1 – Assets (utility)	Value (Reals)		1 – Billing (collection)	% WACC	Values R$ – NPV 10 years		Value R$ – First Year			
Customer Registration	R$	15 992.62	Collection before regularization (2% of billing)	9.00%	R$	413 573.85	R$	64 443.11		
Project Design	R$	14 722.00	Annual post-regularization metered billing (collection)	9.00%	R$	11 383 724.18	R$	1 773 812.92		
Primary Distribution Network	R$	79 437.48								
Secondary Distribution Network	R$	606 675.42	Bad Debt Annual Rate		32%		32%			
Efficient Transformers	R$	105 900.00	Annual Bad Debt	9.00%	R$	3 675 585.97	R$	572 730.14		
			Net Revenue		R$	7 294 564.36	R$	1 136 639.67		

Conventional Transformers	R$	6 309.60	
Coaxial Cables	R$	392 850.00	
Conventional Meters	R$	185 946.86	
Remote Meters and Communication Line	R$	136 800.00	
Labor	R$	529 491.87	
Public Lighting	R$	127 757.97	
Other			
Subtotal	**R$**	**2 201 883.83**	

2 – Customers Connections and Efficient Measures

Standard Material for Connection (box, grounding, fuses)	R$	305 550.00

2 – Subsidies/Incentives

Tariff subsidies for low income households based on average consumption (CDE subsidy) (Reals)	R$	1 106 206.00	R$	172 369.12
Additional Revenue	**R$**	**1 106 206.00**	**R$**	**172 369.12**

Table 10.4 (continued)

Investments			Revenues		
Refrigerators Replacement	R$	298 200.00	**3 – Capital Gain (other monetary benefits)**		
Light Replacement	R$	79 420.95	Avoided costs (saved energy EE plus Reg effect) based on purchase cost and resale benefit (kWh saved)	R$	8 067 695.68	R$	1 257 109.07
Internal Rewiring and Showers (material and labor)	R$	383 134.52	Subtotal	R$	8 067 695.68	R$	1 257 109.07
Other (door-to-door visit, community campaign, lectures at schools, residential mini audits)	R$	102 414.00			
			TOTAL REVENUES	R$	16 468 466.04	R$	2 566 117.85

Subtotal	R$	1 168 719.47

3 – Other Investments

Consumer Survey	R$	67 000.00
Commercial Diagnosis	R$	57 630.30
Subtotal	R$	124 630.30
TOTAL INVESTMENTS	R$	3 495 233.60

Total number of customers considered	4 365 clients

NET RESULTS

NPV	R$	13 261 829.69
IRR		276%
PAY BACK		1.36 YEARS
WACC		9.00%

Source: AES Eletropaulo.

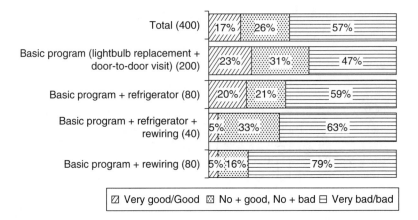

Source: AES Eletropaulo.

Figure 10.15   Participants' assessment of energy quality before pilot project deployment (% of respondents giving a particular answer; numbers of respondents are in parentheses)

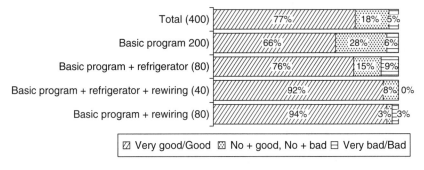

Source: AES Eletropaulo.

Figure 10.16   Participants' assessment of energy quality after project deployment (% of respondents giving a particular answer; numbers of respondents are in parentheses)

LESSONS LEARNED

The results and the financial analysis of the pilot project for electricity regularization have made it clear that, even in pessimistic scenarios, positive financial returns occur within a short period of time. The model adopted in the pilot views the following points as necessary elements for success with the regularization process:

Community Involvement

Community involvement is essential for implementing actions and activities after regularization of the electricity connections. The most powerful arguments that can motivate BOP communities to support regularization are: improvement in quality of life through a safe and reliable supply of electrical energy; easier access to citizenship benefits by having a document (electric bill) that is widely accepted as proof of residence; and the benefits of consumer rights, as set forth by legislation and by the regulator. Damage to household appliances caused by 'bad-quality' electricity supply before regularization are a major financial challenge for these communities, so the virtual elimination of such damage through regularization is considered a plus. The potential for reducing the risk of fire and accidents is one of the items that elicits the greatest interest from residents, for it involves preserving lives as well as property built up over a lifetime. In contrast, if the community does not see an improvement in utility services after regularization, there will be a greater resistance to the process, and sustainability will be more difficult to maintain after project deployment.

Application of Technology

Within the process of changing the community's culture, easy illegal access to electrical networks must come to an end. Technology is an important instrument for reaching this goal. The pilot project focused specifically on the anti-theft (biconcentric) cables and insulated cables connecting to the secondary distribution lines. Although these measures represent changes from the conventional standard, the investments required for revamping the distribution networks are feasible, and these measures substantially reduce the possibility of new illegal connections. In the pilot project, the few attempts at illegal direct connections to the secondary grid were easily identified and eliminated with the use of tapes that armored the cables. This measure sent a strong signal to the community that illegal access to power lines was being eradicated.

Another aspect of regularization that involves technology is finding an alternative to cutting off the power supply to bad-debt clients after all other options for reaching a solution have been exhausted. Communities react strongly to this measure, sometimes threatening the company employees sent to perform the cut-off. Remote cut-off of power supply not only eliminates this problem but also contributes to a change in the community culture. Additionally, finding a new and less dramatic alternative to cutting off the supply is also desirable, so that a good relationship with the community is maintained. In the pilot project, electronic meters were installed in some portions of the pilot area, with remote metering and cut-off features. These meters were equipped with software that enabled small daily interruptions for educational purposes, capping the energy consumption for the month. Thus, the next step would be to implement a 'social cut-off' – that is, to supply only enough energy to meet the household's basic needs, limited by the associated commercial losses. The idea is to create a situation that is uncomfortable enough to motivate people to negotiate with the company and become regular clients again. In other words, this measure is more educational than punitive.

Installation of efficient transformers reduced technical losses and allowed fewer transformers to be used for the same load, since they could withstand a higher load during consumption peaks. This was an important measure, chiefly in areas where the installation of such equipment is critical because of the short distance between the electrical lines and the buildings.

Accommodation of the Community's Socio-economic Status

Due to the socio-economic vulnerability of this population and to a culture somewhat used to dependence on government handouts, the development of appropriate commercial policies adapted to these circumstances is vital to a project's feasibility. The registration of households in the area and the entry of their information into the commercial system should be done in a way that ensures regularization of the household addresses. Frequently, house numbers in such areas are duplicated and do not follow a logical sequence, because settlement of the areas occurred haphazardly. At the time of registration, the houses should be renumbered in order to regularize addresses. In the pilot project, the numbers were painted on the facade of the houses, in easily identifiable places. Ideally, the names of the streets should also be regularized with the municipal administration, and a zip code obtained for each address.

Finding a way to make the new connections at no cost to the customers and without their having to take any action is another key to expediting regularization. AES Eletropaulo's solution was to use institutional funds from the ANEEL's Energy Efficiency Program to acquire the service line material (the standard material for connection) for the customers. If the equipment cannot be provided to all clients free of charge, the utility company should at least find a way to finance its acquisition by households and, if possible, to be responsible for purchasing and installing it.

The most relevant point related to accommodating the low-income status of the community is to offer electricity rates that the households can afford. This generally entails creating subsidy mechanisms that can be sponsored by the government or as a policy of the utility company. In Brazil, 'social tariffs', which provide a subsidy of about one-half of the normal residential rates, are mandated by legislation and regulated by the federal agency ANEEL. Thus, another measure taken by AES Eletropaulo was to assist the population in registering to receive the low-income tariff.

Once an adequate rate is ensured, the next step is to set a transition period during which customers have their bills capped at a certain amount per month so that they have time to come to grips with their consumption levels and the corresponding cost of the electric bill. The population in BOP communities is not used to saving power and usually consumes more electricity than other households. Therefore, an educational campaign must be conducted to help families reduce consumption to affordable levels. In the Paraisópolis pilot project, bills were capped at 150 kWh for six months. During this period, an effort was made to help households with higher consumption levels reduce their electricity use. After the transition period, customers started paying for what they actually consumed, as part of the educational process of becoming regular citizens.

It is important that the distribution company have a physical location within the community, not only to make it more convenient for the residents who find it difficult to go to one of the other established locations for assistance, but also to create a stronger bond with the community. Thus, AES Eletropaulo created an assistance center in Paraisópolis. There, in addition to regular services, the company set up a library and an IT center with free Internet access, in order to strengthen the bonds with its customers.

Finally, after the new regular connections are set up, assisting families with higher levels of consumption or bad debts is a major factor for the sustainability of the process. To address this need in the pilot project, community organizers were set up to visit the area periodically in order to give practical and educational support to the residents. Creating special policies to negotiate repayment of prior debts is another important measure to prevent customers from defaulting again.

Promotion of Energy Efficiency

Education does not always solve the problem of getting families to adapt their consumption levels to their income. Sometimes it is necessary to provide other practical tools to help them reduce energy use and to ensure sustainability of the project in both the medium and the long term. The approach taken in the pilot project was to conduct technical audits of customers' electric facilities and appliances, aiming at finding opportunities to improve energy efficiency. Major opportunities were replacing high-consumption incandescent lightbulbs with highly efficient compact fluorescent bulbs, particularly as these lights were often kept on 24 hours a day because of poor natural light; replacing refrigerators that had poor thermal insulation with new, more efficient ones; after the execution of those action the company proceeded to install solar water heaters to replace electric showers. Such measures provided savings of up to 50 percent in the most critical cases.

Another important company action is to provide lighting in dark streets and alleys so that customers do not need to use their own lights outside their houses to illuminate the passageways. This measure is not only convenient but also brings more safety to the community. After the new lighting system was installed in the pilot project, there was a drop in violence rates in the area.

Social Responsibility

One last pillar in this process must be to enact measures aimed at improving the socio-economic standards of these communities. Social responsibility projects help the utility company build a positive image in the communities, whose culture and values are permeated by a strong sense of payback; that is, it is important that the residents feel that the company is engaged in helping their community prosper, so that they then consider payment of their electric bills to be a top priority. In the case of Paraisópolis, professional training and other educational projects are being deployed in schools, among other initiatives. Such projects must emerge spontaneously in the community in order to create a strong sense of partnership in seeking solutions for problems specific to each community.

Development of an Economic Model

The utility company must necessarily create an economic model so that the entire organization has an objective view of the project's results as an encouragement to replicate the process in other areas.

Broader Lessons

In addition to these necessary actions taken by the company, the pilot project in Paraisópolis revealed broader lessons and practical results for all the organizations that worked together in the project, making it a useful model for replication:

- Project feasibility. The financial analysis shown in Table 10.4 demonstrates the feasibility of the pilot project, taking into account a dramatic drop in theft and energy losses. Payback was estimated at 1.36 years, with optimistic and pessimistic projections ranging from 1.25 to 1.60 years, respectively, or two years if subsidies are not considered.
- Financial resources. Many co-financing opportunities are available from various sources, chiefly from governments, which encourage regularization of illegal electricity connections and energy-efficient projects geared to low-income populations. Use of these resources would further enhance what are already excellent financial returns.
- Community presence. To avoid a relapse to high levels of theft and non-payment in the future, previous experiences with public utility services in Brazil indicate that technological solutions deployed in the pilot project are necessary but not sufficient as deterrents for illegal connections. Continuous company presence and activity, including the ongoing presence of company teams in the community, are some of the crucial elements that ensure the program's long-term sustainability.
- Customer satisfaction. Customer satisfaction with the pilot project was assessed in an opinion poll, showing that most of the families regularized in the pilot area were very satisfied with their access to better-quality electricity and with the measures to help them improve their energy efficiency. Many of the low-income customers, however, said that they would find it difficult to pay their electric bills in the future, despite the measures taken to reduce their consumption.
- Customized solutions. The comprehensive approach pursued in the pilot, encompassing a variety of solutions deployed simultaneously, may be feasible only under special circumstances, taking into consideration the characteristics of the electric grid, the losses in the households due to the poor conditions and inefficiency of appliances, the electricity rates, the availability of government subsidies, the often violent environment of BOP communities, and other conditions. However, some of the pilot project's solutions may be adapted to the specific characteristics of each site.
- Local and federal regulations. The decision of power distribution companies to invest in slum electrification projects and to reduce losses in low-income communities appears to be robustly feasible from a financial perspective, with an attractive return on investment under a variety of conditions. However, the specific situation of each distribution company, according to the regulations in force in each

country or jurisdiction, may strongly affect the company's decision. For example, some countries have tariff subsidies to offset the high levels of losses in the slums, and other countries do not.

THE CHALLENGES AHEAD

The major challenge that remains for AES Eletropaulo after the success of the pilot project in Paraisópolis is to incorporate within its management routines a system to maintain the relationship with the regularized community as time goes by, following up on any changes in community leadership so that the new leaders may be approached and engaged in the process of interacting with the company. In addition, changes in habits require a long time to take root, and educational initiatives tend to wither if there is no continuity. Thus, monitoring the evolution of clients' consumption over the medium and the long term, and maintaining the presence of community agents through periodic visits to the households with the highest consumption levels, are necessary measures to ensure project continuity.

Another challenge is the relationship with the commercial segment. In Brazil, for example, this segment has a substantial presence in the communities but is not included in the existing subsidy schemes approved by the regulator. Yet many commercial customers have high levels of consumption, due to obsolete equipment, poor fixtures and lack of knowledge about power management. This segment must be the object of future action, as it is a major source of jobs for the residents of BOP communities like Paraisópolis, and a major source of revenue for the utility company and thus an important contributor to the viability of company operations in these communities. More generally, seeking solutions to enhance the local economy and to promote human development in BOP communities is a way to improve the sustainability of regularization efforts over time.

NOTES

1. http://www.bmfbovespa.com.br/indices/ResumoIndice.
   aspx?Indice=ISE&Idioma=pt-BR.
2. According to Brazilian standards there is a minimum distance between the electric network and the buildings. Since sidewalks in the slums tend to be narrow, the company has had to adapt the electric network to a compact version – spacer cable – in order to meet the minimum distance.
3. Irregularity of occupation means there is little planned infrastructure and the growth of

slums most often does not follow formal urbanization rules. The occupation of the land changes in an ad hoc fashion. In many cases the homes are constructed over the sidewalks because of the lack of space. Another common situation is the absence of windows in many rooms. The consequence of this situation is the low level of natural lighting inside the homes that requires artificial illumination during most of the day.

11. Conclusions: providing utilities to the poor

Patricia Márquez and Carlos Rufín

The overall message of this book is that effective provision of basic services to the impoverished masses worldwide is happening through novel business thinking, including creative use of technology and human resources, as well as new sets of relationships with both traditional and non-traditional actors. Regardless of motivations and strategies, businesses, civil society organizations and governments in various regions are enthusiastically embracing the pursuit of fresh models for solving the problem of insufficient access to basic services among the poor. More and more, all these organizations operating in the utility sector are coming to realize the economic and social potential of engaging the socio-economic base of the pyramid (BOP) in radically different ways from the past. On their part, there is a willingness to rethink themselves, to experiment and to co-create, where closer attention is paid to the needs of those at the BOP, while seeking to integrate them in commercial ventures as savvy consumers or entrepreneurs.

The experiences analyzed in this book might have high levels of social enterprise in their development. However, it is clear that these are market-driven initiatives. Economic feasibility is essential to sustain service provision. The contributors shed light on what is required to generate economic and social value for different types of utility services and in various regions and contexts. A key aspect is their insistence that value creation has to be evident not only to the firm. Value has to be clearly perceived by the BOP. Only then will the poor be willing to spend their scarce funds on utility services. Given the often tense and even negative history of utilities and the poor in many nations, this is a factor that multilateral institutions have begun to address.

In sum, in this volume our collective effort was about delving deeper into what works in the specific case of utility services reaching out to the BOP through commercial ventures. The chapters speak of heterogeneous experiences with various degrees of success and failure. Nonetheless, they all reveal important lessons for those who will follow. In this final chapter, we summarize key lessons, while highlighting challenges that still lay ahead.

LESSONS

Building business models that bring utilities to the poor involves the development of adequate processes for distributing and selling electricity, natural gas, water or telephone services. This is particularly challenging when one considers the reality that in spite of their massive numbers, those at the BOP have often remained invisible or ignored by many companies in the sector. To serve them, organizations have had to revisit their previous understandings of the needs and expectations of those at the BOP as customers.

Adding to the complexity of this transformation is the strong presence of the public sector in utility industries. As we explained in the Introduction, the particularities of the sector entail involvement of government and regulatory agencies to a degree seldom found in other businesses. But governments are motivated by more than just considerations of economic efficiency. As the evolution of utility industries has shown throughout the world, utilities can be political weapons as well as sources of political mobilization.

Putting these considerations together, we can identify several key challenges that lie at the heart of success or failure when it comes to the provision of utility services for the BOP. First, the organizations involved in this effort, and particularly utility companies, are faced with the need for significant organizational transformations in order to overcome the inertia and preconceptions of the past. Second, cooperation and effective engagement of stakeholders seems essential for these ventures to succeed – the actors engaged in utility supply at the BOP must be structured as an 'ecosystem' that works with a minimum level of consistency, as BOP scholars have pointed out for BOP initiatives in general (Prahalad and Hammond, 2002; Reficco and Márquez, forthcoming).

Beyond these considerations, research about business models at the BOP cannot forget the fundamental issue of scale. It is not enough to attain success in a pilot involving a few thousand families; with rapid urbanization happening in many developing countries (Satterthwaite, 2007), the demand for utility services is growing rapidly, and utility companies that fail to keep up with demand may be faced with serious problems of financial and operational viability due to increasing theft and overuse of existing facilities. Lastly, we need to remember that our motivation for this book is to examine the possibilities for attaining both financial sustainability and improvements in the quality of life for the poor in the supply of utility services. We therefore need to consider also to what extent BOP initiatives reach their social goals as well as their financial ones. In the rest of this section, we summarize and discuss the main lessons offered by the contributors to this volume in terms of the four main dimensions highlighted above: (1) adapting the organization for BOP service provision; (2) building the business ecosystem; (3) attaining scale; and (4) delivering improvements for BOP communities.

The Organization

In this book we find different types of organizations providing utility services. To begin with, there is the corporation. The experiences speak of the need for a shift in paradigm to consider the poor as truly potential customers. There is also the non-profit initiative, fulfilling a social mission of providing information and communication technology (ICT) services in a sustainable way. A paradigm shift is also required here, from treating the poor as beneficiaries to engaging them as customers. There is also the multilateral organization, pursuing the development of governance structures, organizations, and incentives for the effective delivery of utility services. Let us examine the necessary changes and adaptations highlighted by the preceding chapters.

The first theme regarding organizations engaged in the supply of utility services at the BOP is the need for deep organizational transformation. This transformation can itself take place at various organizational levels. Gardetti (Chapter 5) calls attention to changes in the corporate vision, from a focus on the finite nature of company resources to social inclusion as a core belief and a value to be considered in the company's decision-making processes; or even more radically, from a service-centered to a community-centered company that can become a proactive agent of change. Casarín and Nicollier (Chapter 6) allude to a similar concept, when they argue for the need to change the dominant logic that views the supply of electricity to the poor as requiring either cost reductions or cross-subsidies. Such logic fails to grasp, according to these authors, the fact that charging higher prices to wealthier consumers in places like Argentina might actually lead to greater fraud by these consumers. Lawaetz and Smyser (Chapter 7) also show the impact of limited perspectives, writing that traditional company expectations of the poor as consuming very low volumes of services have acted as a barrier to innovation. Innovation has at best been limited to reduce commercial and technical losses, particularly where universal service requirements have forced utility companies to supply the poor. Such a narrow view of service has resulted in a culture of 'stopping at the meter', and failing to realize in fact the potential of innovations such as Codensa's appliance credit program, or AES's efforts to help consumers use electricity more efficiently as a means to make theft less appealing.

What can be done to change entrenched company cultures and limited visions? Veevers-Carter and Russell (Chapter 8) point to the power of rewards and incentives: output-based aid (OBA), by reimbursing companies upon proof of service delivery and thus creating a different form of accountability, changes the culture of service providers. Álvarez and Morandi (Chapter 9) highlight the impact of changing professional norms, describing how hiring professionals from the social sciences with a focus on understanding context and human behavior brought relevant changes to corporate culture. On the other hand, the inclusion of technical staff in the development of BOP initiatives not only avoids the potential for technically flawed approaches, but also brings awareness of social conditions to the technical staff and stimulates their interest in using their expertise to address social problems. More generally, the involvement of different departments in BOP initiatives and the commitment of company leadership in these initiatives can break down internal barriers and resistance to change. AES, in fact, has experimented considerably over the years to become more responsive to social needs: it used a bidding system to change its value chain in rural areas of El Salvador; in São Paulo it established clear and measurable internal objectives regarding cost of service and energy efficiency, and sought to find alternatives to simply cutting off customers who fail to pay their bill. Some of these approaches are echoed in Alampay's analysis of Philippine ICT inclusion programs (Chapter 4), where the 'embarrassment to charge' for services was overcome through basic training of local staff in business management and operations, so that they could run information centers and compete more effectively.

A second organizational theme in the book is the need to pay attention to processes internal to companies engaged with the BOP, beginning with sales processes. Francisco Mejía (Chapter 2) points to the power of value bundling, in order to take advantage of utilities' enormous capillarity, or reach across the population. Innovative processes that tie the promotion and sale of different products around a utility's network have large potential, as Codensa's experience shows. Likewise, Lawaetz and Smyser write about the value of bundling electricity services with other benefits such as credit, education, wiring, safety and energy efficiency, enhancing the poor's control over their own consumption.

Casarín and Nicollier explain how prepayment reverses the entire commercialization process in the electricity sector, changing the cash flow of utilities and consumer behavior. But such a radical change may be limited to BOP consumers who welcome the ability to monitor their consumption and control it more carefully, in contrast to other consumers who remain loyal to the traditional system of payment after consumption has been measured and a bill issued. Gardetti takes the logic of prepayment further when he points out the reduction in transaction costs (for example meter reading, issuance of bills, bill payment) through self-manageable systems. Empresa de Distribución Elétrica de Tucumán SA (EDET), for instance, sought innovations in its commercial processes through a case-by-case methodology that incorporated visits by company agents to BOP consumers. In mobile telephony, Mendes (Chapter 3) points at how prepayment was central to increasing access to owning cellular lines, managing consumption, and having access to additional services such as money transfers. Indeed, the high rates of success led to offering prepayment systems for fixed telephony. It guided further innovations for reaching even poorer segments such as providing smaller increments by over-the-air (OTA) purchases of credit.

The commercial cycle can also be radically reshaped at the billing and collection end, as the concept of prepayment suggests. In fact, prepayment is only one of several possibilities revealed in this book. Mejía argues that a key issue is in fact changing BOP consumers' willingness to pay away from the traditional compulsion-oriented approach. Instead of focusing on the mechanisms for billing and collecting, bundling utility services, which are often intangible products, or products perceived as social rights, with more clearly tangible products such as appliances can create customer loyalty and reduce non-payment and collection problems. This is so because consumers come to associate utility services with more tangible products and even services (such as credit and insurance) that are not regarded as social rights. Other measures that also seek to change the BOP consumer's perception of a utility company are also possible, including: the training and involvement of community leaders who can help the company in sales and post-sales, and more generally in maintaining a presence in the community; assistance to households and local businesses with improvements in energy efficiency; and changing the previous 'punitive' attitude toward non-payment to one of assistance and education.

Often, new processes must be created where they did not exist before in a utility company. For Álvarez and Morandi, this effort begins with truly understanding BOP needs to craft a proposition not just for the individual household, but for the entire community. The proposition needs to change social habits of theft of utility services and of 'unwillingness to pay' ingrained over many years. It can be realized, for instance, through new processes of assistance for households to manage and reduce their consumption, thus lowering households' utility costs. In turn, these processes can involve community agents that create awareness of utility service consumption, access and citizenship on a door-to-door basis.

As the introduction to this volume pointed out, a major question regarding the supply of utility services at the BOP is the role of technology. The preceding chapters provide important, if sometimes contradictory, lessons about the role of technology within the development of organizational capabilities to serve the BOP. On one hand, Gardetti's research in Argentina emphasizes the development of appropriate business models rather than the search for new specific technologies that can 'do the trick'. On the other hand, the chapters by AES executives (Pettersson, Álvarez and Morandi) point to the valuable role of technological components, such as anti-theft cables and appropriate transformers, in BOP initiatives, as well as the need for better payment systems technologies. In fact, Pettersson's chapter (Chapter 10) includes extensive descriptions of the technological innovations deployed by AES in Paraisópolis, including meters that can be read remotely through mobile telephony solutions, and 'telecommand' technologies that allow remote disconnection and reconnection (including a 'social cut-off' providing just enough energy to meet a family's basic needs as an alternative to cutting off all supply of electricity), but also rapid detection and correction of equipment failures. Inevitably, the 'tyranny of the network' means that BOP-oriented utility efforts must involve a significant technology component in order to develop or improve distribution networks. Investments such as these can prevent theft and, perhaps more importantly, by improving quality of service and community well-being (such as public lighting to make streets safer) as well as efficiency, they can increase ability and willingness to pay.

To conclude the lessons for organizational change, many of our contributors call for a new dynamic between organizations and BOP communities. Thus, Gardetti argues that utility BOP initiatives may need to include workshops to educate BOP consumers about responsible consumption and to explore alternative sources of energy; Lawaetz and Smyser show that it is key for companies to learn effective ways to improve relations with communities, and that this can be accomplished by establishing relations that involve not only supply and payment, but also credit, education, safety and, especially, means for families to exert greater control over their consumption of utility services. Álvarez and Morandi highlight the useful role of corporate social responsibility (CSR) programs in creating trust and developing markets, through value-added activities, in rural areas of Cameroon. Pettersson takes these points further as he discusses the need to tailor communication strategies to different audiences, organize local events and involve youths as well, always with a clear message of avoiding relapses into informality and the company's commitment to seeking solutions rather than punishment or compulsion. These new dynamics clearly point at the need for developing different capabilities and organizational culture.

Building the Business Ecosystem

The BOP literature, including our own contributions (Reficco and Márquez, forthcoming; Rivera-Santos and Rufín, 2010), has highlighted the importance of ecosystems and networks in BOP initiatives, particularly in view of the limitations of formal institutions and unavailability of business services at the BOP. This theme receives abundant corroboration in this volume. A first set of participants in the BOP ecosystem for utilities are governmental entities: central governments (Álvarez and Morandi offer a useful contrast between an initiative supported by the government in El Salvador, versus the challenges created by government indifference or hostility in Venezuela); subnational governments (Gardetti); or regulatory agencies (Pettersson's account of the progressive attitude of the Brazilian electricity regulator in promoting solutions for the legalization of electricity services in low-income communities). Multilateral institutions can also play an important role. Veevers-Carter and Russell describe the positive impact made by the World Bank's OBA programs on utility supply at the BOP, including the fostering of public–private partnerships and improvements in the quality of public policy. Finally, there is 'civil society' too, particularly local non-governmental organizations (NGOs) (Pettersson), youth organizations (the Youth Citizen Building program in Brazil and clearing squads in Cameroon, in Álvarez and Morandi's chapter), and local leaders. Youths can play a very valuable role through training that allows them to become instructors and voices in the community (Álvarez and Morandi; Alampay). Alampay, in particular, calls attention to the need for local champions to ensure the viability of initiatives over time. His argument is worth restating, for it differs from the conventional focus of some programs: there is no need to convince communities of the importance of utility services; they are well aware of it and they want those services and more. What companies need is clearly to engage local champion(s) who can keep initiatives going. Champions can range from local entrepreneurs, to local politicians seeking to further their political careers by providing benefits to the community, to youths with the potential to be trained and to take over the initiative and similar ones in the future. Once again, this revealed that new value chains involving community and local champions required a novel set of specific management skills for identification and development of non-traditional commercial ties.

The Issue of Scale

Scalability is at the heart of alleviating poverty. Jhirad and Woollam (2007) believe there are three components for scaling-up in utilities. First, companies need access to project finance. That entails infrastructure but also investing in the development of the BOP markets. Second, an enabling legal, regulatory and policy environment is also necessary for removing market distortions that have been in place for decades. Lastly, companies need to craft appropriate value propositions. What factors did the authors in this volume find to be the main challenges to scale?

A first set of challenges are of a political nature. In Argentina, the fact that the BOP population is already connected to distribution networks means that BOP initiatives turn on the cost of energy and conditions for payment and continuity of service, rather than on investment to create or expand networks. In this context, Edenor has faced a political limiting factor, in the form of the government's preference for instituting a 'social rate' instead of prepayment (Gardetti). For Mendes, government policies and vision were central for the extensive penetration of mobile telephony in the Philippines and the innovations in services provided through cellphones such as banking and information.

Attaining scale may also require sufficient levels of corporate resources to draw upon. Veervers-Carter and Russell point out in their chapter that OBA projects are harder to execute for small players. Mobilizing sources of finance is a challenge, particularly in the absence of tariff reforms that allow utility companies to obtain adequate returns on investment.

Alampay, on the other hand, attributes the difficulties of ICT projects in the Philippines to attain scale less to poverty and market competition (in this case, from cellphone operators), and more to the lack of emphasis on finding and nurturing local champions. Álvarez and Morandi also focus on organizational factors, pointing to the need to track progress on a systematic basis. In this regard, Pettersson offers an assessment framework to measure and replicate BOP initiatives, based on financial measures, acceptability and affordability for BOP populations, and acceptability for the community and society in general. This framework can be implemented, for instance, through financial analyses at the conclusion of pilot projects, assessment of socio-economic impacts among BOP populations, and dissemination of findings. Assessment, however, cannot be limited to financial results. Financial results only speak to the business case, but not to the social one.

Delivering Positive Social Impacts

The last set of results which we would like to highlight concern the impacts of the initiatives reviewed in this volume on the populations at which they were directed. After all, these initiatives have been justified at least in part as efforts to improve the lot of the poor. In their analysis of OBA, Veevers-Carter and Russell argue that its positive social impact is not just in providing infrastructure services to the poor, but also in ensuring the quality of this service, since the indicators used to release aid to infrastructure service providers can be designed to include quality-of-service measures.

Access to utilities generates social and economic inclusion of the BOP. Mendes shows the variety of services that are now provided in the Philippines through mobile phones. The BOP has greater access to information. Cellphones make possible the delivery of health services. M-banking includes access to debit cards or money transfers. In sum, the massive reach of cellphones points at numerous possibilities for greater quality of life among the poor, providing important lessons for replicability in Africa and other poor regions of the world.

In Alampay's analysis of the Philippine case, the main benefit of providing Internet service through community-operated information centers is the empowerment of people at the BOP. The services provided by the centers connect them to the global economy in ways not previously imagined by these communities. For example, those in rural areas can tap into the job market in Manila and abroad, gaining new opportunities at lower costs, and benefitting employers too as they gain access to a broader pool of applicants. Álvarez and Morandi echo the theme of empowerment in their description of the creation of cooperatives to service barrio communities in Caracas, in alliance with the corporation. Through this process, community leaders acquired capabilities and consumers learned about adapting their consumption of electricity more closely to their needs, as well as gaining opportunities actually to practice these lessons through the use of efficient lightbulbs, improvements in wiring, and other measures. As an indication of how dramatic the impact of these changes can be, Pettersson reports that the pilot project in Paraisópolis helped local households reduce their monthly consumption of electricity from an average of 250 kWh to 192 kWh; after implementing energy efficiency improvement measures, consumption was further reduced to an average of 151 kWh per client within the project area. Lower consumption cut electricity bills too, causing the rate of non-payment to fall from 98 percent before the pilot to 32 percent during the first 11 months of the project.

Lastly, the Paraisópolis project also delivered 'empowerment' in the more traditional sense of helping the target population claim their rights as citizens. Registration of households into the company's commercial system led to the regularization of home addresses (for instance, street numbers were painted on houses) and eventually the incorporation of the area's streets into the municipal network, allowing residents to demand the municipal services provided to all other areas of the city. Furthermore, as part of the project, households received help in registering to claim mandated government utility subsidies, which in Brazil can cover up to one half of the cost of utility services.

STILL SEARCHING

This book cannot hope to answer all the questions posed in our introductory chapter, nor did we entertain such an unrealistic expectation when we started out. Our questions were intended instead as a source of themes for our contributors to pursue, and for us to structure our understanding about utilities at the BOP. Our purpose was to expand debate on market initiatives for including the poor in vibrant value chains leading to social transformation, by further uncovering what is needed to provide utilities effectively to the BOP. We pursued the question: How is the provision of utilities different from other BOP ventures? Having reviewed the main lessons from this volume, it is useful at this point to review what questions still remain for future enquiry and initiatives to address.

Are Utilities Special?

This volume has shown that for utilities, success at the BOP does share many common elements with other sectors, notably the need for stakeholder engagement through the development of ecosystems that involve non-traditional commercial actors such as NGOs and local champions, and the challenge of scaling up. Perhaps it is with regard to organizational transformation that the 'tyranny of the network' is most obvious. Interestingly, the contributions to this volume show that this 'tyranny' is most powerful not so much at the technological level, but rather at the level of organizational culture and the mental maps of utility personnel. While this book does not provide evidence of physical networks disappearing any time soon for the delivery of utility services outside of ICTs, it does document a large array of technological and, especially, organizational innovations that soften the constraints of physical networks in terms of cost of supply, such as greater community involvement in network management and investment in efficiency improvements. The greatest barrier to the implementation of some if not all of these changes is possibly the dominance of engineering professional norms in utility organizations, which de-emphasize people-oriented approaches such as the development of close relations with the community. In turn, this suggests some valuable potential contributions of work on utilities at the BOP for the broader BOP literature: the development of processes and policies to transform organizational cultures and transcend professional norms; and the importance of innovations 'at the margin' that have the potential to deliver significant cost reductions as whole even though they cannot alter the dominant technological paradigm of an industry. We leave these for exploration and analysis to be undertaken beyond this book.

Is the BOP 'Strategic' for Utility Suppliers?

Perhaps because our focus was on new business models rather than on political economy and regulation, the present volume only hints at the answer to this question. The experiences of AES in Caracas (Álvarez and Morandi) and of Argentine utilities (Gardetti) indicate that utilities are indeed politically salient and that governments pay close attention to utility supply, particularly when it affects politically important constituencies such as the poor in developing countries. Perhaps for this reason more than for reasons of economic efficiency, utility services are closely regulated in most countries, and regulation is a permanent feature of the institutional environment in which utilities operate. This volume thus confirms that utilities are also different from other sectors because of their political visibility, and not just because of reasons of efficiency related to the operation of physical networks. In fact, the combination of political salience and regulation makes utilities uniquely vulnerable to political intervention, as shown by the obstacles encountered by several companies with regard to the use of prepayment. So while the present volume provides an affirmative answer to this question, what to do about it remains less clear. In the absence of a disruptive technology like wireless telephony, more experimentation and analysis is needed to probe the relation between politics and the supply of utility services to the BOP.

Can Utilities Convince BOP Consumers that Utility Services are Worth Paying For?

The contributions to this volume provide abundant documentation of the elements of value propositions that utility suppliers can make to convince consumers to pay: helping them exercise their rights as citizens (Pettersson); providing them with tools to consume more efficiently or to control their consumption more easily (Pettersson); training and employing people from the community (Pettersson; Álvarez and Morandi; Alampay); or providing them with services that clearly enhance their earnings potential (Alampay). Less clear, however, is whether there is one best way to do this, or whether there is a difference between situations where utility services are seen as rights and where customers have simply come to expect free supply. We also lack sufficient information to understand how such expectations are related to the political risks mentioned above.

What is the Role of Public Policy, Including Regulation?

On the normative side, and particularly with regard to the role of public policy in utility service supply for the BOP, the contributions in this volume offer a variety of answers. Experiences such as that of AES and those reviewed by Lawaetz and Smyser would indicate that utility companies should be given substantial freedom by regulators to decide how much of their resources to apply to supplying the BOP, and especially how to allocate such resources. It is from experimentation with different possibilities that more viable models are likely to emerge. This does not mean, however, that all resources should be obtained from other consumers or from investors. The successful experience with OBA projects (Veevers-Carter and Russell) shows that public funds have an important role to play, not just in terms of mobilizing resources but also to induce more efficient use of resources. The contributions to this volume do not provide one single answer, however, about how much of the burden of supplying BOP consumers should be borne by them alone. Instead, a variety of possibilities seems possible, reflecting the huge variation among BOP communities, conditions and cost of service, business models and even negotiation outcomes across the BOP. The same applies to the closely related issue of the pricing point and structure for utility services, with the additional complication that regulation is likely to limit sharply company discretion about pricing.

In sum, recognizing the BOP as composed of vibrant communities of savvy consumers and entrepreneurs, instead of burdensome groups to be dealt with, opens a world of opportunities for business, governments and non-profit organizations. The contributors to this volume have discussed how the BOP paradigm, has much to offer to solve the challenge of providing utility services to the poor. A growing number of experiences across utility sectors suggest, at the very least, the potential to combine profit with poverty alleviation. In turn, the analysis of these experiences enriches the BOP paradigm, offering new insights into the complexities of the relationship between business and poverty. This book represents an important contribution along these lines.

References

Abrenica, M.J. (2000). 'Technological convergence and competition: the telecommunications industry', *Philippine Review of Economics*, **37** (1): 141–65.

Alampay, E.A. (2006). 'Beyond access to ICTs: measuring capabilities in the information society', *International Journal of Education and Development using Information and Communication Technology*, **2** (3). Available at: http://ijedict.dec.uwi.edu/viewarticle.php?id=196.

Alampay, E. (n.d.). 'Revisiting Philippine universal access policies to ICTs'. Available at: http://www.apdip.net/documents/policy/misc/ph/universal-access.pdf.

Alampay, E., R. Heeks and P. Soliva (2003). 'Bridging the information divide: a Philippine guidebook on ICTs for development', Asian Media Information Centre, IDRC and UNDP.

Álvarez, S.A. and J.B. Barney (2007). 'Discovery and creation: alternative theories of entrepreneurial action', *Strategic Entrepreneurship Journal*, **1** (1–2): 33–48.

Arbeláez, M., F. García and C. Sandoval (2007a). 'El Crédito Fácil para Todos de Codensa: un Programa de Impacto Social para Bogotá', Bogotá: Fedesarrollo and Codensa.

Arbeláez, M., F. García and C. Sandoval (2007b). 'El crédito no bancario, una alternativa para la bancarización y la reducción de la pobreza. El caso del "Crédito Fácil para Todos" de Codensa', *Coyuntura Social*, **37** (December): 89–120.

Asobancaria (2008a). 'Reporte de Bancarización de Marzo'.

Asobancaria (2008b). 'Reporte de Bancarización de Septiembre'.

Bongato, N. (2002). 'Government efforts on rural telecoms development', presentation, Luaremar Hotel, Opol Misamis Oriental, Philippines.

Boyer, N. (2003). *The Base of the Pyramid – Reperceiving Business from the Bottom Up*, San Francisco, CA: Global Business Network.

Brook, Penelope J. and M. Petrie (2001). 'Output-based aid: precedents, promises, and challenges', in Penelope J. Brook and S.M. Smith (eds), *Contracting for Public Services: Output-Based Aid and its Applications*, Washington, DC: World Bank, pp. 3–14.

Brook, Penelope J. and S.M. Smith (eds) (2001). *Contracting for Public Services: Output-Based Aid and its Applications*, Washington, DC: The World Bank.

Castells, M. (2000). *The Rise of the Network Society*, 2nd edn, Chichester: Blackwell Publishers.

Cattaneo, M., S. Galiani, P. Gertler, S. Martinez and R. Titiunik (2007), 'Housing, health, and happiness', World Bank Policy Research Working Paper Series, No. 4214.

Celdran, D. (2002). 'The Philippines: SMS and citizenship', *Development Dialogue*, 1: 91–103.

Celtel (2007). Home page, www.tz.celtel.com.

Chambers, R. (1997). *Whose Reality Counts? Putting the First Last*, London: Intermediate Technology Publications.

Christensen, Clayton M. (1997). *The Innovator's Dilemma: When New Technologies Cause Great Firms to Fail*, Boston, MA: Harvard Business School Press.

Clarín.com (2004). '"Cortocircuito" entre las promesas y la realidad', www.clarin.com/diario/2004/06/07/sociedad/s-02503.htm.

Clark, G. and S. Wallsten (2003). 'Universal service: empirical evidence of the provision of infrastructure services to rural and poor urban consumers', in P.J. Brook and T.C. Irwin (eds), *Infrastructure for Poor People: Public Policy for Private Provision*, Washington DC: World Bank, pp. 21–75.

Codensa (2005). *Annual Report.*

Codensa (2006). *Annual Report.*

Codensa (2007). *Annual Report.*

Codensa (2008a). *Annual Report.*

Codensa (2008b). 'Informe de Gestión', Bogotá: Codensa.

Collins, Daryl, Jonathan Morduch, Stuart Rutherford and Orlanda Ruthven (2009). *Portfolios of the Poor: How the World's Poor Live on $2 a Day*, Princeton, NJ: Princeton University Press.

Consultative Group to Assist the Poor (CGAP) (2006). 'Mobile phone banking and low income customers: evidence from South Africa', Washington, DC: CGAP.

Cooperativa Eléctrica y de Crédito Ltda. de Carmen de Areco (CELCA) (various years). 'Memoria y Balance General', Carmen de Areco.

Crisis Energética (2004). Forum discussion, www.crisisenergetica.org/forum/viewtopic.php?showtopic=2564.

Department for International Development (DFID) (2002). *Energy for the Poor: Underpinning the Millennium Development Goals*, London: DFID.

Departamento Administrativo Nacional de Estadística (2005). 'Censo Nacional de Poblacion y Vivienda'.

Di Natale, A. (2004). 'El Perfil del Futuro Hombre de Negocios', conference held in the second LA-BELL Program Regional Workshop, Alianza Empresa/Academia en la Promoción de Líderes para una

256   *References*

Gestión Sustentable, organized by the World Resources Institute (USA), Instituto Brasileiro de Educação en Negócios Sustentáveis (Brazil), Universidad del Pacífico (Peru) and Instituto de Estudios para la Sustentabilidad Corporativa (Argentina), Buenos Aires, 18 and 19 November 2004.

Di Natale, A. (2005). 'La Base de la Pirámide: Una Visión Empresaria Dinámica', conference within the Argentina Base of the Pyramid Learning Lab, Center for Study of Corporate Sustainability, Argentina, September.

Drucker, P. (1994). 'The theory of the business', *Harvard Business Review*, **72** (5): 95–104.

Dymond, Andrew, S. Oestmann and S. McConnell (2008). 'Output-based aid in Mongolia: expanding telecommunications services to rural areas', *OBApproaches*, No. 18, Washington, DC: GPOBA. Available at: http://www.gpoba.org/gpoba/sites/gpoba.org/files/OBApproaches18_MongoliaTelecom.pdf.

The Economist (2009). 'A special report on telecoms in emerging markets', 24 September.

EDENOR (2004). 'Acceso y Concientización para el Consumo de Energía a Través de Sistemas de Autoadministración', Buenos Aires: Consejo Empresario Argentino para el Desarrollo Sostenible.

EDENOR (2006). 'Casas por + Energía', Buenos Aires: Consejo Empresario Argentino para el Desarrollo Sostenible.

EDET (2007). *Memoria Anual 2007*, Tucumán: EDET.

Elliott, Jennifer A. (1999). *An Introduction to Sustainable Development*, 2nd edn, London: Routledge.

Engvall, Anders and Olof Hesselmark (2007). 'Options for terrestrial connectivity in sub-Saharan Africa', Stockholm: Sida, February.

Estache, A., V. Foster and Q. Wodon (2002). 'Accounting for poverty in infrastructure reform: learning from Latin America's experience', Working Paper, WBI Studies in Development, Washington, DC: World Bank.

Fiszbein, A. and N. Schady (2009). 'Conditional cash transfers: reducing present and future poverty', World Bank Policy Report.

Foster, Vivien (2000). 'Measuring the impact of energy reform – practical options', *Public Policy for the Private Sector*, **210** (May): 1–11.

Foster, V. (2002). 'Ten years of water service reform in Latin America: towards an Anglo-French model', in Paul Seidenstat, David Haarmeyer and Simon Hakim (eds), *Reinventing Water and Wastewater Systems: Global Lessons for Improving Management*, New York: John Wiley & Sons, pp. 63–98.

Galal, A., L. Jones, P. Tandon and I. Vogelsang (1994). *The Welfare*

Consequences of Selling Public Enterprises, New York: Oxford University Press for World Bank.

Gardetti, M.A. (2007). 'A base-of-the-pyramid approach in Argentina: preliminary findings from a BOP Learning Lab', *Greener Management International Journal*, **51** (June): 3–17.

Gardetti, M.A. and G. Lassaga (2008). 'Edenor S.A.: energy and development at the base of the pyramid', in P. Kandachar and M. Halme (eds), *Sustainability Challenges and Solution at the Base of the Pyramid: Business, Technology and Poor*, Sheffield: Greenleaf Publishing, pp. 103–15.

Gardetti, M.A. and G. Quiroga Furque (2005). 'Edenor SA y la Base de la Pirámide', Buenos Aires: Instituto de Estudios para la Sustentabilidad Corporativa.

Garnham, N. (1997). 'Universal service', in William Melody (ed.), *Telecom Reform: Principles, Policies, and Regulatory Practices*, Lyngby: Den Private Ingeniørfond, Technological University of Denmark, pp. 199–204. Available at: http://lirne.net/resources/tr/chapter16.pdf.

Gasparini, L., M. Marchionni and W. Sosa Escudero (n.d.). 'La Distribución del Ingreso en la Argentina – Evidencias, Determinantes y Políticas', La Plata, Argentina: Universidad Nacional de La Plata.

Gertler, P., S. Martinez and M. Rubio-Codina (2006). 'Investing cash transfers to raise long-term living standards', World Bank Policy Research Working Paper No. 3994.

Gillet, Joss (2007). 'Africa passes 200 million connections in Q1 2007', *Wireless Intelligence*, www.wirelessintelligence.com.

Globe and Mail (2007). 'Cell phones play role in fuelling Vietnamese growth', 29 January, Toronto: CTVglobemedia Publishing. Available at: http://www.theglobeandmail.com/servlet/story/RTGAM.20070129. gtcellphone0126/BNStory/Technology/home.

Globe Telecom (2007). *Globe Annual Report 2006*, www.pse.org.ph/html/ ListedCompanies/pdf/2007/GLO_17A_Dec2006.pdf.

Gómez, H., P. Márquez and M. Penfold (2006). 'Cómo AES-EDC Generó Relaciones Rentables en los Barrios de Caracas', *Harvard Business Review América Latina*, December: 68–75.

Gómez Lobo, A. and D. Contreras (2003). 'Water subsidy policies: a comparison of the Chilean and Colombian schemes', *World Bank Economic Review*, **17** (3): 391–407.

GPOBA (2005). 'Output-based aid: supporting infrastructure delivery through explicit and performance-based subsidies', OBA Working Paper no. 5, Washington, DC: GPOBA. Available at: http://www.gpoba.org/ gpoba/sites/gpoba.org/files/OBApproachesWhatisOBA_0.pdf.

GPOBA (2007). *GPOBA Annual Report 2007*, Washington, DC: GPOBA. Available at: http://www.gpoba.org/docs/gpoba_ar_2007.pdf.

GPOBA (2008). *GPOBA Annual Report 2008*, Washington, DC: GPOBA. Available at: http://www.gpoba.org/publications/ar08.asp.

Gradl, C., S. Sobhani, A. Boostsman and A. Gasnier (2008). 'Understanding the markets of the poor – a market system approach to inclusive business models', in P. Kandachar and M. Halme (eds), *Sustainability Challenges and Solution at the Base of the Pyramid: Business, Technology and Poor*, Sheffield: Greenleaf Publishing, pp. 30–50.

GSM Association (GSMA) (2007). 'Universal access – how mobile can bring communications to all', http://www.gsmworld.com/documents/universal_access_full_report.pdf.

Hamel, G. and C.K. Prahalad (1991). 'Corporate imagination and expeditionary marketing', *Harvard Business Review*, **69** (4): 81–92.

Hamilton, J. (2003). 'Are main lines and mobile phones substitutes or complements? Evidence from Africa', *Telecommunications Policy*, **27**: 109–33.

Hammond, A. (2004). 'Unleashing entrepreneurship among the poor', *Sustainable Development International*, **12** (1): 1–3.

Hammond, Allen, William J. Kramer, Julia Tran, Rob Katz and Courtland Walker (2007). *The Next 4 Billion: Market Size and Business Strategy at the Base of the Pyramid*, Washington, DC: World Resources Institute and International Finance Corporation.

Hart, S.L. (2005). *Capitalism at the Crossroads*, Upper Saddle River, NJ: Wharton School Publishing.

Hart, S.L. (2007). *Capitalism at the Crossroads – Aligning Business, Earth, and Humanity*, 2nd edn, Upper Saddle River, NJ: Wharton School Publishing.

Hart, S.L. (2008). 'Foreword', in P. Kandachar and M. Halme (eds), *Sustainability Challenges and Solution at the Base of the Pyramid: Business, Technology and Poor*, Sheffield: Greenleaf Publishing, pp. ix–xi.

Hart, S.L. and C.M. Christensen (2002). 'The great leap – driving innovation from the base of the pyramid', *Sloan Management Review*, **44** (1): 23–33.

Hart, S.L. and T. London (2005). 'Developing native capability: what multinational corporations can learn from the base of the pyramid', *Stanford Social Innovation Review*, **3** (2), Summer: 28–33.

Hart, S.L. and S.Y. Sharma (2004). 'Engaging fringe stakeholders for competitive imagination', *Academy of Management Executive*, **18** (1): 7–18.

Hart, S.L. and E. Simanis (2006). 'Expanding possibilities at the base of the pyramid', *MIT Innovation Journal*, **1** (1): 43–51.

Hills, A. and H. Yeh (1996) 'Using wireless technology to provide basic telephone service in the developing world', *Telecommunications Policy*, **20** (6): 443–54.

Ho, A. (2007). 'Text messaging is still king in Asia', *Philippine Daily Inquirer*, 28 May, p. B9.

INDEC (2002). *Encuesta Permanente de Hogares – Mayo 2002*, Buenos Aires: Instituto Nacional de Estadísticas y Censos.

Information for Development Program (InfoDev) (2006). 'Micro-payment systems and their application to mobile networks', an infoDev Report, http://www.infodev.org/en/Publication.43.html.

Inter-American Development Bank (n.d.). *Opportunities for the Majority*. Washington, DC: Inter-American Development Bank.

Jensen, R. (2007). 'The digital provide: information (technology), market performance, and welfare in the South Indian fisheries sector', *Quarterly Journal of Economics*, **122** (3): 879–924.

Jhirad, David J. and Annie Woollam (2007). 'Energizing the base of the pyramid: scaling up successful business models to achieve universal electrification', in Kash Rangan, John Quelch, Gustavo Herrero and Brooke Barton (eds), *Business Solutions for the Global Poor: Creating Social and Economic Value*, San Francisco, CA: Jossey-Bass, pp. 92–106.

Johnson School of Management, Cornell University (2005). 'Base of the Pyramid Learning Laboratory – meeting notes', February, Ithaca, NY: Johnson School of Management.

Jones, L., P. Tandon and I. Vogelsang (1990). *Selling Public Enterprises. A Cost–Benefit Analysis*, Cambridge, MA: The MIT Press.

Kandachar, P. and M. Halme (2007). 'Introduction', *Greener Management International Journal*, **51** (June): 3–17.

Kandachar, Prabhu and Minna Halme (eds) (2008). *Sustainability Challenges and Solutions at the Base of the Pyramid: Business, Technology and the Poor*, Sheffield: Greenleaf Publishing.

Karlan, Dean and Jonathan Murdoch (2009). 'Access to finance', in D. Rodrik and Mark Rosenzweig (eds), *Handbook of Development Economics*, Vol. 5, Amsterdam and Oxford: North-Holland, pp. 4703–84.

Karnani, A. (2007). 'Doing well by doing good – case study: "Fair & Lovely" whitening cream', *Strategic Management Journal*, **28** (13): 1351–7.

Kim, W. Chan and Renée Mauborgne (2005), *Blue Ocean Strategy: How to Create Uncontested Market Space and Make Competition Irrelevant*, Boston, MA: Harvard Business School Press.

Komives, K., V. Foster, J. Halpern and Q. Wodon (2005). *Water, Electricity, and the Poor: Who Benefits from Utility Subsidies?*, Directions in Development series, Washington, DC: World Bank.

Komives, K., D. Whittington and X. Wu (2003). 'Infrastructure coverage and the poor: a global perspective', in P.J. Brook and T.C. Irwin (eds), *Infrastructure for Poor People: Public Policy for Private Provision*, Washington, DC: World Bank, pp. 77–124.

Lallana, E. (2004). 'SMS, business and government in the Philippines', ICT4D.ph (a project of the Department of Science and Technology and IDRC).

Leffler, Nils and Gudni Dagbjartsson (2004). 'Power to reduce poverty: the direct link between access to electricity and the reduction of poverty', *ABB Review*, **4**: 6–11.

London, T. (2007a). 'A base-of-the-pyramid perspective on poverty alleviation', Working Paper, Ann Arbor, MI: University of Michigan.

London, T. (2007b). 'Business model R&D for new market entry', Working Paper, Ann Arbor, MI: University of Michigan.

London, T. and S.L. Hart (2004). 'Reinventing strategies for emerging markets: beyond the transnational model', *Journal of International Business Studies*, **35** (5): 350–70.

Luz, L.M. (2007). '80% of teachers no ATM, suffer GSIS eCards', *Philippine Daily Inquirer*, 20 June, pp. 1, A13.

Mandri-Perrott, Cledan and D. Patella. (2007). 'Output-based aid in Colombia: connecting poor households to natural gas service', *OBApproaches*, No. 17. Washington, DC: GPOBA. Available at: http://www.gpoba.org/gpoba/sites/gpoba.org/files/OBApproaches17_ ColombiaNatGas.pdf.

MAPFRE (2008). 'Empresas de Servicios Públicos: canales eficientes para masificar los microseguros', presentation at the Microinsurance conference held in Cartagena.

Manroth, A. and T. Solo (2006). 'Access to financial services in Colombia: the "unbanked" in Bogotá', World Bank Policy Research Working Paper No. 3834.

Massé, René, Antoine Merceron, Mohamed Ousni, Mathilde Chaboche, Arthur Jobert, Olivier Normand, Christophe Nappez and Caroline Escoffier (2005). 'L'électrification des bidonvilles de Casablanca: les effets sur la pauvreté. Programme d'électrification de la société Lydec', Groupe de recherche et d'échanges technologiques, France.

Millán, J. (2007). *Codensa Diez Años*, Bogotá: Codensa.

Milstein, M. (2005). 'Transforming BOP from theory to practice: building an agenda', Conference held within the Argentina Base of the Pyramid Learning Lab, Center for Study of Corporate Sustainability, Buenos Aires, Argentina, September.

Milstein, M., S.L. Hart and T. London (2007). 'Revolutionary routines', in Sandy Kristin Piderit, Ronald E. Fry and David L. Cooperrider (eds), *Handbook of Transformative Cooperation – New Designs and Dynamics*, Stanford, CA: Stanford Business Books, pp. 84–106.

Minges, M., E. Magpantay, L. Firth and T. Kelly (2002). 'Pinoy Internet: Philippine case study', International Telecommunications Union (ITU).

Morduch, J. (1995). 'Income smoothing and consumption smoothing', *Journal of Economic Perspectives*, **9** (3): 103–14.

Mumssen, Yogita, L. Johannes and G. Kumar (2010). *Output-Based Aid: Lessons Learned and Best Practice*, Washington, DC: World Bank.

Mumssen, Yogita, G. Kumar and L. Johannes (2008). 'Targeting subsidies through output-based aid', *OBApproaches*, No. 22, Washington, DC: GPOBA. Available at: http://www.gpoba.org/gpoba/sites/gpoba.org/files/OBApproaches22_Targeting.pdf.

Mutis, J. and J.E. Ricart (2008). 'Understanding business models at the BOP – lessons learned from two South American utility companies', in P. Kandachar and M. Halme (eds), *Sustainability Challenges and Solution at the Base of the Pyramid: Business, Technology and Poor*, Sheffield: Greenleaf Publishing, pp. 326–43.

National Statistical Coordination Board (NSCB) (2001). *Philippine Statistical Yearbook*, Makati City: NSCB.

National Telecommunications Commission (NTC) (2003). *National Telecommunications Commission Annual Report 2002*, Manila: NTC.

National Telecommunications Commission (NTC) (2006). *National Telecommunications Commission Annual Report 2005*, Manila: NTC.

National Telecommunications Commission (NTC) (2007). 'Number of cellular mobile, fixed line and internet subscribers 2005', http://www.ntc.gov.ph/consumer-frame.html (accessed May 2007).

Ndiwalana, Ali (2007), personal interview, Directorate for ICT support, Makere University, Kampala, Uganda.

Newbery, D. and M. Pollit (1997). 'The restructuring and privatization of Britain's CEGB – was it worth it?', *Journal of Industrial Economics*, **45** (3): 269–303.

Ofgem (Office of Gas and Electricity Markets) (1999). 'Review of public electricity suppliers 1998 to 2000: distribution price control review draft proposals', London: Ofgem.

PC World (2006). 'Mobile subscribers to reach 2.6b this year', http://www.pcworld.com/printable/article/id,127820/printable.html.

Pertierra, Raul (2004). *Texting Selves: Cellphones and Philippine Cultural Modernity*, Manila: De La Salle University Press.

Philippine Commission on Information and Communications Technology (CICT) (2006). 'Philippine Strategic Roadmap for the ICT sector: empowering a nation through ICT', Manila: CICT.

Philippine Congress (1995). Republic Act 7925. An Act to Promote and Govern the Development of Philippine Telecommunications and the Delivery of Public Telecommunications Services (Public Telecommunications Policy Act).

Philippine Long Distance Telephone Company (PLDT) (2002). *PLDT Annual Report 2001*, Manila: PLDT.

Philippine Long Distance Telephone Company (PLDT) (2006a). *PLDT Annual Report 2005*, http://www.pldt.com.ph/ir/ar.asp (accessed June 2007).

Philippine Long Distance Telephone Company (PLDT) (2006b). 'PLDT Financial Review 2005. Management's discussion and analysis of financial condition and results of operations', http://www.pldt.com.ph/.

Porteous, David with Neville Wishart (2006), *M-Banking: A Knowledge Map*, Washington, DC: infoDev/World Bank. Available at: http://www.infodev.org/en/Publication.169.html.

Prahalad, C. (2005). *The Fortune at the Bottom of the Pyramid*, Upper Saddle River, NJ: Wharton School Publishing.

Prahalad, C.K. and A. Hammond (2002). 'Serving the world's poor, profitably', *Harvard Business Review*, **80** (9): 48–57, 124.

Prahalad, C.K., and Stuart L. Hart (1999). 'Strategies for the bottom of the pyramid: creating sustainable development', draft. Available at: http://www.nd.edu/~kmatta/mgt648/strategies.pdf (accessed 30 November 2009).

Prahalad, C.K. and S. Hart (2002). 'The fortune at the bottom of the pyramid', *strategy + business*, **26**: 1–14.

Proenza, Francisco (2007). 'Enhancing rural development through improved infrastructure and innovative information applications. Philippines country report: applications', FAI Investment Center, June.

Promigas (2008). *Annual Report 2007*.

Ramírez, Manuel and Econometría SA (2007). 'Pobreza y Servicios Públicos Domiciliarios', Departamento Nacional de Planeación.

Rangan, Kash, John Quelch, Gustavo Herrero and Brooke Barton (eds) (2007). *Business Solutions for the Global Poor: Creating Social and Economic Value*, San Francisco, CA: Josey-Bass.

Reficco, Ezequiel and Patricia Márquez (forthcoming). 'Inclusive networks for building BOP markets', *Business and Society*.

Rivera-Santos, Miguel and Carlos Rufín (2010), 'Global village vs. small town: understanding networks at the base of the pyramid', *International Business Review*, **19** (2): 126–39.

Revista Dinero (2009). 'The risk of being successful', 6 February.

Rondinelli, D.A. and T. London (2003). 'How corporations and environmental groups cooperate: assessing cross-sector alliances and collaboration', *Academy of Management Executive*, **17** (1): 61–76.

Rufín, C. (2006). 'The role of government', *ReVista: Harvard Review of Latin America*, Special Issue on Social Enterprise, Fall: 45–6.

Rufín, Carlos and Luis F. Arboleda (2007). 'Utilities and the poor: a story from Colombia', in Kash Rangan, John Quelch, Gustavo Herrero and Brooke Barton (eds), *Business Solutions for the Global Poor: Creating Social and Economic Value*, San Francisco, CA: Jossey-Bass, pp. 107–16.

Safaricom (2007). 'M-pesa', http://www.safaricom.co.ke/m-pesa/default. asp.

Sánchez, P., J.E. Ricart and M.A. Rodríguez (2007). 'Influential factors in becoming socially embedded in low income markets', *Greener Management International Journal*, **51** (June): 19–38.

Seelos, C. and J. Mair (2007). 'Profitable business models and market creation in the context of deep poverty: a strategic view', *Academy of Management Perspectives*, **21** (4): 49–63.

Sen, A. (1999). *Development as Freedom*, New York: Anchor Books.

Shy, O. (2001). *The Economics of Network Industries*, Cambridge: Cambridge University Press.

Simanis, E. and S.L. Hart (2008). 'Beyond selling to the poor: building business intimacy through embedded innovation', Working Paper, Ithaca, NY: Cornell University.

Simanis, E., S.L. Hart and D. Duke (2008). 'The base of the pyramid protocol', *Innovations*, **3** (1): 57–84.

Simanis, E., S.L. Hart, G. Enk, D. Duke, M. Gordon and A. Lippert (2005). *Strategic Initiatives at the Base of the Pyramid*, Racine, WI: Base of the Pyramid Protocol Group.

Smith, Thomas B. (2004). 'Electricity theft: a comparative analysis', *Energy Policy*, **32**: 2067–76.

Soriano, E. and E. Barbin (2007). 'M-commerce for microfinance: the CARD-NGO and RBAP-MABS pilot study experience', presented at the International Conference on Living the Information Society held in Makati City, 23–24 April.

Spiller, P. (1996). 'Institutions and commitment', *Industrial and Corporate Change*, **5** (2): 421–52.

Srinivasa, A. and J. Sutz (2008). 'Developing countries and innovation: searching for a new analytical approach', *Technology in Society*, **30** (2): 129–40.

Tewari, D.D. and T. Shah (2003). 'An assessment of South African prepaid electricity experiment, lessons learned, and their policy implications for developing countries', *Energy Policy*, **31**, 911–27.

Torero, Maximo and Joachim von Braun (eds) (2006). *Information and Communication Technologies for Development and Poverty Reduction:*

The Potential of Telecommunication, Baltimore, MD: Johns Hopkins University Press, published for the International Food and Policy Research Institute.

Touesnard, M. (2008). 'Setting some parameters: defining "BOP"', Base of the Pyramid Learning Lab Network, www.BOPnetwork.org.

Umali, Joel D. and Gigo Alampay (2007). 'Assessing the benefits of innovative payment facility in microfinance: the m-banking value proposition using SMS technology', Center for Art, New Ventures and Sustainable Development, 15 July.

United Nations Development Programme (UNDP) (2005). *Energizing the Millennium Development Goals: A Guide to Energy's Role in Reducing Poverty*, New York: UNDP.

United States Agency for International Development (USAID) (2004). *Innovative Approaches to Slum Electrification*, Washington, DC: USAID.

United States Agency for International Development (USAID) (2007). 'Encuesta de Mercado de Crédito Informal en Colombia', Washington, DC: USAID.

Vachani, Sushil and N. Craig Smith (2008). 'Socially responsible distribution: distribution strategies for reaching the bottom of the pyramid', Working Paper, Fontainebleau Cedex, France: INSEAD.

Vermeulen, P., J. Bertisen and J. Geurts (2008). 'Building dynamic capabilities for the base of the pyramid', in P. Kandachar and M. Halme (eds), *Sustainability Challenges and Solution at the Base of the Pyramid: Business, Technology and Poor*, Sheffield: Greenleaf Publishing, pp. 369–86.

Waddams Price, C. and R. Hancock (1998). 'Distributional effects of liberalizing UK residential utility markets', *Fiscal Studies*, **19**: 295–320.

Waibel, Piera (2009). 'The importance of a bottom-up development perspective when serving the base of the pyramid – concepts, interrelations and usability', paper presented at the Impacts of Base-of-the-Pyramid Ventures, Delft, The Netherlands, 16–18 November.

Weiser, John, Steve Rochlin, Michele Kahane and Jessica Landis (2006). *Untapped: Creating Value in Underserved Markets*, San Francisco, CA: Berrett-Koehler Publishers.

Wheeler, D., K. McKague and J. Thomson (2003). 'Sustainable livelihoods and the private sector: how development agencies can strengthen sustainable local enterprise networks', Toronto: Schulich School of Business, York University.

Wireless Intelligence (2007), Wireless Intelligence Internet Portal, www.wirelessintelligence.com.

World Bank (2004). *World Development Report 2004: Making Services*

Work for Poor People, New York: Oxford University Press for the World Bank.

World Bank (2006). 'Heath, nutrition and population data platform', Washington, DC: World Bank.

World Bank (2008). *Global Monitoring Report 2008*, Washington, DC: World Bank.

World Health Organization (WHO) (2009a). 'Diarrhoeal disease', Fact Sheet No. 330, August, http://www.who.int/mediacentre/factsheets/fs330/en/index.html (accessed 30 November 2009).

World Health Organization (WHO) (2009b). 'Indoor air pollution', http://www.who.int/indoorair/en/ (accessed 30 November 2009).

World Health Organization/United Nations Children's (Emergency) Fund (WHO/UNICEF) (2008). 'Progress on drinking-water and sanitation: special focus on sanitation', WHO/UNICEF Joint Monitoring Programme for Water Supply and Sanitation. Available at: http://www.who.int/water_sanitation_health/monitoring/jmp2008/en/index.html.

World Resources Institute (2004). 'Energy for economic vitality', presented at the conference on Eradicating Poverty through Profit: Making Business Work for the Poor, San Francisco, 12–14 December.

Index